CW00864701

THE CONFESSIONS OF
TIMMY DAY

TIMOTHY J DAY

authorHOUSE®

AuthorHouse™ UK
1663 Liberty Drive
Bloomington, IN 47403 USA
www.authorhouse.co.uk
Phone: UK TFN: 0800 0148641 (Toll Free inside the UK)
       UK Local: 02036 956322 (+44 20 3695 6322 from outside the UK)

Published by AuthorHouse 06/16/2021

ISBN: 978-1-6655-8836-2 (sc)
ISBN: 978-1-6655-8835-5 (hc)
ISBN: 978-1-6655-8837-9 (e)

Print information available on the last page.

Any people depicted in stock imagery provided by Getty Images are models, and such images are being used for illustrative purposes only.
Certain stock imagery © Getty Images.

This book is printed on acid-free paper.

Contents

FOREWORD

Welcome

Whilst I was enjoying my mid-twenties and had already been through so much, by the time I turned twenty-four. I mentioned to friends that I was going to write my biography and it would be ready by the time I was thirty. Well, when I was in my mid-thirties and I had been through so much more, I mentioned to other friends, that by the time I was forty I'll have a book out!

At forty-seven I finally started writing the book, the full story of my life!

I've bumped more vehicles' than a banger racer driver; I've faced more accidents' than a crash test dummy, I've watched as a young mate came to his end and I once found a young girl murdered in my flat. I've spent too many hours' in Police Cells; I've settled down as many time's as Elizabeth Taylor and I've slept with more females' than a part-time porn star.

My son was born with a disability when I was nineteen, and I've had more hospital visits than a regular actor in Casualty, Including being in a coma. I've been through a ton of jobs, from Parts sales to Telesales, from a Taxi Driver to an LGV Driver; from a Barman to a Postman and a Debt advisor.

Through years of accidents', mishaps', dilemmas', and on-the-spot decisions', I just got up and carried on. Sure, I always had my family and friends' to help me through these hard times, Mum would always say,

"You can beat this you're a Day!" Because she is such a strong woman, I became as strong as her and carried on.

By 2018 I'd finally hit rock bottom, I was in a mess and suicidal as my past had come back to haunt me. During my horrible six weeks off work with a breakdown at the end of 2018, I was writing things down as I was told by counsellors, this would help me to get things out. After wasting ink, I thought "hang on get the computer out and write the book." So that I did, before I knew it I was typing my life story. Most years I had a diary for and some I had to scroll ten years of Facebook to work out. I started to feel great about myself and after another suicidal moment passed, I was on a roll and just kept typing!

My stories of things I wish I hadn't done. I've had lot's of regrets' and sometimes low morals', but besides all that, I started playing the drums at four years old, I joined the first band by the time I was thirteen, and now as one of Weston's longest gigging "struggling" drummers, I've decided to tell my story.

Enjoy
Timmy Day.

CHAPTER 1

PRIME TIME

I was born Timothy James Day, in July 1970, in Somerset. For four years, I lived in Cheddar, with my housewife mum Avril, my lorry driving dad Denis, and my three years older, ballet dancing sister Cheryl.

Not long after I had turned four, my mum and dad had their differences. So Mum moved away to Torquay to live with her Auntie Margot, taking Cheryl then seven and me with her. We lived there for almost a year, where Cheryl was schooled and rode horses on the weekend. I was much younger, so I just enjoyed whatever Mum treated me to. Later in 1975, we moved away from Torquay to a Bed and Breakfast that was owned by Mum's parents in Dundry, near Bristol. Cheryl and I went to nearby Dundry School, where the reservoir and woods were just a stone's throw away. We only lived there for a short while, but on weekends, Grandad would take us for long walks through the stone-pile-filled woods to search for fossils.

Every time we went for these walks; I was always left looking through piles of rubble, and I'd not notice my sister and Grandad disappear. By the time I found a fossil, I would look around and be a five-year-old scared boy, as they'd always hide. They'd reappear soon enough, and I'd be happy again. Mum's brother Nick also was living there. He sprayed cars in the garage attached to the house. Around the time we were there, Nick met and married Anne, who already had a young daughter Karyn, who became my cousin. They soon bought a big derelict property in Portbury, which they rebuilt over the years, and he was able to have a spray booth in the garage at the bottom of the drive.

It wasn't long before the three of us moved to Weston-super-Mare; after Mum had started her relationship with Perry, a builder/plumber she knew from Cheddar. We moved around Weston a few times. First, it was a South Road sea view flat with noisy troublemaking Hells Angel's neighbours'. I'd spend my spare time with my mate, Tony Ford, usually climbing around the insides of a derelict old boy's school, which later became a block of flats.

Instead, we moved to a quiet rural bungalow in Bleadon on the outskirts of Weston, where I became friends with the Davies family. They lived over the road from us, and they had a big outdoor swimming pool; I became friends with Scott and Lisa and spent that summer splishing and splashing about.

We finally settled in a three-bedroom family home in Milton Weston. Perry was a keen fisherman, and he often went fishing later at night. There were many occasions when I came down to the kitchen in the morning, to find a dead fish staring at me when I opened the fridge!

I did give it a go one evening. Perry and I went to Knightstone Island, (a popular fishing spot), we'd cast a couple of times but no action. It was time for me to cast again; I did everything right, swung the rod, and I let out an almighty scream! What happened was the hook had somehow pierced my finger; once I was at the full cast the hook made root, working its way around the bone. With me still crying in pain like a nine-year-old would, Perry loaded the fishing gear and me into the car and drove us to the nearest casualty department. A butterfly stitch was put in after the doctor worked the hook out, I've not been fishing since!

We enjoyed family weeks away mainly to Dartmouth, where at that time we had a family chalet in Norton Holiday Park, right next door to Nan and Grandad's chalet. We went crabbing a lot as it was safer than fishing. After their divorce, Mum and Dad sold their chalet, so we stayed next door in Nan and Grandad's.

During the house moves, Dad would still come and pick Cheryl and me up every Sunday without fail, whether it was a long drive to Torquay, a bit closer drive to Dundry or a short drive to Weston, as he lived in

Cheddar. Nan and Pop lived in Cheddar too, as did my auntie Val with Uncle Barry. It was fun on Sundays through the years, as other relatives, Uncle Maurice and Auntie Josie, Auntie Hilary, Uncle Rich, and Auntie Maggie all lived nearby in Wells. I'd get to see my cousins, Jon, Simon, Lisa, Martin, Steven, and Alison on occasion.

Most Sundays after the family visits, Dad, Cheryl, and I, would spend the late morning and afternoon in the Legion, Bath Arms, Butchers Arms, or any other pub my dad would frequent. Sis and I would play around whilst Dad downed a few pints. He'd have the occasional scrap; I saw a couple. He always had a roast ready to eat, or Auntie Val and Uncle Barry would do us lunch, as Dad would be asleep on the sofa. But I always got to watch The Dukes of Hazzard and The Muppet Show before Auntie Val took us home.

The Grandparents sold the Bed and Breakfast in Dundry and bought a house in Locking on the outskirts of Weston. We'd spend many weekends there, and Grandad, Cheryl, and I would go for long walks in the woods, at Windmill Hill in Hutton; through to Bleadon. Again, they'd hide and leave me scared, but by now I was nine and started getting used to it!

My last year at Walliscote School was very memorable. All the pupils in my year were singing backing vocals, to Tim Rice and Andrew Lloyd Webber's, Joseph and the Amazing Technicolor Dreamcoat at The Playhouse Theatre. I've still got the audio tape for that show, and it brings a tear to my eye every time I play it. In 1981, I started my first year at Wyvern Secondary School.

By the time I was four, I'd already been bought my first kid's drum kit. Obviously, I didn't have a clue about playing it, so I just made lots of noise according to my mum!

Mum, who'd become a secretary, and her now fiancé Perry, bought me a junior drum kit for my eighth birthday. I spent every spare hour playing and finding the rhythm. It was when I was nearly twelve, that the memories really started for me. Cheryl came home from school one day and informed me, that her friend Neil, was selling his drum kit for a hundred and fifty quid. Well, as it was nearing my twelfth birthday, I got on the phone to my dad, requesting that he buy me the kit. Thankfully he said yes and the purchase was made.

I was in my element. I'd gone from a twelve-inch bass drum to an eighteen-inch bass drum, a tom and a floor tom; not two drums fixed to the bass drum; and a proper snare drum. But best of all, I now had, two separate cymbals and a set of hi-hats, instead of what sounded like a set of old paint tin lids I was whacking before. This kit, from memory, was what can only be described as a Ringo Starr looking kit, an Olympic (pre-Premier) kit. By this time in my life, I'd seen pictures of The Who and heard their music; I was in love, but now I wanted more drums like Keith Moon!

So by the time I was thirteen, I'd taken the bus from my home town, Weston, to Bristol as often as I could. I'd get off at the bus stop right outside the drum store, which was opposite the SS Great Britain and then spend about thirty minutes checking out a selection of well-used drums. I'd leave with a drum for no more than ten quid, I'd get back on a bus and go home. So from January to about August, I'd bought a further four drums, from ten to eighteen-inch, and makes from Olympic to Premier. These drums were all different colours, so it looked a bit peculiar when set up as one big kit.

There wasn't a lot to do in the early 80's; so one of my new-found friend's, Richard, who's parents' owned a local hardware store, sold me five metres of white Fablon. So with a screwdriver, scissors, a duster, and the roll of Fablon, I spent the weekend stripping down the seven multi-coloured drums. I recovered, cleaned, and rebuilt the kit. Now it finally looked like a drum kit and not some car boot classic.

Between all this collective drum building and reconditioning, I did have other hobbies, like taking my BMX to the local stunt track. Ok, so I wasn't as good as a couple of my schoolmates, Rob Hill and Matt Stevenson, but still I had fun. There was a cycle shop near the track that I often passed, on one particular day cycling home, I spotted a rather pretty well-dressed modette. I casually drifted her way and stopped for a very brief chat. It was made brief as the guy in the cycle shop came bounding out. He was a well-dressed mod with attitude; "Oi, fuck off chatting my bird up," he yelled. Off I pedalled, and not looking back or even knowing who the cool-looking couple were.

During the six-week summer holidays in 1983, I spent nearly every day with my best school mate Alex Ashman, whether it was playing tennis (badly) in Grove Park Tennis Courts or just hanging out around Weston. Well, this one day we must have spent the best part of three hours, following two young girls of the same age everywhere they went. After a while, they stopped and we talked, one was Melanie Peters, and the other was Traci Flamson. I took a shine to Traci, and we exchanged phone numbers; I walked away a happy little boy. I phoned her later, and we met up and became a boyfriend and girlfriend, first proper school love, even though she went to Priory School and I went to Wyvern.

I'd also met other new friends from Priory and Worle School, other schools in my end of Weston, they too were mods, and they all lived around Milton and Worle. We spent many evenings, and late nights hanging around in Ashcombe Park. They were Miles Dolphin, Dave Payne, Craig Tildesley, Gavin Cox, Justin Pang, James Fox, Julie Williams, Mel Pudney, Mel Peters, Traci, Lisa Brown, Tyrone Quick, Dean Cooke, Nigel Webb (aka Spider), Dave Hawkins and Paul Venn. More often than not, we'd drink a bottle of ScotsMac or homebrew wine I'd pinched; from Perrys under the stairs stash and all of us getting wasted on one bottle. Of course, Perry did realise this was going on, I got the roasting I deserved, as if the hangover wasn't enough! There was always the older mod, Alan Bussell, you know the type; all the right expensive clothes, the shiny black new Vespa, with chrome side panels; a chrome front rack, with lights' and mirrors'. Everything us young mods dreamed of. Traci was also into the mod scene, so I now had a modette girlfriend, more mod friends, and a half-decent drum kit.

I wasn't into football or sports in general really, so rather than spending time watching TV all day on the weekends; apart from Happy Days with Arthur Fonzarelli of course! I'd set my drums up in the garage on the back of the house, I'd take out my big old record player too, I'd stack the centre spindle up with Perry's Beatles albums, then I'd spend all day Saturday and Sunday practicing. It was at this time that Dean Cooke, an ex-Walliscote school friend and Ashcombe Park buddy, phoned me one evening, he informed me that his older brother Reeves, was in a band and they were looking for a drummer. Now, being thirteen, and within the last year had found and become a mod, I was in my element, as I knew Reeves was also a mod.

A meeting was arranged at my house for the weekend, the weekend came and the doorbell went; I remember it like it was yesterday. I went to the front door to see two six-foot mods stood there; the one I didn't know was wearing a black and white pair of Jam Gibson shoes, black stay press trousers, a white Fred Perry T-shirt, covered by a black V-neck jumper and a parka. Reeves had on a pair of plain black bowling shoes, dog-tooth trousers and a dark trench-coat. I already knew Reeves, but I didn't know the other guy Nick Cavill; I was a bit nervous to meet him for the first time. To break the ice, I made them both a coffee, then we went into the back room where the drums and record player were.

I hadn't been a mod for long, so my record and tape selection were very limited; one particular record I did have, also one of my most played at this time of my life, was The Jam's "Start," an easy song to play along with for the audition to play in their band, after a chat, the record span and I played the beats. Nick and Reeves were happy with what they heard, and practice was arranged for the following Thursday, at nearby Worle School. I actually went to Wyvern but lived in Milton near Worle.

I finished school on Thursday and after tea, I loaded the drums into the boot and back seat of Mum's Morris 1100, then went off to meet the rest of the band. I was both nervous and excited, I'd not long been a mod, so being part of a mod band was awesome. I'd already met Nick, who played the lead guitar and Reeves with his bass guitar; there were two other members, Steve Wilkinson on vocals and Jo Matthias on the rhythm guitar. They had "Atom," an acoustic band they'd formed during their school years, after leaving school and being best mates, they decided to keep the band idea going. Rich Southcombe was also there, he was Steve's best mate, so he took all their gear down in the Southcombe's Hardware Sooty Van, as he was the only one with a driving licence. They were still friendly with the headmaster at Worle school, which was how they were able to use the social wing for rehearsals. So after a meet, greet, and chat, and discovering that Steve was in fact, the cool mod from the cycle shop, we assembled the drums and amps and the practice took place. It sounded pretty good for our first time together. A few songs were agreed and rehearsals continued, we covered songs including, Jam classics, "In the City," "Art School," "Non stop Dancing" and "Butterfly Collector," The Who's' "My Generation," 9 below Zero's "Got my Mojo Working" and "Woolly Bully," Squire's "Walking Down the King's Road" and The Safaris "Wipeout." We also wrote a couple of our own tunes, "Last Train to Bluesville," "Takin' my Time" and "Can you tell me why."

After a couple of months, the rehearsal room was being renovated so a new venue was on the menu. It didn't take long to find a new place, for thirty pence each a week, one-pound fifty for three hours at St George's Village Hall, about two miles down the road. So rehearsals continued, and also in my garage on the occasional weekend. We also had our great friend and backing vocalist Sean Farr, he went out and bought a microphone and he came to all the practices' but I don't ever remember him singing!

Towards the end of 1984, I was knocked off a pushbike whilst doing my evening paper round, by a VW Beatle; I was thrown some distance and finally stopped when I head-butted a tree. This caused an ambulance trip to the hospital and a few week's rest with a very swollen forehead. When I recovered, a couple of small gigs had been sorted, playing family barbeques' and a one-off 18th birthday party for Sally; a friend of the other band members. I was only fifteen and spent the night gigging in a front room on the Bournville estate, to about twenty drunk teenagers', I met a rather lovely young lady that night Claire Brown, she was hot and looked stunning in a blue dress.

During 85, we added a new member with Gareth "The Harp" Edwards, bringing some harmonic melodies to the sounds, at the same time, we organised to go into a recording studio to record our first two-track demo. Conveniently for us, there was a studio Horizon West, owned and operated by Brian Monk, within a mile of all our homes. We spent a full Saturday and Sunday recording the separate bits and laying down the tracks, "Can you tell me why" and "Takin' my Time," the sound was great, two typically 80's mod style love songs.

We purchased several copies' of the cassette and proceeded to send these off to various destinations', like a Bristol Radio Show and a couple of different modzine's. One particular was "In The Crowd," written by Derek Shepherd and Jackie. Inner City had previously posted them a small article, which had been printed in an earlier copy of In The Crowd. It was after Derek heard and fell in love with the demo, that he decided to get in touch with us for a full-page interview. The demo also got great reviews in a couple of other modzine's, as well as on the Bristol Radio Show where it was often played.

Of course, my life wasn't just about being in Weston's only mod band, through the years I'd gained quite a variety of friends. Wyvern Comprehensive School was separated into two sections, the first two years being on a main road, whilst the last three years were about a mile and a half away, on the outskirts of a housing estate the Bournville. In the first two years, age eleven and twelve, I'd gained some awesome friends, Alex Ashman, whom I went to Walliscote school with, Sean Thomas, Darren Thomas and Steve Coombes to name but a few. I would guarantee to be enjoying a nice cold soda stream around Alex or Sean's house over a hot weekend, or a nice cream cake on a Saturday from Steve's mum; Pat's bakery. Steve was younger than me and had an older brother Mark; Mark was in the year above me, our paths didn't cross at school for a year, as we were in different halves of Wyvern.

When the term ended and it was time to progress to the upper school; where my mum worked as the Head Master's Secretary, I was looked out for by Mark. We became good friends; I then started my school life hanging out with the guys in the year above, obviously Mark, Jon-Paul Jones who was also a mod and Darren Gibbs, Aaron Fear, Paul "Hurman" Roberts and Geoff Kingcott. They were all into the Psychobilly and Teddy Boy lifestyle, and outside school, these guys spent time with an older bunch of Psychobilly mates', Mike Cotterell, Paul Pavlo, Kelvin Palmer, Neil Middle and a couple more.

On many week-nights and the occasional weekend, my gang of new-found friends and I would spend our time running from, and now and again taking a beating or throwing a lucky punch, with the Oldmixon skinheads. They were a large gang, with many bald heads and shiny Dr Martens with a big reputation; some were at the same school as me, as the Bournville was next to the Oldmixon; it caused the odd Wanderers moment but nothing too savage. Jon-Paul and I often hung around with another Milton mod and fellow Sea Cadet Paul Burton, it was at Paul's house with Jon that I first watched the classic Who film, Quadrophenia. Jon-Paul preferred the Psychobilly style more, he went on to grow a flat-top and through the years gained many tattoos'.

Reeves and Dean lived across the other side of Weston, yet they both went to Worle School near where I lived, and I went to Wyvern, which was over the other side of Weston nearer their house. Dean wanted to go to the Worle school disco on this one particular evening and as it finished late, it was suggested and organised that Dean would have a sleep-over at my house. I didn't go to Worle school, so I wasn't allowed to go to the disco. Things were different as far as school's were concerned back in the 80's, a lot of school differences, gangs meeting up and fights breaking out, especially at the disco's! I'd spent the last couple of years, making new and great mates with kids from both Worle and Priory school, and I went to school the other side of town. So, to stay out of trouble I stayed at home that night, and agreed to walk over to the school by ten o'clock, to walk Dean back to my house.

That was sorted, we met and we made our way back to mine, whilst I listened happily to Dean's tales of his night. It was getting late now, for a couple of young teenager's dressed like us, in red, white and blue mod shoes and both wearing parka's to be walking the streets, but we weren't alone!

We'd been walking for ten minutes and were only fifty yards away from my house; We could see my house porch light, that's how close we were! We spotted a group of older youths' at the bus stop, the same bus stop I caught the bus to school from every day! I recognized a couple of them, and keeping my head down I said to Dean; "don't look just walk on by." With that, two of the bald hard looking lads came running over, one of them was Steve; we vaguely knew him, the other guy we later found out was Paul. Well, after ignoring my keep quiet request, Dean stopped walking and said hi; I however, was being confronted by Paul and I was quite nervous about what could happen.

By now, Dean had turned around and started running, as it turned out that Steve wasn't coming over for a chat. I was now alone, and worried as I'd never seen Paul before. Paul threw a punch and it made contact, I was a little nervous, as I'd only really been in fights with skinheads' I knew; sure, I'd seen Quadrophenia, but I wasn't expecting it on my doorstep. Like a fool, I made the stupid mistake of throwing a punch back, then it just got nasty. Paul punched me again, but this time in the gut; as my body folded from the pain, I got a kick; a boxer boot straight in the face; I fell to the floor, Paul grabbed my head and thrust

9

it into a wall; then it just stopped. Me through blood filled eyes, saw Paul running after the bus, which by now had pulled off and his mates were making gestures at him out the rear window, Steve had got on the bus by then too, but Dean was nowhere in sight. Luckily, two passing neighbours, Julie and Charonne who had also been to the school disco, realised my pain and ran to my aid; they helped me to my house, as blood poured from the two-inch gash in my forehead.

Mum and Perry were out for the evening and still weren't home. So whilst I was covering the kitchen sink with blood, Julie, also a good Ashcombe Park friend, went through the family phone book to find my sister. I knew Cheryl would be with her boyfriend, so Julie found his number and contact was made. Cheryl couldn't drive at that point, so her boyfriend's mum drove me to the hospital. I had five stitches and waited for Mum, to come with Dean and take me home.

I still spent time with my other younger mates, Sean, Alex and Steve, and also another bunch of lads, Tony Ford, Tony Coram and Richard Johnston; We'd all been mates since Walliscote Infant and Junior School. I'd also joined the Sea Cadet's, where I learned to play the Bugle and the Bell lyre; marching in Carnivals' and remembrance parades'. In 85, I was privileged to play the Last Post on the bugle, for the remembrance Sunday that year in Grove Park, I was also certified as one of the Southwest's top Buglers'. I had also gained certificates for my Bosun's Whistle playing; some very special proud moments for my family and I.

In the early 80's, Dad had met and moved in with Trish, in Hutton on the outskirts of Weston. She had three sons, Steven, Rob and Chris, and a daughter Angela, they were as good as my second family for many years. Angela was with a guy nick-named Deal, who she later married. There were other Hutton people I got friendly with, John and Sarah De Bruin, John Seiger and Zoe who I briefly dated.

July the 13th 1985, Nick Cavill and myself walked from Milton to Hutton, just so we could spend the day; my 15th birthday by the way; watching "Live Aid" at my dads, with all Trish's family and their friends. It was ace, the patio doors were open and the BBQ was cooking in the back yard; drinks were flowing all day and I don't even remember the walk home.

So, since I'd turned thirteen, Cheryl, had settled down with her man Darren, who was a DJ in Charlie Browns at weekends, and he also ran the arcade record shop, a shop that aided me building my record collection, and finding more areas of the scene, like ska and soul. Cheryl moved out of the family home, and in with Darren, leaving me the bigger bedroom. I'd also purchased my first scooter, a Vespa 50 Special, that I was able to buy from a modette friend Sarah Dwerryhouse, for two hundred and fifty quid. I actually bought the scoot in February, but wasn't sixteen until July; so some weekends, I'd push it to Reeves's house in North Worle, well, I actually pushed it until I could no longer see my house, then I'd pop my helmet on and have a quick spin to Reeves's, sorry Mum! Reeves, Nick, Steve, both Rich's and myself, would spend the day riding our scooters round a field, that's now a housing estate. Of course, my first time riding a scooter or at least attempting too. Was when Miles Dolphin turned up at my house one Sunday, he was pushing a multi-coloured Vespa Rally 200 that he'd bought cheap from his neighbour. I sat on it as the engine ticked over, then he showed me how to put it in to gear with the clutch in, he then said, "just pull the throttle back and let the clutch out." But, what he didn't say was; do it slowly! So there I was, doing a wheelie up the drive and into the main road, luckily there was no traffic, so after that, we'd push it over to Worle School on Sundays and ride it with mine around the car park all day.

I'd started my first relationship; I'd built up a bigger drum kit and I'd joined a mod band. By this time, I'd also left school in May, with a couple of CSE's in English Literature, English Language, Maths and Physics.

I'd also landed myself a job as a Caravan Fitter in Hewish, just outside Weston where I started at the beginning of June. That was a good job, I was fitting water pumps' and heater system's into new caravans' and tow bar's onto cars'. Before this, I'd worked in a local petrol station a couple of evenings a week, as well as doing paper rounds every morning and evening, saving every penny I could to buy my scoot; as well as ordering my clothes from Carnaby Street favourite's, the Melanddi or Cavern catalogue. I'd pop into see Mark Jones at Our Price Record shop every Friday, pick up a couple of mod records'; then I'd pop next door to

WH Smiths for a Golden Oldie single and then onto the Arcade Record Shop, to see what special freebees' Darren had put back for me.

Later that month and approaching my sixteenth birthday, Inner City were asked if we'd like to play a gig on Weston's Birnbeck Pier; obviously the answer was yes and a weekend gig was arranged. It was with two other local bands, The Frame and The Unknown. It was a busy two night event which sounded great. The Unknown (who organised the event) didn't play, so The Frame did a few numbers and Inner City head lined which was awesome. Until the plug was pulled on the second night due to the volume of under age drinkers; Oops. Still a great time was had and a fantastic memory was created. I was finally on the road for my birthday, which is another great memory for me. I sat up on the 13th of July until midnight, as soon as the clock changed my insurance kicked in, so I jumped on my scoot and rode to Bristol and back, in just over an hour because I finally could. I passed my work place thinking no more need for buses.

Traci and I had our first lovers tiff; we split up, so I dated Claire instead for a couple of weeks, I met Claire at the party Inner City played at. I soon made it up with Traci and we resumed our relationship!

Now back to the band basics, things were on the up, we had a cheap rehearsal room, gigs were more frequent and the set was starting to grow. We added a couple of non-mod songs', including "Goo Goo Muck" by The Cramps and attempting to reproduce classics from the 80's scooter rally favourites, "Colonel Kilgore's Vietnamese Formation Surf Team." Unfortunately, things were about to make a change; Jo the rhythm guitarist was a college student and was leaving us to head to university, at the same time, we'd been given sad news that the village hall was being sold and demolished, a new rehearsal venue was again needed. Luckily for us, a great friend and budding guitarist Gavin Cox, was only too pleased to step in as the new rhythm guitarist and backing vocalist, practice continued at the village hall; but only for a month or so.

The local YMCA was sourced as a good place to rehearse, there was also a drum kit set up and ready to use. Which was just as well, my drum kit had slowly started going missing from the village hall bit by bit, yet no one knew who was taking it. There was very little left of the original kit, I was gutted!

For a short while, I had been part of forming a mod club, "The Inmates MC." We'd all meet at The Hobbs Boat Inn, at Bleadon, one night a week and discuss mod stuff. September and we as a club, took the train to Exmouth Mod Rally Weekender. It was a brilliant weekend, with mates Chris and his sister Karen Woolley, Steve Lewis and Sean Curry, whom I both went to school with, and Andy and Eddie Horwood from Cheddar. The train was quicker than taking the scooters, as I had a 50 Special and they all had PK 50's, they were even slower than mine. Although, mates Sean and Ben had rode their PK50's, we did beat them down there. We also spent the weekend with Pete, from Hounslow London, we became his new friends along with Alan Dando from Bridgwater. We saw "The Reaction," and "Bryn Gregory and the Co Stars" Live at the Pavilion on the sea-front. There was also a custom scooter afternoon. A mod version, of "The Wanderer's" Vespa won the best ridden Vespa, and a Lambretta with the reg MOD 18 F, I think won best Lambretta. We had a safe return on the train and when I wasn't busy, we'd spend the odd Saturday night getting drunk at Karen and Chris's house in Worlebury.

Rich Southcombe, Rich Lewis, Reeves, Nick, Tina Ninnis, Steve and I, decided we'd go for a Sunday afternoon ride to Cheddar, it was a lovely ride, first through the village and up through the gorge; we had a stop at the top for a quick fag and then made our way back home. Of course, young novice rider Timmy Day, took one of the gorge bends too fast and went off road; straight up a mound and into a rock and tree. I wasn't hurt but my mirrors were everywhere, so I straightened them up and made it safely home.

Mid-October and Top Gun had just been released at the Odeon, I rang a mate Miles Cuthburtson and a date was made for us to go and watch it that evening. I was on my 50 Special all modded up with lights' and mirrors', by that time I'd also added a bigger kit, converting it to a 90cc. I took the not so busy top road, making my way to Miles's house so we could catch the bus in to town. I'd just gone over a brow and was now approaching a small build up of cars, cars parked on the left, cars parked on the right, a Morris Minor coming from the opposite direction and a Porsche in front of me letting the Morris through. By now I was travelling at speed and hitting the brakes hard, a decision needed to be made, "do I hit the rock solid moving Morris head on," or "do I rear end the stationary Porsche?" With no real time to make that decision, I sailed straight into the left-hand rear of the Porsche, spinning the scoot round and causing it to damage the entire left-hand side of the once shiny nine-two-eight.

The Porsche driver heard the noise and no doubt felt the bump, he was desperately looking around to see what the hell that was, up popped my head, my little embarrassed face grinning from my black open-face helmet. The bloke jumped out and to be fair, he didn't care about his car on this occasion. I just bounced, not even a bruise; details were exchanged and off went the now dented nine-two-eight. I however, had to do a quick road side repair job and pull the now bent frame away from the brake pedal, so I could continue my journey. After a bit of kicking and a bit of pulling I was ready to get going. There was no electric start in those days, so kick start it was. I kicked and I kicked and I kicked, but nothing, by this time I was getting a bit more stressed, not only was I worried that this slight delay might mean I may miss the bus and the film, but because there was a little old lady constantly yelling over at me. I was ignoring her as I had enough to worry about, until I finally snapped; "What?" I shouted whilst glaring angrily at the lady; "Is that yours?" she yelled back pointing towards the gutter. Now, due to me recently stripping and rebuilding my engine to fit the 90cc kit, I'd failed to screw the fuel tank back in; so, what the (trying to be helpful!) little old lady was pointing at, was in fact the fuel tank from my scoot. After a quick apology and a fuel tank re-fit, I was off to see Miles and the great movie.

Within a week, a friend of mine Phred Steer, had come to the rescue as he had a frame sat in his back garden, the same as the frame I'd just written off! So with Rich and his Sooty van, the frame was collected and I proceeded to re-spray it yellow and re-build the scoot. But this time, adding a Lambretta mudguard supplied by Rich Lewis, cut-down by Kerry Stark and chromed by Nick Taylor, along with the new Fresco exhaust from Bob Wright.

November was one of my favourite memories, as me and an Ashcombe Park pal, Dave Hawkins, decided we'd go to the Buckingham Palace Mod Weekender. Loads of venues and loads of bands, including

The Purple Hearts at the all-dayer on the Sunday, at The London Hippodrome. It was all great, as Dave's Auntie and Uncle lived in Uxeter in London, so we had somewhere to sleep and eat all weekend. We caught the tube all over the place, there were scooters and mods everywhere. The Sunday was what we were really waiting for, as we couldn't wait to see The Purple Hearts. I was able to get my camera in, as I had a 80's Disc camera and it wasn't noticed; cameras' were banned, so I got lucky and got some great pics'. When the weekend was over, we got on the Bakers coach and went home.

By now and approaching the end of 86, another local band that also used the YMCA to practice, "March of Time," were playing a gig in a local hotel pub, Chaplin's. They were covering songs from The Alarm, Stiff Little Fingers and many other punk favourite's. Lead singer Mike Headington, asked if Inner City would like to support, well of course, five boys got over excited, as it was about to be our first proper pub gig. It was a Saturday night and in a busy pub with a happy crowd. It was mainly friends, but I was also starting to meet new musicians, as well as Mike Headington singing, there was Steve Kearns on the guitar, Rich "Rat" Scott on Bass and Ross Davidson on drums. By this time Inner City had a slight genre change and had started adding more known favourite's to the set, like various tunes from The Housemartin's, The Vapours "Turning Japanese," The Buzzcocks "Harmony in my head," The Cult's "She Sells Sanctuary" and The Smithereans "Behind the Wall of Sleep."

Now well into 87, rehearsing in a dark and dingy rather damp, smokey basement at the YMCA, things started to change. As well as Steve electrocuting himself with a damp microphone one night and him having a fall out with Nick, we started writing more and more original material. We'd started frequenting Charlie Browns, the best pub in Weston, the only pub you could guarantee to find a member of the 13th Valley Scooter Club and usually, a full scale Duke's of Hazzard stylee bar brawl. But all the same the landlord's, Russ, Andy and Noddy, asked Inner City if we'd like to play a gig in Charlie's. This became our gig venue for the next two and a half years. The only thing was I had no gigable drum kit, so a friend, Tony Steele, came to the rescue and pointed me in the direction of a young lad Clive, who lived near

Charlie Browns. That was both brilliant and handy. Every gig, Rich in the Sooty Van, would round up the lads, pick up the drums and drop us off for the night of entertainment. They were total non profitable gigs mind you, as the sound had to be awesome when we performed; a PA hire was sourced, Alan would turn up from Swindon, with a system big enough to power Wembley and all for a hundred and fifty quid. Cheap enough, but we only got paid a hundred and twenty, plus the drinks we'd consumed during the night. It was all for fun so it really didn't matter, it sounded great and was also recorded. We played a couple more Charlie Browns gigs', alongside other local bands, including a great Soul and Blues outfit The Orphan's; Renegade Flight and Matt Purslow's Ancient Bewilderment, (featuring Alan Van Kleef), to name but a few. Due to band politics and fights starting to break out during the gigs, and expensive equipment started to get knocked, Inner City gigs became a lot rarer and the band was put on the back burner's with very little (if any) action.

We still carried on our friendships, as well as the occasional visit to Carnaby Street, to purchase some multi-coloured shoes or a Paisley shirt or maybe a two tone suit. We were Saturday Kids on a Saturday afternoon, drinking coffee or coke in the Monte Carlo Restaurant, with our other friends and their scoot's parked outside. Steve with his Vega, Nick and his SX Lambretta, Reeves's (built that morning) LI chopper and Rich's self squiggled Servetta. There were a couple of other close Milton boys, Rich Lewis and Kerry Stark; Rich had many Lambrettas', including Frustration, a red and blue GP 200, his orange self-built racing Lammy; and his custom GP, "House" the horror movie. Kerry had many scoots too, but more memorable was his yellow Lammy low-rider.

I turned seventeen in July, and it was time for a bigger Vespa. So after a trip to Bristol Six Scooter's with my dad and Reeves, we signed the documents and I bought a brand-new PX125E on HP, for six hundred and ninety quid, and on the road to take straight away. I still had two weeks to wait for my age change, so Reeves rode it back to Weston for me. I then went on to do my part one bike-test, in Winterbourne Bristol, that August with Jon-Paul, and I passed part two in November in Weston. A local Vespa dealer, Bob Wright, had a Vespa PX engine with a 180cc conversion, with a nice new fuel guzzling 28mil Dellorto

Carb; when he asked me if I'd like to swap my brand new 125 engine for this one, I jumped to the chance.

I rode my now quicker Vespa to the Isle of Wight that year, with Spider an Ashcombe Park buddy on the back. We didn't take things like spare clothes or tooth brushes back then, so all I had bungeed to the front, was a tent and two sleeping bags and a drunk Nigel Webb on the back, with a twenty-four pack of lager, that he consumed the majority of before we even got there. That year was more memorable than a lot of them, as it was a wet weekend all weekend. The camp site entrance was a mud pit, with one wet plank of wood to try and get a grip on, there were muddy scooterists' everywhere. On the Saturday night some crazy scooter nut, from another club had pinched a Mark one Escort, drove it on the camp site and set alight to it. We had a food fight in a supermarket and everyone scrammed when the old bill turned up, a fantastic weekend was had.

Now into 88, the band lads all had different jobs, and some had started getting serious in relationships'. So we concentrated more on recording new original material, at a newly found recording studio, The White House in Kewstoke Weston, owned and managed by Martin Nicholls. We laid down some classic self-penned numbers, "Mr Mystery Man" and "Where's the Hammond," on the second occasion at the same studio, we recorded a four track tape with "Runaway," "Prime Time," "The Evidence" and "Aunt Alice." By then we weren't gigging as often, except one particular gig. Gavin at this time, worked in Weston's biggest music shop, Hamlin's, and he worked with a guy called Dave. Dave was in a band "The Long March," he asked Gavin, if Inner City would like to play The Bierkeller, one of Bristol's biggest music venues, so in March 88 Inner City did just that; with two other bands, "The Long March" and "The Curve." It was a very busy night and a quality gig. I took and passed my driving test in June that year and for my eighteenth birthday was bought a mark one Escort 1300 for a hundred and fifty quid. Traci passed her test a few months later and she also bought a mark one Escort.

13th Valley Scooter Club was formed in mid 88. Of course, we'd been mod and scooter friends' for many years; so we were a strong, and large group of young Lambretta and Vespa enthusiasts; who had travelled the country together, got drunk together in many destinations', from Devon to Scotland, some times caused havoc with the occasional arrest, but all in all a tight club that would always be there for each other no matter what! Club fun on sunny Sundays', would sometimes involve a group ride out, usually within a twenty mile radius, one certain Sunday it was agreed that a ride out to Cheddar, and up through the gorge was where we would go. Off we went, ten to fifteen scooters' and we made our way to Cheddar. After arrival and heading up through the gorge, a crazy motorcycle rider, zoomed past us sticking his fingers up and shouting abuse. As we turned the next bend, we see the same rider sat in the lay-by, with a grin on his face, whilst giving us the middle finger. Within seconds, the guy was surrounded and one of my lot jumped off his scoot, he proceeded to punch him the best he could through his helmet; someone else grabbed the keys out of the bikers ignition and threw them into the hedgerow. We all jumped back on our scoots and made our way back to Weston, and then spent the next couple of nights in Charlie Browns, excitedly talking about our Cheddar antic's.

Although, over the next month things started happening to the scooters parked in the car park, wheel nuts were being loosened and key scratches started appearing in paint work. I was leaving the pub with John and Steve one night, we saw a lad on a motor-bike kicking a scooter, the three of us jumped on our scoots and gave chase; we caught up with him and gave him a mild beating. Things like this continued! But now other drinkers in Charlie's were getting involved; now, these guys were not the guys to be messing with, from scrap yard owners to builders and bouncers, and known hard-nuts; as well as being friends with all the other Weston known bad boys.

Before we knew it, there were forty plus people, guys and girls heading for Cheddar on a Saturday night. It was mayhem, windows were shattered, punches were thrown, baseball bats and planks of wood, bodies falling everywhere. One little local police man, was trying his best to control the now sixty fighting youths, but instead he was being swarmed. One brave lad, jumped on the car and kicked the light off the roof, of this now bouncing side to side Police Metro. One lad got stupid and slashed someone with a knife, it wasn't long before reinforcements started arriving and everyone scrammed, it was like a scene from Quadrophenia.

A mate Skids, was able to wave some friends down in their passing car, so we jumped in with Heidi and Ashley and made our getaway back to Weston. Unfortunately, sixteen Weston people weren't so lucky, as they and one Cheddar lad were arrested, fined and charged with affray. I did however have my front tooth broken that night!

I didn't get caught for being at Cheddar, but on a Saturday night a few weeks later, Steve, Dave and myself had been out and pinched a cheap car stereo; from a car parked in an industrial estate.

Dave went home, so Steve and I cruised the Saturday night streets in my Escort. With "Henry the Wasp" in big white letters across the boot, and music popping out of a cheap stereo I'd just robbed. We drove down Richmond Street at about two thirty, where all the night clubs' were just kicking out. Passing the clubs and entering a T-junction, we spotted some mates; so I gave them a toot and a wave, and I hit the accelerator. Little did we realise due to showing off, the pizza delivery van that had pulled out before us, had actually stopped to let a couple of people cross the road; "Bang;" I drove straight up his arse, sending him through the opposite window, but instead of pulling over and giving details or even seeing that the driver was ok; I decided to floor it and hope to get away with it. Unfortunately, due to about fifty witnesses, two days later I was arrested and charged; with wreckless driving, failing to stop after an accident and failing to report an accident!

Weston scooter rally was in September, and I drove Steve and myself around all weekend, as both of our scooters were off the road. A great idea for the Saturday night, was to park the car on the beach, walk to nearby Charlie Browns, get as drunk as we liked, then sleep in the car which we left our sleeping bags in ready. We had our fun drunken night and slept in the car as suggested. "Tap Tap," on the window was what woke me up at about nine-thirty on the Sunday morning. After slowly crawling out from my sleeping bag, I was greeted by a persistent police man, standing with his leather glove, tapping the glass and requesting that I step out the vehicle. After a quick spot check when other coppers arrived, they found a stolen stereo, a baseball bat and a fuel siphoning kit. So after a day in the cells, (me, not Steve) and a house search to my poor mum and Perry's terror, where nothing was found, I was released and charged with theft.

The end of October 88, and things took an unfortunate turn for me and the scootering fraternity. The recently purchased Escort that I'd got for my birthday, had broken down due to a knackered water pump; it was off the road as was my scooter. But great news, scooter buddy Steve Bowen had a Black, mark one Escort practically identical to mine, but not taxed or insured, and he hadn't passed his test. So I thought it would be a good idea, to put my Escort number plates and tax disc on Steve's Escort. Typical teenage stupidity really.

It was Saturday the 30th of October, Steve, Mark Coombes and myself went for a drive; I was driving as the car had my plates on it. We did the usual, pop in to Charlie's to see our mates', then we did the around town cruise. We took a drive around an industrial estate, but didn't realise there was a copper parked up; can you imagine the panic when his blue light came on. I shit myself, when he got out of his car and pranced over like a little fat fairy. Due to the past couple of month's, my registration was all over the police department; luckily the car was in a not bad looking state for a 1977 Escort. As I was driving the car with illegal plates, I carried all my documents with me and I shoved them in his hand like a cocky teenager would. He took a quick look at the car and scanned the documents and sent us on our way. "Phew," we got away with that, the donut didn't even notice the documents stated four door saloon; we were in fact in a two door!

After a laugh and giggle and pleased with ourselves, we took a drive up to Weston woods, where we met with a couple of other passenger filled cars'. It was now that I decided, as we were off the main road Steve could have a drive around and he loved it. I however, was feeling every bump, as was Mark in the back. Picture if you could, an old car with self lowered suspension, no rear seats, just a blanket and no stereo; so I was sat with my feet pressed against the dash board, with a 3D BIG stereo on my lap and The Jam blasting out. Eventually, the three cars all parked in a line; with us as the middle car, facing into the woods and the passengers' all chatted happily.

As it was approaching bonfire night, it was possible that fireworks may go off in the woods at any time, well this was that time. A loud bang came from the trees and everyone panicked, the two outside cars shot off first, Steve then quickly hit the accelerator and span the car round; he didn't give me a chance to get behind the wheel; so he proceeded to drive at speed out of the woods. The dodgy suspension and being on rough terrain, meant that Mark and I were now being bounced around the car like a pair of raggy dolls; both of us screaming for Steve to slow down and with The Jam still booming from the beat-box. Then came the end of the rough road and a ridge up to the new tarmac road, where one of the other car's was waiting. Steve twitched the steering wheel right to avoid the waiting car, but as we hit the ridge the car started bouncing across to the other side of the road, it was now travelling and still at speed, with the two left-side wheels on the road and the two right-side wheels still on wooded terrain. We could see the lamppost directly in front of us, Steve was desperately trying to steer the car back on to flat road. The two front wheels finally touched down on the road, as the Escort smashed, drivers side into the lamppost, throwing me from the car and trapping Steve and Mark.

Passengers from one of the other cars ran to help; one lad, Yankee was his nickname, jumped on the boot of the wrecked Escort and smashed out the already damaged rear windscreen, Yankee and I then fought to pull Mark from the rear; the roof had cut into his head, causing him to be unconscious and his foot was trapped under Steves seat. There was no way we could get to Steve, I could only reach his shoulder but he was motionless.

I stood by the trashed Escort sobbing and screaming, unfortunately, the visions are so fresh that it could have happened this morning.

Nearby homes had heard and seen the accident, so fire and medical teams' were quick to arrive; Mark and I were rushed to hospital, but with the shock of the crash it didn't seem right, that I only had a few cuts and bruises, and Mark had a mild concussion. Unfortunately, it was a sad moment to be told that Steve didn't make it. If only, the copper that stopped us earlier in the night had done his job properly, we would've never made it to the woods. If only, I'd of been more sensible and not put my plates on the car. If only!

The morning after the accident, I took a walk round to Caroline's house, to give her and her family the sad news, she was Steve's girlfriend and she'd seen us the night before. Caroline and I then took a walk round the corner to see Gary Watts, another of Steve's best mates, it was a very sad time as I'd lost one of my best mates, who had just turned eighteen and he had left behind his lovely parents, Maureen and David, and his younger brother Carl.

The funeral was what Steve deserved, scooter friends from all over the UK had come to show their respects. After a memorable church service, literally a hundred scooters' followed the cars, carrying both the coffin and Steve's family to the Crematorium, a couple of miles away. The police, had even given all riders' permission to ride their scooters' with no helmets on.

After the funeral and a few months of sadness, I went to court for a bucket load of driving offences. Including wreckless driving, failing to report an accident, and failing to stop after an accident, for the pizza van incident. Fraudulent use of tax disc, fraudulent use of number plates, and no MoT for the tragic accident; and just for extra measure the car stereo theft too. I went to court for all the offences on the same day, and was fined six hundred quid and given eighteen points. After a panic, my solicitor put things straight in my head, and informed me, that I only actually received five points on my licence; great my licence was safe; but taking home sixty-eight quid a week, and paying fifteen pound a week on HP for the scoot, meant I needed to change my job. I soon applied for a position as a Parts Person, for a Mercedes Benz commercial vehicle company, WSM Motors, which I got. It was better money and with better prospects. My relationship with Traci had briefly ended, as I was spending a lot of time with Caroline. To be fair we did start dating, and we spent that Christmas together at her family's house in Bristol. On New Years Eve, Caroline decided to end the relationship, probably not a good idea on this particular day, as myself and a large majority of 13th Valley Scooter Club, had been in Charlie Browns all day drinking gallons of Fosters; you can imagine what state we were all in by the end of the night!

After going on a New Years Eve pub crawl, and drinking anything from a pint to a shot, chanting rubbish as we burst through Weston streets, we headed back to Charlie Browns for the midnight chimes. Marching through the Dolphin Square shopping centre and through the glass panelled arcade, I was being rather loud, I'd punched anything or anybody that got in my way all night; I'd had a lot to drink, lost my best mate in a car crash and not been able to help him, and Caroline had just dumped me. So then I was punching the seven-foot square window panels, they quivered but only a little, so someone shouted, "use your elbow," so what do I do; I use my elbow; there was an almighty crash and I went flying into the Iceland freezer store; but not for a late night shop!

No alarm's sounded, but still I panicked and scuttled my way out from the small splinters of glass, and now messed up freezers. It was as I was pulling myself free from the shop, a large panel of hanging glass dropped on my head. With my adrenaline on a high I just got up and ran. Heading for Charlie's with my mates behind, shouting and cheering about my window shopping conquest, I felt a stinging in my head and I rubbed my crown whilst still fast on my feet; it felt damp, warm and sticky; I looked at my hand, it was now covered in blood. My pace slowed, as I knew by now things weren't looking good. I collapsed outside Charlie's, and panic took place. Great mate Andy Coles was a hero, as he ripped off his woolly jumper and wrapped it round my head. Thankfully there was an off-duty nurse in the pub, she was able to come out and calm the situation, until the ambulance arrived to whisk me and two mates; Jon-Paul and Darren Gibbs off to the hospital. Several stitches did their work to repair the damage, a bandage was wrapped round my head, and the three of us left the hospital. Whilst walking home, me in my blood stained clothes, Dan and Lisa Stokes pulled up in their van and gave me a lift home. Darren and JP walked; Happy New Year indeed!

When arriving home, I rang the door bell and Mum came to the door; she took one look at me in a turban and burst out laughing! Being the end of the year celebration night, meant that Mum and Perry had a good reason to annihilate a bottle of Sheep Dip. After a minute or so of laughter, she finally realised, that I wasn't dressed up for a New Years Eve giggle; it was then that the drunken Spanish inquisition started. I made up some lame story, that I was pushed by someone in fancy dress; "Donald Duck Did It." Sorry Mum! Time went by and the stitches were removed, and my relationship with Traci was soon back on track.

Now into 1989 and Inner City had come to an end. Despite earning more money and pestering my dad, I wasn't able to replace the drums I once had; Inner City was over but the friendship was still strong. I now had eleven points on my licence, as I'd also had a couple of speeding tickets and was paying hundreds in fines. If that wasn't enough, there was the altercation at the traffic lights, when road rage took over and I got out of my car and beat another driver until he drew blood! So now I had an ABH charge to deal with. Luckily after a Crown Court hearing it was reduced to Common Assault, so I ended up with a hundred and thirty quid fine with conditions.

It was time for me to start calming down a bit, and be a bit more responsible and not such a wanna be bad boy. My mark one Escort ended up at the scrap yard, so I bought a powder coated red mark two Cortina, from Martin at work for sixty-quid instead. That was actually paid for by Dan Stokes, as I'd spent the weekend in my garage, fitting a shed load of electrical items, to his recently purchased side-car on his Vespa. I eventually blew that car up racing Alfie in his Escort mark two Mexico, down the A38 one night, so I sold it to Burt at WSM Motors for ten quid.

I went on to learn a martial art Ninjutsu, with friends Jon-Paul and Mike Cottrell and by now, I'd bought a mark two Escort 1600, from my boy racer buddy and old school mate Chris Kitching. 13th Valley had also had a disagreement and split, a few mates and myself formed The Breakaway's Scooter Club; but that club slowly drifted apart too. I still went on the occasional more local scooter rally, in Newquay, Exmouth, Weston and the Isle of Wight, until I blew a hole in the piston of my 180 Polini; by then cars were my main toy.

My driving standards had hit another glitch. As I worked selling parts for Mercedes Benz lorries, on occasion I had to go out on deliveries, be it in a company car for a quick small delivery, or the van, which was more likely if the happy regular van driver, Scottish John was off. It was March and John was off, so I was on deliveries all week. One particular day, the deliveries were going well and I was on my way back to Weston, after my last drop in Illminster; I was in the company 307D van. It was a long straight road, and about a mile ahead, I could see I was approaching a hump back bridge, at the same time, I was fumbling with my box of cassettes' on the passengers seat, so I could change the tape in the stereo.

I accidently knocked the box onto the floor and did a quick box pick up; it goes to show how quick things can happen! By this time, the van was already on the upward slope of the bridge, and travelling at about fifty mph. After only, two to five seconds of ducking low enough to pick up the tape box, I lifted and looked, to find that I'd just gone over the brow of the bridge, and there was a forty-five degree bend. Then "Bang," Straight into a wall; the van stopped dead, sending the fuel tank into a field and me face-butting the window, splitting my lip and gum and causing a five-mile tailback, for the best part of four hours. After a very long day, I went home to recuperate. I only got a police caution for that accident, no points and no fine but a roasting from my boss.

I carried on through 89, spending my nights driving Weston sea front, with my new group of friends. In May, I swapped my mark two Escort; for a five door Mark three 1600i Escort, with full body kit with Chris Kitching. I fitted a new expensive, bought and paid for stereo and amp, from Richard at Paul Roberts Hi Fi, and a hoofing great 200 Watt Sub Woofer, I bought from long-time friend and scrap yard owner Dale Burrison. I'd put my scooter and band times behind me, but kept my piston blown scooter anyway and became a boy racer. Even my taste in music took a turn, playing chart classics like, SL2's "On a Ragga Tip," or Ce Ce Peniston's "Finally" and many other popular tunes of that era.

June was a memorable time, as most nights were spent with Chris Kitching, cruising the seafront or sometime's the Bristol streets. We spent most Saturday nights out on the town for a very drunken session. Well, on one particular Saturday we decided not to drink, but instead go to Bristol for a cruise. Traci and I were on one of our break ups', which as you've read happened from time to time! Just before we were about to leave for our drive, I nipped into Mum's for a quick wee; it was then that Mum informed me, that Traci needed a chat. My first thought was, "already, we usually split for longer before we get back together!" I gave her a quick call and she said she needed to see me. I told her to be quick, as Chris and I were about to go to Bristol, I got back in the car with Chris and waited. About five minutes later, she pulled up in the passengers seat of our friend Karen's van, but further down the road, we both left our vehicles' and met in the middle. I was waiting for her first words to be, "I love you and want you back." But instead her first words were, "I'm pregnant!" We didn't go to Bristol in the end, instead we went out and got extremely drunk!

After a lot of thought and family discussions, it was decided that I'd move in with Traci, and her mum and dad, Sandra and Dennis. So I moved in and kept busy driving Mercs about for work, I took and passed my forklift test, I carried on with the martial arts and worked my way up through the grades, and was happy with my pregnant girlfriend. I still had video nights in Chris Kitchings static caravan with Stubbsy and I still socialised on weekends, usually with Traci.

Besides my boy racer and family man life, in October, I took a long drive to Milton Keynes, for a week long Mercedes course. It was a fun week, clubbing most nights at "The Pyramid," what a venue that was! Different music on all the floors: ska on one floor, rave on another and chart music on another. I got my certificate and came home to my mum to be.

In March 1990, in the very early hours of a Saturday morning; I'd been out the night before so I was still tipsy, and was woken by a screaming Traci about to go into labour. After running into Dennis and Sandra's bedroom and shouting for them to get up, we all went straight off to Weston Hospital. After several hours and still no baby, it was suggested we have the birth in St Michael's Hospital Bristol; Traci was rushed off in an ambulance, I followed close behind in my Escort. By eleven thirty Saturday morning, Darren John Day was finally born, weighing 6lb 9oz.

Inner City early practice 83

My first Vespa 50 Special in 86

CHAPTER 2

AMAZING JOURNEY!

Now starting a new chapter in our lives. Traci and I were both nineteen when Darren was born, so we spent the first couple of months of 1990, preparing ourselves for parenthood. My dad bought us a new pram from Boot's and we did the usual shop for bottles' and baby-grows'. Our nights were usually spent with me watching a video I'd rented, from Video Vision or Whirlwind videos; whilst Traci was reading her selection of "Your first baby" books'.

After the birth and when Traci had come home, things were pretty normal! I'd go off to work every morning, as would Dennis; Sandra had recently been made redundant, which was unfortunate but helpful, as it meant that Traci wouldn't be alone all day.

The night times however were a different story! When it was late and time for our beauty sleep, Daz would be awake, screaming and not keeping his milk down! We'd spend hours awake, and sometimes drive miles to calm him down; it did work but once we'd got home and put him back in his crib, he'd wake, and those tiny lungs would scream louder than Big Ben!

My sister, within the last year had split with Darren, and eventually had started a new relationship with Mark. Traci and I decided to look for a flat. A nice three floor, two bedroom flat was sourced in the centre of town, and we moved into our new first proper family home. It wasn't far from my work so I could walk if Traci needed the car, as she'd sold hers by then. Daz was still suffering, but by now he'd had tests' and was on a different milk to help.

As well as many trips to Bristol Children's Hospital for tests, we still made time, and sorted Darren's Christening to take place in September that year; St Marks Church was booked; a Christening gown was made and the invites' went out. During all this, I borrowed a van from work and took a drive to Draycott near Cheddar, to purchase our first washing machine; a twin tub, do you remember them? It was great, it did it's job that's all that mattered!

One late evening and not long after my 20th birthday; I was sat on the twin tub, trying to keep the thing from bouncing round the kitchen. Traci was doing whatever she was doing upstairs with Daz, then the next thing I heard, were several loud bumps and then another of Darren's almighty screams; I'd not heard him scream that loud for a while. I jumped off the washing machine, and across the lounge to the stair entrance, to find Traci in a heap at the bottom of the stairs with Daz in her arms, but he was still screaming and now changing colour.

We jumped in the car and rushed to hospital; Daz was rushed off, and Traci and I paced the waiting room in anticipation. We had to deal with the Social Services sticking their noses in, but it didn't matter!

We were eventually told that he'd actually broken his leg! Poor little dude had had more hospital visits than me, and he was only three months old. They were still doing on going tests on Daz in Bristol, so we were back and forth a lot; but as he was so small, he had to stay in Weston General for six-weeks, in traction. The Christening was in five and a half weeks so panic was on! I carried on working and spending every spare hour at the hospital singing Daz to sleep at night.

During Darren's hospital time, my sister moved in with us as she'd split with Mark. A month or so later and she introduced us to Drew, the man she'd recently met. Time was ticking and it was approaching Darren's Christening; luckily for us, he was out two days before. Traci's family came down from Newcastle, my family too were all there. It was going lovely, until the pre bought booze was starting to run out. Now, this was the very early 90's, nothing was open. Supermarkets' closed at four as it was a Sunday, what were we to do? No problem, as Cheryl's new male friend happened to be at that time, the manager of a popular off licence chain; so Sis got on the phone to Drew, he turned up within twenty minutes, like a knight in shining armour with a new stock of everything; top man, he was a keeper!

Christmas came and went, and Traci turned twenty on the 30th of December, the new year turned and Darren's first birthday went with no problems. Cheryl and Drew took their relationship a step further and moved into their first flat together in Milton.

Popular back then on Sunday nights was Prom night at Mr B's Fun Pub in Richmond Street. A bunch of mates and I would frequent this establishment; it was easy for me as I lived in town, and could be home ten minutes after leaving the pub. Bearing in mind, that the pubs closed at ten thirty on the dot on Sundays' in those days.

One of those Sunday nights, a group of squaddies' on their R and R, felt the need to throw rude comments our way all evening. We ignored it to some extent! Half past ten came and everyone left the pubs', the streets were busy, people started queuing for taxis' and the kebab house was packed in minutes. The off-duty army were still giving the abuse, a couple of my lot had a scuffle in the road, the police were close by so it didn't last long. Six of us walked one way, whilst the others walked the other way; we made our way through a bus avenue, then, three of my mates went off in another direction, so the remaining three of us, Garry Griffiths, Jamie Gatti and myself, headed off to take a final short cut home.

As we approached the end of the cobbled lane, four lads (the squaddies' from earlier) appeared, but this time, each of them gripping a three foot long, piece of two by two strip of wood. "Shit," was the first thing to go through all of our minds. Although the three of us, were reasonably high up the grades in Ninjutsu; being drunk was no time to try and be a Ninja, so we turned and started running. Jamie went first, Garry was close behind, but as it had been raining and I had trainers on, my feet litteraly had a slow motion run on the spot moment. "Crack," a piece of wood hit me, straight in the right hand side of my now stinging head. It didn't knock me out but it did send me eating concrete cobbles! I curled up in a ball covering my head; as my T-shirt lifted I felt every slap of the wood on my skin, until it suddenly stopped and I heard them running off! Thankfully, Garry couldn't leave me behind to take a kicking, so he picked up a massive boulder and threw it at them. My back was blood red with bruises and I had a ringing in my ear, as I'd been caught a couple of times in the head. I walked through the door at about eleven thirty and Traci wasn't happy; I immediately burst into tears and lifted my T-shirt, then she realised why I was late home and the pity started.

It wasn't long into the year, when Cheryl and Drew's house they'd been waiting for became available, so Traci, Daz and myself, were able to move to Milton into their old flat, better parking and no more narrow and very dangerous flights of stairs'.

Things were good, I'd been in the same great job for two and a half years, we had a lovely flat in the same area I'd grown up in, so our family and friends were nearby; I was still in love with my first school girlfriend and we had a gorgeous baby together. I still had the 1600i mark three Escort, I went to the gym once a week, and I did Ninjutsu about three nights a week. My not ridden for some time scoot was parked in our small front garden. Southcombe's Hardware was just across the road, so my best mate Rich was on tap if I needed his help. Even though there was no band we all still hung out together, Steve married Gill, Nick settled down with Diane and Rich had also settled down with Rachael. Reeves had started his own photography business, so we didn't see as much of him as he was starting to travel around for work. It was also around this time, that I took Traci for a meal and popped the question! She said yes and the preparations took place. Dennis put a deposit down at the Seaward Hotel for our reception, Traci, baby Darren and I, would spend a few Sundays' at Mead Vale Village Hall, for a Sunday morning church service; that was the Vicar sorted. Then it was just the wait, until Saturday August the 31st for the special day.

It was during June that Traci and I were asked to see a specialist in connection with Darren. We made the call and the appointment was made; it was after the last year and three months of tests, that they finally had a result for us. It was then, we were told that Darren had Williams Syndrome and a heart murmur! We were told, that by the time Daz was seven, he would have to undergo open heart surgery, to reopen his aorta, as it was slowly closing. Obviously, neither of us had heard of Williams Syndrome before, and the questions started. We also visited another family in Sandford, their child also had Williams Syndrome, it was a very upsetting time for us all!

But still, we stayed positive and happy and got on with our lives. Family and friends rallied round when we needed it. Dennis and Sandra looked after Daz for us, so we could get away for a short break on occasion; usually to Newquay for a Fat Willy's Surf Shack T-shirt. We also got our first kitten together, I named her Splinter from the Ninja Turtle film.

Cheryl, now three months pregnant and Drew, had their wedding in June in Kewstoke; I was able to borrow Ernie Loving's white 190 Merc for the day with ribbons and everything, Cheryl and Drew hired a white Jag with a driver. I turned up in a nice shiny Merc with my mum and the bridesmaids' and it was a lovely day. About eighteen months previous, my dad had been laid off from Michael Fowler's as a lorry driver, he'd been there for years and years; on the day of my sister's wedding he got a job at BWOC, driving tankers', that made it a better day!

My twenty-first birthday was nearing, so when family members started asking what I wanted for my birthday, I just said, "why don't you all get together and buy me a good mountain bike." As far as I know this took place, and in July I was presented with a brand-new yellow/green bike. I was well chuffed, as I was right into keeping fit as well as keeping on top of the Ninjutsu. By now Traci and I had talked, and decided we wouldn't get married after all but stay engaged; deposits were lost and I was frowned upon for a while; but still we stayed happy.

For a weekend at the end of August, myself and three other Ninjas', Mike Cotterell, Rowland Phillips and Rich May, from "The No Respect Dojo," spent a full Saturday and Sunday training in Twickenham London, with Grandmaster, Masaaki Hatsumi from Japan, it was then I got my 1st Kyu belt.

Every day I'd get up nice and early and cycle to work, I'd cycle home for lunch to see the family and eat, I'd cycle back, then home again Monday to Friday every week; it was helpful, as Traci could have the car as often as she wanted.

On the afternoon of August the 30th, after leaving the flat to head back to work after lunch, things ended badly!

I was crossing a busy main road, with cars coming from both

directions; then it cleared from the left, and apparently the red car approaching from the right, was indicating to turn into the road I was coming from. As I started pedalling, and by now had started to enter the road, the little red car changed their mind and went straight on; hitting me so hard that they caused my right leg to bend the bike frame. I apparently flew far in the air, after bouncing off the windscreen and then landed head first in a heap on the road. The car at first sped off, but someone gave chase and stopped the woman, who at this time was in a state of panic.

Paramedics were quick to get there and they rushed me off to Weston General Hospital. Apparently, I flat lined for a minute or so but I guess I wouldn't know, so after revival they sent me to Frenchay Hospital in Bristol with severe head injuries. There, I underwent Brain Surgery for Subdural Haematoma (blood clot of the brain). Mum, Dad, Perry, Cheryl and Traci, were told that I was in a bad way, and had very little chance of survival, and if I did survive the op; there would be a very large chance I could be left handicap. After a successful operation performed by the late Brian Cummins, it was time for the waiting game. I was laid up for four weeks, the first week in a coma, then semi-conscious for the remainder; with only family and two of my best mates, Steve and Rich visiting me daily. I was un-recognisable as Steve and Rich have since informed me, it took them a while to find me in the ward, as I looked a mess and was covered in tubes.

After the first week, I finally started to wake from my deep sleep. I believe as Mum has informed me, my first words were in fact, "I've gotta fucking headache." I practically fell out of bed, and started downing water after pulling flowers from a vase; no one cared, they were happy I was awake at last. I stayed in a semi-conscious state for the last three weeks; any noises' or moves' I made whilst people were talking to me, were noted in a yellow book next to my bed.

Once all the piping was disconnected, they whisked me off in an ambulance back to Weston General, where I spent a further eight weeks.

It was like being in a hotel. I was treated like a god; family would sit with me all day bringing treats', friends', work colleagues' and people I barely knew would come and visit me. There were a few memorable moments', one being, the old retired age man in the bed opposite from me, I forget his name now, but he had a haulage company in Blackmore Somerset, and I used to sell him parts' for his lorry so I knew him. Well, this one day he went off his nut! He started pulling the tubes out of his hand, then the crazy old fool grabbed his catheter and started yanking on it. I was shouting for nurses and any other able person were shouting for nurses; then with blood squirting everywhere he started heading for my bed! I couldn't go anywhere, I was connected to tubes and had a catheter too. Thankfully, it didn't take long for help to arrive, but he started throwing nurses around, and was finally sedated before he made it to me. "Phew," they moved me then into a more placid wing round the corner, so that was nice.

Another memory being, and I still cringe when I think about it now, was my catheter removal day; whatever trolley I was holding when they pulled that tube, went long distance I can tell you!

Another funny and now laughable memory, was the fact that I was only allowed limited fluid at any time to drink. Well, my mates would all bring in a four pack of Coca Cola, more often than not, Chris Kitching would bring in a three litre bottle of Coke. I wasn't supposed to be drinking anymore than a couple of pints of hospital water per day, so once it was lights out at night time, I'd grab a can from the bedside cupboard and wait for that vital moment. You see, the guy two beds away from me, had a very loud cough, after a while you could practically set your watch for the times he coughed, as soon as the ten 0 five cough went, "Psst," I'd pull the ring off the can in one quick move; whilst trying not to spill the coke, as by now the can was also under the covers for extra silence. I now had a new power after my operation, and found that I could drink litres' of fizzy pop or water (the colder the better) very quickly, so it didn't take long to down all my coke thank's to coughey cougherson next door.

December came and it was time for me to leave. All the coke was gone, nurses' Shelley and Tina stood and waved goodbye and now could get back to normal, I did nothing but harass them both but it was all in good fun, and we're still friend's now.

Things were tough for a while once I was home, I wasn't allowed to drive for a year, my eyes were all over the place, I had trouble with distances and nearly got run over trying to cross roads on my own; I'd lost my sense of smell, and I was drinking anything up to twenty litres' of fizzy pop a week. I'd also lost a ton of weight, so I had the body of a fifteen year old boy, and I was getting constant headaches that no tablet was able to shift.

I had to try and focus my eyes as I was constantly seeing double, I had to learn who people were again and my little yellow book helped me put things together, I was also shown loads of photos of my past to remind me of things!

Nearly every night, many friends or family members would come to see us. On one of those nights, we had a flat full of friends, and one of them pulled out some pot from his pocket and asked if he could roll a spliff. Now, before my accident I only smoked cafe creme cigars myself, but not being a boring person, I agreed for him to have a smoke. So, Jamie lit his spliff and we all carried on chatting, he passed it to any people that also liked a toke and then he offered it to me! Sure, I may of had a puff in the past but only to show willing, so I took it from him and thought, why not I've died once already this year. After taking only a small drag, I coughed a little, then took drag two, by the third drag, the headache I'd had for the last few weeks had finally disappeared. So from that point, any time I had a bad headache, I'd ring Jamie and he'd come round for a smoke and my headache would go.

There wasn't things like there is now; "Had an accident at work, you can make a claim." I was in touch with a solicitor, but they basically told me, as no witnesses had come forward and I'd lost my memory immediately, that it could have ended up costing me hundreds and maybe thousands to get a claim. So I had a life changing experience and still suffer to this day with stress, headaches, no sense of smell, and I'm a financial mess. I didn't get a penny for my injuries!

As the year came to a close, it was Traci's turn for her twenty-first birthday, so Mum, Perry, Dad, Trish, Dennis, Sandra, Cheryl, Drew and I, went for a lovely carvery at The Catherine's Inn in Bleadon; it was also a celebration of me being home and surviving the accident. It was all so surreal, as our wedding day would've been on the 31st, the day after my accident so it wouldn't of taken place anyway. Dennis only lost a deposit but it could've been a lot worse.

It was whilst we were sat around the table enjoying the night, that

I mentioned to my Dad, "in my little yellow book that I read every day, you said you'd buy me that drum kit that I wanted so bad, if I come out of this coma." Well, I was out of the coma and then asked when I could have it.

The following Saturday, Cheryl, Dad and myself went to The Drum Store in Bristol, a shop I'd not been to for a while; after a five minute chat with the shop owner who remembered me from eight years before, went on to sell us, a brand new black Pearl Forum five piece kit, two cymbals, a set of hi-hats, a stool and a couple of pairs of sticks. He threw in a full set of cases for it all, a Pearl T-shirt, a cap and a key-ring and all for four hundred quid. We took it home and then all I had to do was put it together, and learn to play it again as often as I could!

Cheryl and Drew gave birth to their first baby, Abbie Fay Elkins a couple of days before Christmas; after what I'd just been through, it was a happy ending to the year!

So, through January I'd gained a new drum kit and I was able to pick up where I left off reasonably quick; I hadn't actually played the drums for about two years as it was, so after brain surgery as well, I surprised myself. My friends still came to visit often but best mates Steve, Rich, Nick and Reeves would be more often.

There was always talk of "Getting the Band Back Together," now I again had a drum kit we could look more into it. Reeves at this time, worked for an audio cassette winding company, he also worked with a young lad Barry Newman, who was a major Jimi Hendrix fan and a budding guitarist. We organised a weekend visit to the Castle Batch Village Hall for a rehearsal.

February 1992 and only four months after I'd come out of a coma, I was back behind a kit with my best mates, Steve, Nick, Reeves and now new rhythm guitarist Barry. Neither of us had done anything together for some time, although Nick and Steve had got together and written some lyrics and guitar riffs. To be fair, although it was only a trial run practice it went quite well, at first we called ourselves "Gigantic," doing only original songs and moving away from the mod covers band we once were. By April we'd gone into a studio with Brian Monk, at his new Horizon West Studio, to lay down our first four track demo, "The Gigantic EP." Nick was unable to be at the mixing night, as he and

Diane were busy with the birth of their daughter Paige. Shortly after the recording, we decided on a name change and became the X-Men.

I'd been out with the lads, for a night on the town one Saturday, and returned home about two AM on the Sunday. I climbed into bed and cuddled up to Traci, no sooner had I dropped off and the home phone started ringing, I leapt out of bed to answer it before it woke baby Darren, it was my sister, in tears, and saying she was coming to see me! It was three in the morning, what could she possibly want? I was worried, so we made a coffee and waited for Cheryl's arrival. About thirty minutes later she arrived, but she was pushing the pram, with three months old Abbie sleeping inside, I was worried that Drew had thrown her out. After a massive hug and another hot drink made, she informed us, that when we were young and going fossil hunting in Dundry with our grandad, and walks in the woods at Hutton a few years later; when they were playing hide and seek, he was actually being a paedophile to my eight to twelve years old sister. Oh My God, I couldn't believe what I was hearing, I was so angry, I just wanted to get my dad and go round to sort him out. After my sister calmed me down and Drew came and picked her up, the long process took place to get him nailed; he ended up with a two-year probation order and a fine, they should have castrated him! Thankfully he died years ago!

During March and April, Traci and I had a few too many differences, I was being a hard person to live with after suffering with my head injuries, I was bad tempered and arguing constantly; although it was advised to me that I shouldn't drink alcohol, it seemed to be the only thing that kept me going, as well as the occasional spliff to ease my headaches'. We split, I moved out and found a cheap bedsit on the outskirts of town for thirty-five quid a week, it was ok, but a bit full once my drums were in there. In April, I also swapped my car with Chris Kitching again, but this time for a two door black, mark three 1600 Escort. I finally said goodbye to the Vespa, as I had nowhere to keep it and my old school mate Steve Coombes bought it from me. I delivered it to him and put it in the front room of his house.

I did start seeing Debbie Newbury, who I worked with at WSM Motors for a couple of months'. Here's another mad story. Debbie shared her flat with a friend, who was dating Danny Murphy, the flat under

Debbie's, was shared by Dave Chamberlain and Kevin Hood. One night we were all sat in Debbie's flat and someone asked what was up in the attic? They didn't know as they'd never looked, so Dave went and got some step-ladders and he took a look. He returned, with a dust covered box full of paperwork, claiming that he, (who wrote it all) Jonny Rainbow, was indeed responsible for Helen Fleet's murder in Weston Woods, a few years before. We immediately phoned the police, and to be fair they did turn up quite quick, they had a scan, left the flat with the box and we never heard anymore about it. Soon after, I called it a day with Deb's.

I had to quit Ninjutsu as my head was unable to cope with it. That was typical, I'd just got a high grade and the week after was put in hospital. It didn't matter by now though, I was back in a band with my best mates, got my own pad and a new car.

In June, the X-Men were booked to play in good old Charlie Browns for our first gig. Rehearsals continued hard and fast, people were happy that we were again working together, and we were constantly being asked what covers we were doing? Well, none was our response; this didn't go down too well, so we decided we would do just one cover. We weren't going to pull any of the old favourites' we once did out of the bag, that's like going backwards; so for a laugh, we prepared "Deeply Dippy" by Right Said Fred. It certainly was a surprise for everyone, it was our first gig in a couple of years and sounded great, with a huge happy audience. We even managed to source Alan and his huge PA again, so we've got that on tape!

It was during July, that all the staff at WSM Motors were informed, that by the end of August, the Weston depot will be closing down. This was new, I'd never been laid off before! It was all done properly and we were all issued our redundancy cheques. I was happy with that, as I'd not long turned twenty-two and I was about to enjoy living a life of work free leisure, with just over a grand in the bank. I'd never heard of things like, "four weeks lieu pay," it turned out, that it meant I wasn't able to make a claim for the dole for four weeks, by the time I'd found out what that meant, half the money was gone. I'd already been to London, for a day out with a bunch of mates, Chris Kitching, Mark "Howold" Steer, Phil Manville and Nathan Lister, we caused havoc in Harrods and got thrown out, as Mark had pressed the emergency stop on the escalators. I got grabbed and dragged by security, in a Virgin music store for pinching a CD, I sorted that and left pretty sharp-ish and blew about a hundred and fifty quid all day. I also went to Newport for a day of fun and Go-kart racing with another group of mates, Lee Hawkins, Jonathon Old, Chris Fry and Nathon Lister, again we got kicked out of just about everywhere we went that day, but we still made it memorable and Lee was a pro kart driver so he won.

Darren Gibbs married Lisa at the end of August, and conveniently the church was right opposite my bedsit; so I got to see all my old Psychobilly mates and a few old-school mates' too.

By mid-September the money was nearly gone, I'd paid my rent for the month and had food in the cupboards and fridge. My car insurance and tax was about to run out, the car had also had a front tyre blow out so I couldn't drive it anyway. It was about three weeks after being laid off, that the money was almost gone and now I was starting to worry a bit. I still had a week before I could claim dole and then I still had to wait for the claim to go through. As I was popping into Charlie Browns now and again, for the odd pint; I decided to ask for help. Darren (ex-Charlie's DJ and Sister's ex) was now the manager of the establishment, and thankfully for me he still looked at me like I was his younger brother, so he let me work a couple of nights a week, behind the bar for a few quid. This was awesome, but it also caused a few problems. You see, even if I wasn't due to work, I'd sit in the pub all day anyway drinking and on the weekends, Darren would shove twenty quid in my hand and send me off clubbing so I didn't miss out.

It was ladies pool night on Tuesdays', I was needed that night as it was always busy; Pam always worked the Tuesday and sometimes weekend shifts with me. Pam's other half was Gorilla, one of Weston's well known bad boys. On one Saturday night whilst pulling pints with Pam behind the bar; I needed to pass her, so I squeezed past, but Gorilla being the other side of the bar didn't like that move. He grabbed hold of me, pulled me towards him and head butted me, I saw it coming so was able to back off a little, he only caught my chin, it still hurt and I backed off big time. He just wanted to pull me apart, he then made his way towards the bar entrance to get me, Leigh stood in his way and he knocked him straight out! By this time my own Clark Kent, Darren, had heard the commotion from his office and came dashing out, fair play, he kept Gorilla calm, he shouted for me to have the rest of the night off and get the hell out of there! I was gone like a shot! I got a sober apology a few weeks later and I was happy with that. I'd also become friends with the bouncers at Mr B's, Burt Skidmore and Darren Bevan as well as the owner Samir, by now I had new nightclub drinking buddies too, Jason Binning, Wayne Nelson and Chris Jessop as well as many others and things weren't too bad.

But then I received news, Traci had gone on a date to Longleat Safari Park, with Daz and one of my oldest mates. Of course I wasn't at all happy with that, I myself am not a fan of breaking the bro code. When I found out that a mate was trying to get in there, I turned nuts! I wasn't allowed to see Daz as I'd become an angry young man, I was drinking a lot, and to be fair, glad I never bumped into my so-called mate!

For a month or so, I basically became a stoned, alcoholic, speed freak, that would spend every night fighting with someone, whether it was inside or outside Charlie Browns, or outside the clubs on weekends'. I took a different girl back to that bedsit every time I went out, even Hugh Heffner would be proud. There was Alexandra, she worked at Next in Dolphin Square, we dated for a month, Louise, Caragh from Cheddar, who I did date for a month or so; Alison, Lisa, Tina, Katie, Laura, Hannah, Natisha, Cindy, Chantelle and a few more. I'm just glad Jeremy Kyle wasn't about then, I would of probably ended up as a regular on his show. Oh, I forgot about, I think it was Paula, my Quadrophenia moment behind Olympia arcade, a lane of rubbish one late drunken night.

I did start seeing one of the boy racer's girlfriend's, Liz, she'd often pop round, and eventually got a flat two doors down from mine, so we became friends with benefits and she ended it with her boyfriend. Si and I weren't great mates back then and we hadn't known each other long; but years later and we're great mates now, I haven't seen Liz for years.

Every day I'd sit in Charlie's, and turn to see who'd walked through the door every time it opened, just hoping that it may be Traci and Daz. By now I'd stopped shaving, I was clean but I didn't look too healthy, I drank more than I ate, I was smoking pot and I was snorting a line or two of speed daily. It was around this time I also found poetry and started writing dark poems, they were all sad and depressing about sex, drugs, alcohol and death.

I was sat at the bar in Charlie's one afternoon, looking like a hobo and having my usual daily intake of Newcastle Brown Ale and the door went; I turned, and to my surprise it was my two-year-old boy Daz, I'd not seen him for about a month. Traci came over and said I looked a mess and took me straight to McDonalds as I needed to eat, then she took me back to her flat, so I could have a bath and shave. We gave it another go, and I was thankful to her for getting me out of the rut I was in.

We were now a family again. I managed to get my car moved from the Bedsit to Milton in our back garden, but as I was still unemployed I couldn't afford to drive it; Traci had bought a mark three Escort after we split, so we did have transport. I kept the bedsit though just in case, even though we were working it out, I'd still had freedom and wasn't sure what I wanted in life at that stage!

Drew, had changed his job from the off licence trade, to be an estate agent instead; so in May, he offered us a huge first floor flat in Orchard Street, in Weston's town centre. We moved in, I sold my Escort for a hundred quid as we needed money, now all I had to do was find a job. For a couple of days, I attempted to sell double glazing in a supermarket doorway, until the entire staff at the Job Centre decided to go for lunch at Asda; I was still claiming, so I got in the car and never looked back! In February, I landed myself a job with Severn Cabinets, boy racer mate Si Hooper worked there so that was good. My first day was spent at the NEC in Birmingham, Ardene Stoneman, Jim Griffiths and myself, spent the day erecting a stall for a show; otherwise I would help make and deliver bedroom furniture; that was only four weeks work! So I went across the road to Systems furniture, this time making and delivering office furniture, with other mates Steve Parker and Tony Steele, again this job ended four weeks later, as every day was becoming a fourteen-hour day, and for very little money. Whilst I was at Severn Cabinets, I was able to buy a C reg Vespa 125 from Jim, for two hundred quid and could pay him anything up to fifty quid a week. I got the scoot after the final payment, that was great but I'd been laid off before I'd finished the payments, for a couple of weeks, I had to walk daily for an hour, just to get to Systems Furniture and an hour back, creating sixteen-hour days. It killed me for a bit, but once the purchase was made there was no more need for walking.

Traci had got her first council flat by May, so we moved out to Worle and I got rid of the bedsit. At the same time I was asked by Pentagon Mercedes Benz in Weston, if I'd like to do a months work. They'd just purchased a mass of stock that needed putting away and stock controlled. As that had been my last proper post and also for Mercedes, I was the man for the job. I started immediately, and by June I was properly employed as a Parts Sales Executive!

"Bad Manners" were live at Stars night club in June, so I took Traci to that and we queued up after for half an hour, just to get Buster's autograph.

The X-Men were still rehearsing and had played a couple of venues, but by August and after several band disputes, again we came to an end.

During September a blue Vauxhall Cavalier was selling at my work place, a part exchange for only three-hundred and fifty notes. I snapped it up, my first automatic car, the first time I owned a car with power steering, low mileage and very clean as there had only been one old man owner from new. I sold the Vespa to a work mate of Mark Coombes for two hundred quid. I was on the move once again, as the end of September saw me walking away from Traci; but this time was the very last time!

With Dad and Pop Day at Cheryl and Drew's wedding

Nanny Day with her great grandson Daz

CHAPTER 3

SLOW DOWN!

S eptember 93 and I was on my own again. With my David Banner bag and only my clothes with me, I moved in with Kerry, as he had a not bad sized sea view flat-let. He was a good mate, and his brother Jonny lived in the next door flat. My drums', went to Cheryl and Drew's new bought house in town; as there was plenty of room and I hadn't used it for a bit. I bumped into Sarah one night, a friend from old and I walked her home as she lived near Kerry. We had a quick stop, in the public toilets' on Marine lake promenade, but not for a wee. We had some naughty quick fun on the floor of a dark and dingy toilet and then continued on our way.

During a night out, with the Mercedes lot in Neptune's Nook, and also a few of the WSM Motors Bristol, and ex-WSM Motors Weston staff, I got friendly with Julia from the Bristol depot. From that night on, we started seeing each other as often as we could, but it wasn't easy as she was married and going through a separation. A couple of nights a week, I'd drive to Bristol and meet her on Hotwells Road by The SS Great Britain, she'd be in her little mini and she'd hop in my car, then we'd spend about two hours having some fun on the Down's. We had to keep it quiet from all the other staff, so I became Tom Davies and had to put on a silly voice when phoning her at work daily. She had the final split from her husband and moved in with her parents in Kingswood. I did a stock check, at the WSM Motors Yeovil depot one weekend, I earned some great money, so I treated Julia to a weekend away in Weymouth. We had a great time and spent most of it in bed as far as I remember. It was whilst on this break, I decided I'd have a complete turn around and move to Bristol or Bath, so we could be together properly. I applied for jobs that way, and landed a job with BMW in Bath, to start two weeks later.

I was about to start a new chapter, but realised it was all going too fast; as did Julia and she ended the relationship. I didn't take the job in Bath so I stayed single at Kerry's.

On a night out with mates in November, I bumped into a female friend I'd not seen for a while, Louisa. The last time I'd seen her she was living with Alan, but since had split with him and was then single, so the charm went on and we started dating! Within a couple of days, I moved in with her above the laundrette in Baker Street Weston; her dad and her uncle both owned the laundrette so rent was cheap!

We'd not long been together, when late one night, there was someone outside kicking the front door in. I leapt off the sofa and ran downstairs, to find a drunk Alan wanting to kick my head in for dating his ex-bird. I'd known Alan for some years as he went to school with Traci, I tried talking to him first but then he threw a punch. After a roll around in the road and a few small head-butts and punches, we got up and shook hands and off he went!

On a Sunday evening in early December, my dad had been in touch as he was visiting his dad, my pop in Weston Hospital. Pop had been suffering with cancer for a while but at this time he'd become a lot worse. We went along and it was very sad to see, that Pop, someone who had been there through my youth, could barely talk, just cough and spit. We gave our love and I kissed his forehead; we left and we went for a drink to discuss how sad it all was.

I was sat in my office at work the following day, when a huge BWOC tanker rolled into our car park; I looked to see it was my dad and straight away I knew it wasn't going to be good news! I was right, Dad had come to inform me that Pop had passed away during the night. After a week of things being sorted, Pop was laid to rest at a big service in Cheddar on the 16th of December. Rest in Peace Pop!

We had a lovely Christmas spent at Lou's mum and dads big house by Worlebury golf course, her two younger twin sisters were also there.

On February the 10th, I gave Lou a kiss goodbye and went off to work all suited and booted. Mr Perry's Mercedes, needed collecting from Ashcott as it was due a service, and no one was free to go and collect it. Off I went, in the company 190D, even though it was early, I got through the morning traffic with no trouble, I soon arrived at Mr Perry's office and we swapped cars. I started my journey home, now in a two year old J reg 230E. After crossing the motorway bridge, I found the M5 was grid-locked and knowing the car had to be back as soon as possible; I thought otherwise and decided to go back via the A38 from Bridgwater. It was going great for the first three miles; I was in a turbo fast car and the roads were clear. I floored it down a long straight reaching speeds of eighty to ninety mph, it was only a sixty limit, but there were no speed cameras in those days.

As I was approaching the end of the long straight, I eased off the gas as the road had a slight bend to the left. Still travelling at about eighty mph, I hit black ice right on the bend. The brakes weren't working now and I was already crossing to the right-hand lane, panic had set in; as I now seemed to be speeding up and heading direct for a Ford Sierra coming towards me. I was desperately hitting the brakes and steering the car in all directions to avoid the oncoming car. The car started spinning, then "BANG!" As the Merc span; the rear end had hit the other car; causing the Merc to start the rolling process. Three times it rolled, from side to side and finally stopped on it's passenger side down, with the non-existent rear end in the trees.

The engine was still roaring, until it just went crack and stopped. I was now passenger side down, with me dangling like a raggy doll looking up at the sky. I'd done some damage to my right arm and couldn't lift the door to get out; I wore a sovereign on my left middle finger and during the roll, my hand must of smashed against the gear stick, causing it to cut into my finger. By now I was yelling; "Help, Help!" Suddenly, the door flew open, and a passing body builder pulled me out the car; he then laid me down. By this time, there was traffic queued both ways and debris spread everywhere.

I was confused and in shock, people came from all the cars to help where they could; one helpful off duty nurse did the necessary procedures that needed to be done and made me comfortable. My neck really started to hurt by this time, all I could see standing over me, was a woman screaming, that I could of killed her, her friend and her little girl. Thankfully, all three of them were ok, just shook up. I however, had blood pouring from my middle finger, a right arm I couldn't move and a neck that felt broken. The ambulance came and whisked me off to Taunton Hospital, where I spent the best part of five hours. I had a badly bruised right arm, I had to have my ring cut off my finger and I had a bad case of whiplash!

I was picked up by the service manager Gary, and as far as I remember we didn't speak for the entire trip home.

I wasn't charged with anything for that accident, but I did spend the next month having Physiotherapy on my neck twice a week. The boss at work was just glad that I'd survived and he gave me a warning!

As we entered March, I started having a fling with Trudy; naughty I know but this is how I rolled now! Within a couple of days Louisa found out and she kicked me out, so I moved in with Trudy by April. That was a fun relationship while it lasted! You see, I still smoked the weed in the evenings at this point; her Grandad and landlord of her flat was a copper, he also had the habit of letting himself in when he wanted. I nearly got caught on more than one occasion! So I started going out more often, until then we'd spent all our time together, except when we were at work of course. A change was noticed and she soon got fed up with that and kicked me out by the end of May!

Auntie Val by this time, had split with Uncle Barry and moved from Cheddar to Weston, she eventually met Graham who was a property owner. I got on the phone to him and a bedsit was sorted for me, it was a tiny place but it did me. I couldn't fit my drums in the room, there was a bed, a sofa, a small black and white tele, a small cupboard, a tiny chest for my clothes', a sink, a fridge, a cooker, a record player and my record collection, there was barely any room left!

I was out on a Friday night and I ended my night up Hobbits Nightclub. I left in the early hours with Karen; I'd not seen Karen for a few years, and we'd dated for a few weeks back in the late 80's, as she too had a scooter, and she was in The 13th Valley Scooter Club. We went back to her flat in Clifton Road, and to be honest, she looked amazing, in her Dr Martens and checked skirt. We had a fun night and in the morning, I gave her a kiss and left. I said I'd ring her and meet her later that night. Well, on the Saturday, Cheryl and Drew were re-newing their marriage vows'. I planned to go out and meet Karen, later at Hobbits. That didn't happen though! After a great day and a big wedding, a night do was organised at Dance Scene. A great night was had and I left with Kate, one of Cheryl's dancing friends. We weren't really a couple but we saw each other a few times'.

They say it comes in threes, well here's the proof!

Part one.

Saturday June the 2nd and I was out on the town with my pals and I took a fancy to a girl about my age, she was with her mate and looking over so I made my move. I found out her name was Debbie, I bought her a drink and we spent the last few hours of the night talking and snogging. When the clubs kicked out, she got straight in a taxi and waved goodbye, I was gutted, we'd spent the best part of two hours getting friendly up Mr B's and there she was, gone!

Me in my drunken state and remembering that she mentioned she lived in Winscombe, about eight miles outside Weston, like a fool I thought to myself, "Winscombe's only a small place and just down the road, I'm gonna go and find her." Big mistake; I jumped in the car and became the person I hate and drunk drove to Winscombe. No problem getting there, but it was then I realised it was a bigger village than I first thought and I'm drunk and shouldn't be driving the car. So I immediately turned around and made my way home. As soon as you leave Winscombe, you enter a mile long straight, with a slight left hand upward bend, I was in an automatic, easy to drive Cavalier and I fell asleep! Not taking the slight bend, I went off road, over a mound, across a back lane, bottoming the car out at this point and waking me up. I was grabbing the wheel tight and bursting through trees, until coming to a very quick stop after hitting and knocking down a big metal farm gate.

I jumped out the car, dressed like someone from Miami Vice with my White Chino trousers, a cream shirt and espadrilles on my feet, I realised with both the front wheels pointing horizontally, that the car was going nowhere! So now, I was about seven miles from home with no way back! I walked to nearby Banwell, phoned a taxi and went home! Sorry Mr cab driver, I was about eighty pence short of the fare, so I dumped a hand full of change in his hand and ran!

The next day, I lied to Mum and one of my best friends Chris, and told them my car was pinched, I went to the police station and told them the same, they knew where it was; so I was able to go and collect it with Chris. After seeing how bad the damage really was, that car wasn't going anywhere without a crane. Chris was the man, and got on the phone to Dave Harris who turned up, took it away and stored it at his work unit until the insurance was sorted. Sorry Mum, Chris and Dave!

Part two.

On Thursday the 8th of June and the end of my working day was close, I finished at five. Well, at ten to five, my boss Gary asked me to go and pick up a car from the tyre depot. Even though Winterstoke Tyres was only about fifty yards away, I wasn't happy about that request, I was about to finish work and just wanted to go home as I was meeting up with Debbie from Winscombe.

After a bit of moaning I quickly scuttled off, out the yard to pick up the car. It turned out to be a brand-new, very, very expensive car, it had just had new alloy wheels fitted, and unbeknown to me the loose steel wheels were now in the boot! It was five o'clock on the dot, so traffic was absolutely manic. I was also pulling out on to a very busy dual carriageway, the car was automatic, so no problem for a quick pull off. There was a gap, so I hit the gas and was gone, immediately having to cross into the right-hand lane, to enable myself to go round the loop road, get back on the opposite dual carriageway and then round a big roundabout with a sharp left, back into work. It was all so quick, I didn't even notice the trip took place!; I dropped the car in the workshop, said goodbye and walked home. I spent that evening with Debbie; she drove to me as I no longer had a car, it was the first time I'd seen her since we first met, so it was really only for a night of passion and then she went home.

Eight thirty the next morning on arrival to work, I was confronted by Gary and he was wearing the face of a man on a mission. Before I could even enter my office and make my first coffee, he led me out through to the workshop, at the same time, asking me a ton of questions to do with picking the Merc up the night before. I was still confused, we entered the workshop, to see a massive dent in the rear side of the brand-new Merc! Gary pointed to it and informed me that I was responsible for the damage. What had in fact happened, was when I was going round the bend and roundabout at a fast pace, it sent the tyre-less steel wheels flying around in the boot; causing there to be a wheel shaped dent in the panel work! All the lads at Winterstoke Tyres said the same thing, that I'd driven out of there like a maniac. Gary then told me that Michael would be coming down from the Head Office in Aylesbury as he needed a word, I'm not stupid (well not totally) and knew that I was about to lose my job, and I did on the 9th, as this and Mr Perry's 230E was enough damaged caused!

On Friday the 15th of June and feeling down, I was out on the town for a usual Friday night session, I'd also found out by this time, that Debbie whom I'd only seen once since I met her, actually had a boyfriend. I guess as I'd never been to her house I would never of known!

I was dancing away, being my usual helping the bouncers out self and I bumped into the recent ex-Trudy, by the end of the night we went back to her flat and got on it in the bedroom. In the early hours of the morning, through squinted eyes and facing the big window, I spotted under the ledge; nicely laid out on the carpet, a perfectly neat poo! Suddenly I was wide awake, I looked at Trudy fast asleep, or was she? I looked at the poo, I looked at Trudy again, I looked at the poo and now I was starting to sweat. What if she wakes up, how the hell am I going to explain this? I quietly slid out the bed and crouched by the poo; I picked it up between my finger and thumb from the centre; as I raised it, both ends sagged, it then looked like a gone off croissant! Now it was getting it from the bedroom to the toilet, and being careful not to wake Trudy! Or worse still before I drop it in the wrong place. It was a tricky manoeuvre, but I did splosh it in the bog in time! I scrubbed my fingers and crept back into bed, after spraying some perfume around the carpet. We woke a bit later, had some more fun and off I went! Nothing more was ever said, and to be fair, it could've been her poo!

So, within two weeks, I'd written my car off whilst drink driving, and lost my job for rough driving, really, how much worse could things get?

Well, I'll tell you how bad things got!

Part 3.

On Saturday the 16th of June and again out on the Newcastle Brown Ale, the night came to a close and I was stood outside Mr B's, chatting with a great mate Andy Griffiths. Suddenly, Debbie appeared, she wanted to have a chat. After repeatedly stating that we never really worked, I grabbed her hand anyway and we walked. I was telling her to just get in a taxi and go home, as our relationship had been a nightmare from the start! She was adamant that it was over with her boyfriend, so we made our way back to my bedsit. We had our safe fun, and in the morning, we walked hand in hand down Locking Road like a pair of love sick children, we talked about our next move, and she arranged for someone to come and pick her up. As her car was apparently off the road, I sorted it with a good boy racer mate Steve Brookes, to drop me in Winscombe later that afternoon.

On arrival, I knocked on her door but no one was home, I waited for about twenty minutes, then walked down the road to her friend Lisa's house. Lisa informed me that Debbie's son was at his dad's so she may have gone out. At this time I started thinking things weren't quite right, she'd told me her car, was broken down on the drive only that morning; yet there were no cars on the drive when I got there. Knowing the last bus from Winscombe back to Weston was at a certain time, I left Lisa's house and made my way back to Debbie's for one last try before I got on the bus. As I approached her house, I could now see there were four cars on the drive, my immediate thought was, her boyfriend who she said she'd split with, may be in the house with a gang of his mates, waiting to beat me up; so I walked on by and headed for the bus stop. I checked the times and walked to the nearby phone box to give her a ring, I told her, "she'd taken the piss out of me for one last time and to not bother me again!" She answered and got all; "Oh Tim please don't go, I'll meet you at the bus stop before you get the bus."

I sat on the wall and patiently waited, to be honest, I was preparing myself for a one man battle with a gang of blokes. About ten minutes later, and literally five minutes until the bus was due; a police car screeched up and two cops jumped out, they said my full name, the cuffs were slapped on and I was bundled into the back of their car. I was being arrested for an alleged rape!

Sunday I was arrested, Monday I was charged, and Tuesday I faced the judge, my friends and family were there for me, as they all knew this wasn't me. Perry's mum had also passed away the same day I was charged.

My great auntie and uncle lived in Whitchurch, on the outskirts of Bristol, I was able to spend my six weeks on remand with them rather than Horfield. Mum, Perry, Cheryl, Drew and occasionally my boy Daz, my best mates Rich, Steve, Nick and Barry, from the X-Men would regularly visit me, as would Trudy and I'd meet with my ex-Louisa most day times too, as she worked in Bristol. She'd treat me to dinner, and then leave me with enough money, for Newcastle Brown to help me sleep at night. Trudy came from Winscombe, and her mum Kerry still lived there at this time; Kerry would ring me to keep me posted on what Debbie was up to, like wearing mini skirts and being happy with her boyfriend; hardly the actions of a rape victim! The cops also had my filo-fax, don't laugh, yes I had a filo-fax; if you remember I also dressed like Miami Vice man too!

Anyhoo, the filo-fax had every name and number, of the last few years of sexual conquests I'd had, so they got in touch with them all, and thankfully they all said the same thing, "Tim didn't do it!"

I had to sign on at the cop shop every day in the centre of Knoll West, that was easy enough but I wore a lot of bling and it was such a hot summer I looked Caribbean! Walking through Knoll on a daily basis, I got to know where the dodgy families and houses were! Every day I'd always get dogged up by one bunch, but one afternoon I noticed they weren't there. I continued walking, but this time a bit more relaxed than usual, then suddenly I heard, "GET HIM," coming from behind me, I turn to see about twelve kids coming at me, from six to twenty-years old.

I was fast on my feet and I was gone, only to get rugby tackled by a younger lad, the rest just joined in. After thinking I've got to do something quick, I gained all my strength and leapt up like a super hero doing the chicken dance, I was punching kids but they could've killed me. After running to the cop shop and begging for a lift back to no avail, I sat and waited until they got bored and went; the police wouldn't take me home but they did escort me just in case.

During my six-week ban from Weston, Banwell and Winscombe,

I turned twenty-four. My sister to my surprise, had gone to the courts with my dad, and they'd got my ban lifted for one day and night until midnight. On the 14th of July, Cheryl and Dad picked me up and drove us to Cheddar. After turning into Westacre Road, where my nan lived, it was clear that a surprise party was set up for Dad and I. There were bright green, and yellow paper signs stapled to the telegraph poles, with Happy 50th Birthday Denis and Happy 24th Tim in big letters, all the way down the road. Dad's birthday was the day after mine, so it was easy to do it as one party. Plenty of family members' and best friends Rich and Rachael Southcombe were there, they'd also had cakes made for us, and I made it back to Whitchurch by midnight!

I also went for a nice picnic with Mum, Perry, Cheryl, Drew and the kids at Ashton Court, but my sister let me down on that day. Next to where we were picnicking was a group of boy and girl racers, as I'd not had any fun for a few weeks, I thought I might go and show my presence, well thanks to Cheryl that wasn't going to happen; as she saw what I was up to, she threw her arm round me and acted like my girlfriend. So I turned around and went back to the family instead. Uncle Stan once treated me to a day trip on the SS Great Britain and a boat trip up the canal, that was nice.

Auntie Eileen and Uncle Stan's son and his wife Stuart and Cherie, are sound engineers, with their own PA sound system and they were always in charge of the sounds at The Ashton Court Festival. That year, Auntie Eileen and Uncle Stan gave me a lift to Ashton Court, as I was spending the afternoon with a bunch of mates I'd been in touch with. Finding them was another story, a couple of thousand bodies' and I was looking for eight people. After climbing up on Stuart and Cherie's sound deck, I finally spotted them! They had cans of drinks so I was happy, and with a bunch of mates, a couple I'd spent a lot of time with over the last ten years, like Rich Lewis and Kerry Stark, Colette Chambers who I went to school with, and Dean Harvey, who was a known scooterist, I don't remember who the other four were!

It was one mad rush at six o'clock, I was on curfew and had to be back in Whitchurch by seven, I said my goodbyes and ran! No one was helpful outside the gates, I'd had a great day, but was now worried that I wasn't going to get back in time and then find I'm going to Horfield

Prison tomorrow anyway! I managed to flag down a taxi and that cost me eleven quid, luckily, I had fifteen on me and walked through the door at five past seven. I didn't have a mobile phone, so I couldn't ring ahead to my auntie, who was pacing up and down the hall way when I wasn't home by seven. It was like being twelve all over again!

My hearing day arrived early September, Mum and Perry brought me a suit up and took me to Weston Magistrates Court, my first visit in four years, to be told by my solicitor that Debbie had indeed dropped the case and the CPS had also thrown it out. I could have gone on and sued her, but I just wanted this chapter of my life to end!

I was back and things needed to change! I moved back into the bedsit that by now had a new door fitted, as the police had wrecked the last one. Whilst on Her Majesty's holiday, a female friend Louise (not Louisa), had rung my mum for Auntie Eileen's number and got in touch with me; we stayed in contact all the time I was away. Within four hours of being back in my bedsit, Louise came round and we didn't leave the bed, apart from to go to the toilet or to shower for three days, life was good again!

I'd told Graham that I had to move from the bedsit and wanted something bigger; a nice sized flat-let became available, in a nice area of Weston and I took it. At the same time, Mum and Perry's good friend's Sue and Wayne, offered me a job working in a freezer store in Portbury, I took the job and started in October. Slowly things were becoming better! Four weeks into working in the minus twenty-six freezer, picking the stock with my battery operated pallet truck; I had a black out and was found flumped upon box's of fries. After being carried out and warmed up I came too! I phoned my doctor who at the time was always there as I'd not long had brain surgery, he asked me to go straight to him; so a work mate, Lee Mcdowell drove me home and to the doctors. I was informed, that working in such a cold environment was shrinking my skin, apparently my head was still healing, even three years later, so I was signed off sick and not to go back to that job!

Entering November and jobless, I was passing on foot one day a Janitorial shop, a business a friend I went to school with Jamie owned. I popped in to say hi and tell him about my recent dilemma; to which he offered me a job as a sales rep, it was fun, but I only did it for a couple of weeks as I wasn't making too much out of it. I did however work and become friends with Marcus, as well as dating Kelly for a couple of weeks, I'd chatted her up in the hospital after trying to make a sale, as by now the relationship with Louise was over and it was only for a couple of weeks of fun anyway. I was on the sick, living in a new flat, with no car, no scooter, and not knowing where to go from here. With what had just happened to me, I was in a bit of a mess if truth be told! I'd had the brief relationship with Kelly, and I dated Debbie's friend Jenny, after a night out and bumping into Debbie who I worked at WSM Motors with. We only dated for a couple of weeks. I caught up with old mate brother's, Kerry and Jonnie, who still lived next door to Kerry and we'd hit the town on a regular basis; as well as sitting in one of our un-employed flats, getting stoned and pissed on cheap Tesco stripey cider.

In-Shops, was a popular coffee drinking place and on occasion, we'd sit and drink Louis and Andreas's coffee all day, served by another great mate Andy Hudson. Kerry and Jonnie's older brother Richard, worked on a handbag stall, with an older than me chick Nadine, I'd often look over and catch her checking me out. Her best mate happened to be Dora, the sister of Louis and Andreas, well, one day she came over to me with a hot drink and said, "Tim can you pop this over to Nadine for me please?" I obliged and spent that night and six other nights, with a thirty five year old nymph; I was a mear twenty-four and was in heaven. That didn't last long unfortunately, as her ex-husband came back on the scene.

Still in November, we were sat at Jonnie's flat one night, that he shared with his sister Katie; Katie and I had slept together once before, but that was just so I could rub it in her ex-blokes face, as he was the guy who grassed me up in the late 80's for splitting his lip. There was a friend of Katie's there too, Mel her name was, I got chatting and flirting and before we knew it we'd hit it off straight away!

I had a night out at the Winter Gardens later that month, with just about all the skinheads' that I was fighting with ten years before, we skanked the night away to "Buster Bloodvessel" and "Bad Manners," it was another great Manners gig.

At the start of the year, I gave up my flat-let as I was never there, so I moved in with Mel. Cheryl and Drew were moving around the same time, so my drums had to come with me to Mel's. It was a tiny flat so it took up a lot of space and it wasn't even set up. My pot dealer was just down the road, and Mel worked in Huckleby's, a small coffee shop next door to the Playhouse in Weston High Street. I made some new mates, but admittedly, I also saw some things I never want to see again. Like an old scooter buddy I'd not seen for some years, living in a crack den, smacked up and looking ill and he'd become a stealing druggie, it was so sad to see.

We were offered a newborn kitten, so we named her Chi and she was lush. As I wasn't working I spent loads of time loving that cat.

By March 95, after searching for work, I finally landed myself a part time job pulling pints at The London Inn, for Ken, Jon and Gregg Dudd; as a grave yard shift barman, right next door to Huckleby's. Also in March, Mel and I got a coach to Plymouth for her sisters wedding. In April, Rich Southcombe, Steve Wilkinson and myself went to Devizes in the Southcombe Sooty van; to see blues legend's Nine Below Zero, and the gig was awesome as they always are. After the show, I got the lads to chat to the bouncers; I snuck around the back and headed for the changing rooms. I didn't even knock, I just walked straight in and there they all were, Dennis Greaves in his underpants, and with a grin on his face, in his Cockney accent says, "Alright son, autograph yes." Me grinning like a Cheshire cat replies, "Yes Please," then as casual but as quick as you like, he tore a small empty page from his diary, he asked my name and then scribbled, "To Tim all the best" and signed it, the other three lads were quick to sign too and then I was gone! I passed the confused looking bouncers and gave them a cheeky nod and grin, then I headed for the lads, proudly waving my signed piece of paper. "How the hell did you manage that?" was the response I got. I didn't care, whilst I was on remand, Nine Below Zero played in Clevedon, but I couldn't go for obvious reasons. That night there was a big football game on, so the band sat in the pub before the gig watching the game, with Rich, Nick and Steve. I was well jealous! I've followed this band since they performed, on the first episode of the Young One's, playing their classic Eleven plus Eleven in 1982.

At the beginning of May, and having a hundred quid or so hidden away for emergencies, I decided I needed transport! I really needed to get a full-time different job with better money! It was around this time, that I bumped into a mate Cavey, and he told me that his brother Ardene, whom I worked with at Severn Cabinets, had a PX Vespa that had been sat in their garden for a year gathering rust. I was offered it for fifty quid and I couldn't get there quick enough, I pushed the very rusty and holey scooter to my lock-up a few miles away, and stripped it down to salvage what I could. The piston was blown and seized, the floor panels were full of holes, so it was nowhere near rideable.

I was with Mark Coombes one night, and we went to visit his brother Steve. Steve was very sick and he also suffered with MS, Steve turned to me and said, I could buy the Vespa back that I'd previously sold him for fifty quid. To be fair he'd not actually touched it, since I dropped it there a year or so before. Mark and I dismantled it, put it in Marks car and dropped it at my lock up with the other scooter.

During May and June, I'd walk about four miles each way to my garage and back on my days off. Once there, I'd clean, sand down, re-spray and rebuild, two scooters into one half decent scoot. I achieved this, as well as visiting Ray Pangs Gym in Whitecross Road three days a week, where I became great friends with John Lees, and I'd also swim twice a week.

By July, Mel and I had moved to a bigger flat in Milton, right next door to George Hardwick Motorcycles, the biggest and longest going motorcycle MoT garage in Weston. I got the scooter back to our new pad with the van we used to move, so I could do the finishing touches at home. Barry Newman from the X-Men, married Nick Cavill's sister Rachel, at St Peters Church. That was handy as it was just around the corner from my flat, the evening do was at Westland's Football Club and a very entertaining night was had. By the end of the night, newly wed Baz and myself were topless, and were synchronized dancing with the DJ, to Whigfield's hit, "Saturday Night."

Unfortunately, due to our new flat being on the main road wasn't good. Chi had got out one afternoon and was left for dead, I found her when I got home from work one night. Thanks to a passing car, we were able to get her to the vet, but unfortunately she didn't make it; we were very upset for weeks!

I still worked in The London, but our relationship had seemed to change after the move and my mood wasn't the best after losing Chi. Working the afternoon shift, I got to meet a lot of different people: office workers would often come in on a Friday, for their end of week tipple. There was one particular Friday regular that I took a shine to. Sharon would often spend more time at the bar than any of the others, I'd flirt with her, then she'd flirt with me. After a couple of weeks of flirting, she handed me a piece of paper with her phone number on it; I smiled and said "thank you," she looked me straight in the eye and said "ring me." Obviously it was difficult, as I was living with someone and we had no phone. My scooter was finished, and it passed the MoT, so I was finally on the road. Rich Lewis's then bro in law, Andy Spry, would often pop in for a drink on a Friday too, and during general chit chat, he mentioned to me, that he was leaving his job and he could put my name forward if it would help. So that he did and I started there a week later.

By mid-August, I'd been a paint sprayers labourer at Dunfil Engineering for about a month. Money was good and I had my scooter, Mel and I were arguing more than usual, and one night it all just got too much. I jumped on my Vespa and sped off, I made the call to Sharon and within a week, I moved from Milton to not too far down the road to Montpelier with Sharon.

It was her own bought, one bedroom flat; it was cosy and we were happy, my work mate Barry Rowlands lived near me; so I got a lift to work everyday and no need to use the scooter. We had a spot on relationship and financially things were good.

Mum and Perry, had received a sum of money after his mums passing, so they purchased a nice little boat in Dartmouth. There it stayed, for them to use as an escape when they needed a break, and with me as their son that was quite often the case!

Traci and I received some sad news in October. We were told, that our boy Darren's aorta, had closed further than expected by the age of five! An appointment was made, and Daz, like a little boy soldier went for his operation on the 30th of October.

The open heart surgery was on a Monday, and Traci was at the hospital too. I worked all day and made my way to see them in the evening, it was a sad occasion to see so many tubes and my little boy who could barely move or talk. All he'd keep saying was "water water," the poorly little dude was so thirsty, but he was only allowed a few mil's a day, I had to keep telling him no, it was so hard. By Tuesday he was already a lot brighter, although this time he was allowed more water but refused to drink it. By Wednesday, he was wanting to be out of bed playing with the toys, by Thursday he was! By Friday he was running the ward and ordering nurses about, and by Saturday, he was allowed home. Then he spent the next year showing everyone his scars!

Christmas came and went, Barry and Rachel had had their first baby Beth on Christmas Eve. In January, I received a call from my mum, to let me know an ex-school friend Shelly, had been in touch. She was asking, if I was still friendly with any of my old-school mates, as she was organising a ten-year school reunion. I'd not seen or spoken to her in ten-years and when I was about twelve, Shelly was my brief school girlfriend. I gave her a call, so we met and she gave me a list of all the old-school mates, and the addresses they lived at when leaving school. I immediately got in touch with anybody I was still in touch with, and the reunion took place. I was gutted really, as only about fifteen girls and seven guys turned up.

The night was still enjoyable. Sharon came for a short while, then left me to go clubbing with the school lot, during the night I did get friendly with one of Shelly's friends Paula. She was a couple of years older than us, but reasonably fit. As I was happy with Sharon, nothing took place with Paula, but she stayed on my radar all the same!

April came, and I was still with Sharon although things had become stressful between us, I was still at Dunfil, but now was in a small parts office ordering paints, metals and other metal fabrication stock.

A great friend, Mike Lewis, who occasionally bought and sold the odd car, phoned me one day and asked if I was interested in buying, a nice low mileage, silver A reg Vauxhall Cavalier. I bought that and was happy to have a car again! Sharon did have a car, so I didn't always use the scooter, but during May we split. So I moved out and temporarily moved in with my mate Kerry.

I was now back in touch with Shelly from school, and at that time, she'd not long been dating one of my longest known Ashcombe Park buddies, Jimmer Fox. I was now seeing a lot more of them and I again became friendly with Paula, whom I'd met at the school reunion. We started dating and I stayed living at Kerry's. We did the usual family stuff, I took Daz, Paula and her kids to Brean for a day out during the lovely summer. I remember being sat on the sofa one evening, watching "Take your Pick," with Des O'Conner; I spat my coffee out and yelled "That's my sister." Fair play to her she did go on to win a holiday to Rome, but as she was very pregnant, she got money instead, as they wouldn't allow her to fly preggers.

I found out within a week or so, that Paula was still seeing her ex behind my back, so I walked away from that relationship! By the 28th of June, Cheryl and Drew had their first baby boy Ryan.

Mike Lewis had a flat in Exeter Road in Weston, and the flat underneath his, became available to rent; It was a nice sized, two bedroom flat and for a good price. It wasn't a good start mind you, as the ex-tenant and landlord, decided to give it a complete revamp the week I moved in! It was a nightmare, when I came home from work on the Monday, I couldn't use my lounge, as he'd put everything from it into my bedroom, sofa, TV, literally everything. I could hardly breathe from paint fumes and I couldn't use my bedroom, let alone see my bed. "But it's a two bed," you're probably thinking! Guess what? that was his paint storage room! Oh yeah and to top it off there were "BOOBS" all over the lounge floor. The Daily Sport was his chosen daily read, and he must of kept every paper that he ever bought, they were everywhere, can you imagine if I'd of brought my mum round to check it out; or worse still brought a woman home. Which brings me to another date. As I was now working in the stores at Dunfil, I'd often answer the phone, on one occasion and taking a call, a rather sweet female voice asked for Carol, the boss's wife. They weren't there at the time, so I took the necessary details and then turned on the charm. She was only in Burnham and I don't remember her name, we made arrangements for her to come to Weston that night and we went for a drink at The Ship, in Uphill. She was ok, she turned up in a mini skirt and a low cut top, it was pretty clear that she didn't drive ten miles just for a coke; the best thing was she made the first move. I just supplied the one night love nest, she went home and I never saw her again.

When it came to paying the first months rent, I disputed it as I couldn't stay there for the first week due to the painting and decorating.

He got all silly and told me to go, so I paid him nothing and moved straight into my dad's flat on the Oldmixon, as by this time he'd split with Trish!

Have a Hart was a charity event held in Burnham, It was an all day event on a hot August Saturday. I went with a work mate, Steve Ballard and met up with loads of other mates' when we got there, there were scooter mates', martial art mates', pot mates' and some general Weston drinkers'.

70's Glam Rock favourite's, "Sweet," played live early evening, they were fantastic but by the time they'd finished, I'd lost Steve and he had my house keys! After a forty-five minute walk back to Weston, I finally found him in Sands Nightclub, whilst I was in the club I met Debbie, every night from then on I spent with Deb's and her two kids.

It was around this time, I went on a road trip to Dartmouth with Daz. Mum and Perry were on their boat for a short break. Cheryl, Drew, and their kids were also there for the day. It was a beautiful, very hot day and Perry took the boat just out of the River Dart, to a small pebble beach and dropped anchor. I'd say it was about half a mile to the beach, so Drew and I decided we'd take a swim over and back, we jumped in and did just that, but, "Holy Shit!" Yes, it may have been a blistering hot day, but the water was bloody freezing. After about a minute or so, we got our breath back and we proceeded to swim, only then, we found we were now swimming in amongst hundreds of jellyfish; we made it to the beach without being stung. At that point, we decided we were not swimming back! When we looked back at the boat, to wave Perry to bring the dinghy and pick us up, we realised then, that Cheryl had by now, entered the water to swim to the beach too; she too realised that there were jellyfish everywhere and tried climbing back into the dinghy. That wasn't happening; you see, as she had literally just had baby Ryan, there was a little after birth weight, so she wasn't able to. She paddled along with Perry to the beach, we all climbed in and made it safely back to the boat! We spent the rest of the day enjoying the sun; even though mum had made sure that we were all wearing plenty of sun cream all day, I was starting to suffer the burn on the journey home, getting Daz back to his mum's. For the next few days, I was off work sick with sunstroke, but I had Deb's looking after me so it was all good.

As I'd asked Drew to keep his eye out for a cheap flat for me, one was soon found. It was a nice little one bed flat in Worle High Street, so I moved straight in and it also had a garage, so I could put my scooters' in there and stick with the car.

Debbie and I soon split and for a couple of days, I stayed single. My new neighbour had a younger sister Christine; I happened to bump into her on a night out and we became a couple for a month or so. It didn't last long but it was a joint decision. I still went out all the time and went through a couple of very short relationships with Geraldine, Jo, Hayley and Melanie.

By October, I had left Dunfil and got a job at Comet in Clevedon, at the Delivery Control Centre. That was better, a nice clean job, in a nice big warm office, on the phone from one PM to nine PM, Monday to Friday and every other weekend. I was happy with that, I had Daz every other weekend so was able to work it well.

In December, I had the pleasure of driving Rich Southcombe and Steve Wilkinson to Earls Court, we went to see my most favourite band, The Who, performing Quadrophenia live. It was awesome, Billy Idol appeared as The Ace Face and PJ Proby was The Godfather. John Entwistle was still alive at this one, so three out of four was great. Although I'm a major Keith Moon fan, Zak Starkey (Ringo Starrs son), did an awesome job behind that kit!

Breezer photo shoot

My trusty steed P200

CHAPTER 4

TWO FUNERALS' AND
A WEDDING

Now into 97 and through January, I did telesales for a cable company; also in Clevedon where I attempted to sell Electrical Cable. That was a fun job, I only worked the mornings' and then would work the afternoons in Comet. In February, I left that part-time job and went around the corner, to be an early morning Post Room Clerk instead; I was delivering mail to personnel in a two-story office block at Clerical Medical and again was able to work the afternoon to evening for Comet.

Now, this is another memorable time for me, after I decided I was working too hard; I left the Post Room job and just stuck with working at Comet. As I didn't start work until one, I would often pop into town, at about eleven o'clock and enjoy a cup of coffee in Gardens Restaurant, I'd sit in the window and just watch the world go by.

After leaving the High Street one day and walking back to my car, I spotted a lady; she looked a couple of years older than me and was wearing a short denim dungaree suit, she climbed into her Escort Estate and at the same time checking me out. I gave her the Timmy Day smile and drove off, with her close behind. It turned out she was heading the same way as me, which was nice. Once I entered Worle High Street and still with this chick close behind, I looked in my mirror to see her indicating left; she then waved and turned, I waved, but she was gone! Straight away I was thinking, "hang on I can't just let her go like that!" Knowing the next left would loop me round to the road that she just turned up, I span into the next left, only to come face to face with the same chick. How happy was I, as it turned out that her thought pattern was the same as mine and she'd come back to find me, well, I had to go and do a shift at work so then wasn't the time for any heat. Her name was Amanda, we exchanged numbers, and had plenty of fun as often as we could. It was difficult as she had young kids, it was fun whilst it lasted but we soon fizzled out.

I was out on a Saturday night a few weeks later; after the clubs closed a few of us made our way home, stopping at Tina's family guest house for a night-cap. Well, Tina and I spent about ten, maybe twenty minutes having a very uncomfortable quickie in her downstairs toilet, whilst the other three or four people were sat in the front room only a few feet away; what a great night.

A few of us took a trip on a Sunday in April, Miles Dolphin was driving Danny Stokes and myself to Gloucester. It was Lambretta's 20th Anniversary Custom Show, there were loads of stalls, custom scooters', and plenty of Southwest scooterists'; that was a great day. Although the night before, I'd been up Hobbit's Nightclub and left with Pamela, heading back to my place for some fun! I was woken in the morning ;by Miles and Dan outside in the car beeping! They'd come to pick me up, but Pamela and I were still wrapped up in the duvet. So we jumped out of bed, got dressed and I quickly dropped her off home. I came back and had a quick shower, thankfully Miles waited and a great memorable day was had.

Rich Southcombe, drove Steve and myself to Kettering in the Sooty van mid-July, but this time it was Lambretta's 20th Anniversary Rally. Edwin Starr and his full band played and sounded awesome, it was a great weekend, plus Steve and I managed to get our sweaty, sun tanned heads in the Scootering magazine whilst watching Edwin.

Sometime during the summer months, I was walking down Severn Road when I bumped into Barry Newman, the rhythm guitarist from the X-Men, he was carrying little Beth on his chest and I'd barely seen him since his wedding to Rachel. He went on to tell me, that he had started teaching a workmate at his work Smurfit, Micky "Rambo" Evans, the bass guitar, and did I fancy getting together for a jam some time. As he was now Nick Cavill's brother-in-law and teaching someone the bass, we saw a band in the makings.

Sure enough, the practice was organised at a little village hall not far from my house; it was great to be working with Nick and Barry again and now Rambo, we spent about three hours playing the Bill Withers classic, "Ain't no sunshine."

The practice's continued, we called ourselves Strangebrew and went on and added a few more covers, like "Parklife" by Blur and Ocean Colour Scene's "The River Boat Song."

August bank holiday was spent at the Isle of Wight Scooter Rally, which I attended most years. As I had no scooter on the road, I often borrowed Kerry Stark's, grey primer PX125, with a 180cc conversion and a massive fuel-guzzling carburettor. I ran out of fuel on the way down and by the time Rich Southcombe had ridden for miles, bought a fuel can and filled it up and rode back, I had very little money left; but my mates made sure I still had a drunk and enjoyable weekend. Kerry is a great long-time friend and would lend me a scooter should I be stuck for transport when working in Clevedon.

I carried on working for Comet through the year and by September, I'd started dating a nineteen-year-old bird Sue, who also worked at Comet. She'd apparently come from a troubled home in Wolverhampton, after deciding to leave she found cheap accommodation in Clevedon a few months before; she soon moved in with me as she only had her clothes.

My dad eventually started dating Margaret, the landlady and owner of The Walnut Tree Pub on the Oldmixon; on the 25th of October they got married. As Strangebrew had just started, we had very few songs, but still, my dad asked if we'd like to play their wedding. Being our first gig we said yes, we turned up at the Walnut Tree; where there was a big Marquee set up in the car park; we set up the equipment and the gig commenced. No sooner had we started playing the second song and Dad asked us to stop; as there were a rather large volume of older people, they couldn't stand the noise; as we didn't do any Sinatra or the Chicken Song, we packed up, Barry took my kit home, I stayed and got drunk.

Shortly after the wedding, Dad handed his notice in as a lorry driver and became a landlord with Margaret.

Barry and Mick's Smurfit workmate, had asked them in November, if Strangebrew would like to play a gig at The Anchor, a pub in Bleadon. We literally had a set of about eight songs, but we said yes anyway. Strangebrew turned up and played to an audience of about twelve people and the same songs were repeated, over and over again, until about one-thirty in the morning. Poor old Rambo's brother, Andy, had come to pick us all up and he got there at eleven, so he had to sit and wait patiently bless him.

Shortly after, I was informed that a Post Person job had become available; I'd applied to be a postie in the past and I changed jobs in late November. At that time, my bro-in-law Drew was also a part-time postie as his business had only been going a short while. Sue and I, had seen some kittens advertised in the local paper and decided we'd get them, so we went to what was the RAF camp in Locking and picked up two gorgeous little one-year-old sister cats', named Mo and Max. Sue also wanted a pony and we found one of those as well; we sourced a nearby stable and she spent my working hours with Dinky, her pony. Her mum had sent her money for the pony and it's extras.

By December, I found that she was spending more Saturday nights out than me, and not coming home until four in the morning; the clubs' closed at two-thirty. When she came home in the early hours one Sunday morning, her stuff was in a black bag on my doorstep, she was out of my life. About a week after I kicked her out, I got my BT phone bill; I found that whilst I was out posting mail on a daily basis, and she was supposedly at her horse all day; she was in fact at mine, ringing her mum in Wolverhampton for hours on end; the bill was about three hundred quid!

I knew I wasn't going to see the money from her, as she'd left Comet as soon as I started as a postie as she could no longer get there. I did ask for the money back and as expected she said no chance. She did ask if I would spend New Year's Eve with her so she wasn't alone. I said I would, but instead spent the night with Mandy (not Amanda from before).

Four months into being a postie and starting 1998 as a new man, my scooters' were in the garage gathering dust, so I stuck with driving the car.

I was having my hair cut, early one February morning at John and Marcus's Barber Co, no one else was in the shop; so I whipped my T-shirt off after the cut to blow off the hairs. As I was stood topless, two young ladies' walked in with prams and started giggling; I got Claire's number, then went home.

I later phoned Claire, to find out that she was a single mum and living in temporary accommodation at Maysfield House on the Bournville. Now, anybody reading this book, that had anything to do with Maysfield House over the years and up to the late 90s, will know what an un-healthy dump this place was! So Claire stayed at mine with her very noisy little boy, nearly every night as I didn't want her staying there. We only saw each other for a month or so, as she was about seven years younger than me and she wanted different things, like soldiers!

My nanny Day from Cheddar passed away in May; it was a very sad occasion, I hadn't been to such a large gathering at a funeral since Steve's funeral in 1988. My nan Ethel Day was a very well-known, popular lady, so I think the whole of Cheddar, Wells, and surrounding areas' turned up to show their respects, it was very overwhelming. After the funeral, Dad and I made our way to The Lamb Inn, in Worle, to get drunk and commiserate together. It was Dad's mum and he was really upset as you'd expect. I couldn't drink like my dad, so I left when I'd had enough, I only lived down the road from the Lamb so I staggered home and got upset on my own.

By June, I'd gone on to the night shift at the Post Office, I was also working overtime delivering mail after a night of sorting it. Around this time someone was selling a rough-looking P200 Vespa; they were only asking for a hundred and fifty quid for it, so a week later it was mine. It was a matt black looking monster, with big bits of metal welded in place; in time I was offered another frame in good condition and was sold it for thirty-five quid. It turned out to be Alan from Ashcombe Parks old frame! See, good things do come to those who wait, although now it didn't have chrome side panels, lights or mirrors.

So with my complete, but slowly rotting 125 in the garage, and the old holey frame and other various engine bits from my lock up, I now had this frame and a complete P200, so I was able to build, a really nice shiny black P2, with a Vespa T5 front end. Gary who lived in the flat downstairs, had a compressor so he sprayed it for me; I'd prepared and sprayed it with grey primer aerosols the week before. There was also a paint distributor that I used when I worked at Dunfil in Banwell; I bought a litre of black paint and some lacquer and whilst I was there, I popped to my chroming man next door; Nick Taylor, with a load of bits and a hundred quid, so when the scooter was ready it looked extra shiny!

I had a week off work sometime in July, so I thought I'd have a drink in town one afternoon; I'd bumped into Jon-Paul who was on his way to the job-centre, I joined him, took a seat and waited. Whilst waiting, two young ladies had entered and straight away caught my attention; I immediately turned on the charm and got chatting, inviting them for a drink with JP and myself. We probably only spent an hour or so drinking a few drinks, then we left, JP went one way and the three of us went off hand in hand; to catch a bus back to mine, well that didn't happen! I got on one bus and they got on another.

That night I had band rehearsals so no plans were made, the next night however was a completely different story!

As we'd exchanged phone numbers, we arranged for JP and I to visit the girls in Kewstoke one evening; JP turned up on his black Vespa P200 and picked me up. On arrival, we were greeted by the two girls and a young lad; my first thought being, "great one of them has a boyfriend!" But no, we were soon told that he was one of the girl's brothers. Now things just got weird, as we entered a practically empty smoke-filled living room, honestly, you wouldn't believe it, there was a sad 1970's looking chest of drawers, with a really old sad looking television sat on top of it; an armchair with it's back towards us and on the floor in front of that, was a dirty bucket filled with water. The brother, after quickly kneeling down, was now playing with the bottle that was sticking out of the bucket and loading a socket up with tobacco, then he asked if we wanted one? After realizing that sat in the armchair, was in fact a very old lady, who was soon to have a pot filled bucket! I looked at JP and he looked at me, no thanks was our response so the girls then led us away, asking if we'd like a coffee; well after seeing the state of the kitchen we both chose not to. After walking up an un-hoovered set of stairs, we all entered a room, and JP and I were left alone. The room was disgusting, yes, it was clear they shared the room, there was a double mattress dumped on the floor; no wardrobe or curtains and what I can only describe as, every item of clothing, underwear included, that they both wore; just randomly thrown everywhere! It was shocking, there was even graffiti all over every wall and the ceiling. I looked at JP and said, "I'll use the loo and we're out of here," he agreed and we made our way to separate loos'. I used the upstairs and he used the downstairs, well guess what? That was disgusting too! There was no kiss goodbye, and JP couldn't have started that P2 quick enough! We were gone, and spent a few occasions laughing about it after; that was a lucky escape as that was unclean!

Cheryl and Drew had their second boy, and third and last baby Adam, on the 25th of October. We decided Strangebrew needed a name change, so a meeting was arranged at The Imperial; a few names were jotted down, from "Indygo" to "The Jones's'". It was as we were thinking about this, one of the guys spotted a bottle of Bacardi Breezer on the opposite table, from that point we became "Breezer." We started covering more songs, from Elvis Costello to Joe Jackson, from The Jam to The Who, from Jimi Hendrix to Dodgy and many many more. Barry and Nick had also been working together writing songs, so we banged out a couple of originals too, "Up All Night" and "You make me happy". Through September and October, we played a couple of gigs in Cellar's "Basement" Bar. It was a tiny pub but it guaranteed a big audience, there were no windows, just a stairway down to the bar, we could see as everyone entered, and Barry would only be a couple of feet away from the audience; which by the way was mainly Smurfit staff. I had Christmas with my family and New Years Eve with my friends; I'd been single for a few months and that night met Jayne, we had a very short two-week relationship, made difficult as her ex-husband and father of her kid worked at Smurfit; it was just awkward so we called it a day.

Now into 1999, Breezer started the year off in Cellar's again, it was a great gig as a lot of friends' had turned up; it was at that gig I started dating Veronica for a very brief time. She was about ten years older than me and we had very little in common, instead I started dating Emma who worked at the Walnut Tree. We had a month or so together, but that ended too. As I had some spare hours to fill, I started frequenting the gym in Sunnyside Road. There I became friendly with Helen; she looked great working out in front of me, she did have a partner, but was enjoying my company and she soon left her guy. We had a fling for a couple of weeks', it was fun but it didn't last! By mid-February, Breezer were asked to play a gig in The White Hart in Weston town centre, I don't think a band had ever played in there and don't think a full band has since. It was packed and very loud, but all the same we were suddenly out there.

Whilst I was at Rambo and Sarah's one Sunday afternoon, their neighbour had left her house. I gave her the chat and she told me her name was Sheryl, followed by her number and then we were soon dating. Only for a couple of weeks mind as we didn't seem to work, but it didn't matter as Breezer became busy. We started playing gigs every weekend, from Jack Stamps in Weston, to Finnegan's wake in Bristol in March, and O'Malley's in Weston, to the Old Pier Tavern in Burnham, in April and May. Cellar's was a pub in the past and now it's been closed for years.

We played a gig in the Market House mid-April, and what a gig that was. My sister had come along with her friends and our usual followers joined us too; my ex-Sharon who I lived with in the past was also there, with her work friend Sheryl (Rambo's neighbour), as well as Helen from the gym. When we had our ten-minute break between sets, I didn't even have a chance for a wee, after talking with my sister for a minute; I was suddenly grabbed hold of and snogged by Helen, then I was pulled by another hand, the hand of Mandy (I'd known her for years); then we were snogging, then Helen pulled me again and this went on until Barry, was behind the microphone shouting for me to put the girls down, and get behind the kit. So after playing a Breezer blinder, I took Mandy home and we became a couple for a month or so. Mandy shared a flat in town with her friend Carly, Carly had a boyfriend Colin Smith, we became great friends.

Now Dad was in the pub trade, and Margaret already had another couple of pubs in Torquay. They decided in May to move to Goodrington near Torquay; I was asked if I'd like to go and work with the new Managers, Rich and Jo at the Walnut Tree. I did the afternoon graveyard shift, from two in the afternoon, until seven in the evening. I only did it for a couple of months and only a couple of days a week; I was still working nights as a postie and I'd also started to deliver Chinese food a couple of nights a week too. I'd kept Mo and Max since I split With Sue and now Max had become pregnant; so a few weeks later and six gorgeous little balls of fluff were born. After the six weeks wait, they went to various people, one particular little brown tabby, I happily gave to a good mate Mike Lewis. The flea problem had become massive during the six weeks and I was struggling financially, I had to let Mo and Max go in the end. I cried as I handed them over to The Whitehouse Kennels and Cattery in Mark, just outside Weston.

During my afternoon stint as a barman, I met a guy who worked landscaping for the Council, he was a friendly enough guy and two of them would come in together, they'd both down about four bottles of Newcastle Brown Ale, then they'd get in their truck and drive off; I couldn't believe it, but there you go.

We became mates and I got his number, he was soon leaving the Council to landscape on his own and I soon left the pub, as it was miles away from my house and doing all the other jobs was enough.

I carried on as a postie and delivering food and on my annual leave times, rather than a holiday I would go and work landscaping; it was great doing that in my spare time, a few hundred quid cash in hand, whilst learning a new trade at the same time.

One particular job we did in Southmead Bristol, was re-laying the grounds of a church with different sized slabs. It was hard work and heavy lifting, but the goal was achieved in two weeks and it looked great, it was a two-man job well done.

The only thing that bothered me big time, and I got very angry with him about it, was that on the last day and several times, he would say things like, "shall we go over there and rape a chick!" Now, over there was a long lane, that went through a wooded area, and various people would walk or jog through all day; it was boiling hot so ladies were dressed down. We argued on the journey home, as I reminded him that I'd been falsely accused in the past, and how sick he was to think it. Once he dropped me off I never phoned him or worked with him again!

I was still single and always busy; Breezer were playing a Saturday gig, right in the centre of town, at Jack Stamps (now The Tavern). I had nothing to do after work, so I went home, showered and shaved, and made my way into town. I spent the day drinking at the bar in Jack Stamps. I'd given Barry a spare key to my flat, anytime Breezer played a gig in Weston, I would spend the day in whatever pub we were playing in. Baz picked my drums up and brought them to Jack Stamps, bearing in mind, I'd been in the pub since one o'clock and by now it was six, I was very drunk. We always played a blinder of a gig and because of my drunken loud and frantic playing, I would usually break a drum stick or two. Anyhoo, during the gig, I noticed a female at the bar, she was wearing a black skirt and jacket and a pair of knee length boots. After the gig, I took Rachel home and we dated for about a week.

By the end of June, Breezer had played more gigs, from the Foresters in Weston to Finnegan's wake again in Bristol; we also played another date in June at O'Malley's, I remember this one well. I fell asleep playing the Oasis classic "Wonderwall," as the kit was set up so snug in the corner, I was able to sit back and relax whilst playing. As I'd been on nights and not slept that day, I was very tired, I stopped playing on the break where I should've, but by then had dropped off, so I didn't come back in, until Barry shouted at me and I woke up!

The same night, I noticed a lady about my age, looking at me all night. After the gig we got talking and I took Caroline out on a date a few days later; she'd not long left her husband, she had a baby daughter and lived in a nice house with her parents; they'd converted the garage into a big room for her and her baby.

One day my sister, Caroline and I went to London. Cheryl drove, and we went to see our Cousin Martin. He at that time lived in Wimbledon and he worked in a high-tech job, we all had a lovely day together. Martin showed us his work office which overlooked the grounds of Buckingham Palace, and we saw the London Eye before it was erected. We travelled on packed busses, we were all loved up in Trafalgar Square, but then the day drew to a close and we all went home! It was the first time in a long time, I actually felt like I was in a proper relationship, we never mentioned love but it was going great.

Things were great from June. Breezer had played a load more gigs, I had a lovely partner and was earning with the Post Office and delivering Chinese food. Mike Lewis and I took our scooters for a ride to Goodrington in mid-July, and we spent a drunken night with my dad and Margaret. As Dad's birthday is the day after mine, we did a double celebration, but of course, it was a beautiful hot day when we rode down so neither of us had waterproofs. We woke up on Sunday, and it was chucking it down with rain, we got drenched going home. Thankfully it didn't rain when I went for my weekend away on the Isle of Wight scooter rally in August, with the usual mates Dan and Lynne, Wayner and Cath Fleming, and many others.

My flat was one of five, within a house with three entrances, two around the back by the garages and one locked front door, that led up the stairs; to my flat on the left, another on the right and a flight of stairs in the middle, leading to the roof flat.

If anyone was coming to see me, I'd know so I'd wait and then go and let them in. This one Monday afternoon, there was a tap on my flat door, assuming it was my neighbour Jenny, I jumped up and opened the door, to find the landscaping guy stood there.

I'd not seen him for a couple of months, he then went on to tell me that he'd had an argument with his woman in Banwell and didn't know where else to go, as he originally came from Newcastle. Me being the sympathetic caring type, let him stay with me on my sofa until he could sort things; at the end of the day he had cash so that's all that mattered.

That same evening a female friend Kerry Harris had popped in to say hi; she was only a friend as I knew her through other friends, her dad Dave, picked up my drink driving car for me.

Kerry worked in a hair salon and would pop in to say hi on occasion on her way home from work, my new temporary lodger had a big, more up to date phone than what Kerry had and she took an interest in it. She said she'd buy it, but wouldn't have the money until Friday, so she arranged to pop in then and do the deal.

Best mate's Rich and Steve, had both just had their first children with their wives around that time; they'd asked if I'd like to come to The Borough Arms, to "wet the babies head's." I said yes and as Kerry had come to buy the phone, we all went along. A great night was had with plenty to drink and we got taxis' home later. Rich and Steve went one way and we went the other; dropping Kerry off at home before we went back to mine. It wasn't until the morning, we woke to realise that the deal hadn't taken place for the phone. It was obviously a good night!

The Saturday afternoon, I arranged for Kerry to come over in the evening and sort the phone out. She turned up at seven-thirty, at the same time Caroline had turned up in a taxi, it was her 30th birthday and we were off into town to celebrate.

As Caroline lived at her parent's house and they were looking after her baby, we literally had to plan our night to go into town until eleven-thirty, back to mine for a bit of fun, giving her enough time to clean up and get back to her mum and dad and not too late. I'd already mentioned to my lodger that this was my plan, so he said he'd go out and not come back until after one o'clock.

Kerry stayed to sort out the phone, I climbed into the taxi with Caroline and went off to start our night of celebrations. We met up almost straight away with Breezer fans and great mates, Sean, Sash, Gary and his daughters Donna and Kelly. We had a great night and mini pub crawl; a bit of live music and a burger on the way to the taxi rank. The usual wait for a taxi took place and we shared it home with a big fella; I don't remember his name, he used to be the doorman at Charlie Browns back in the day.

We got dropped off first, handed him some cash and he went on his way. We stumbled happily and a little tipsy through the main front door, making our way upstairs. My flat door was a different lock; it wasn't like the front door yale key, it was a long boney key with no catch. As I approached my flat, I realized that the door was already open; straight away I wasn't happy, he'd gone out and forgot to lock my door, anything could be gone, my drum's, my record's or my CD's. I stepped in and immediately panicked and became sober. I pulled the door closed and was being a little sick; I tried yelling for Caroline to not go in, but it was too late, she just wanted to get in the flat; she pushed past a shaking and still urging me and said, "I don't care if it's messy, just get in there please." With that, she came face to face with what I didn't want her to see.

Kerry had been brutally murdered, her clothes had been stripped off, and she'd been sexually assaulted, with the handle of the lump hammer that she'd been beaten to death with. We didn't stop long enough to see if he was still in there, or if there was any small chance she was still alive. I couldn't even make her head out with all the blood, to be honest, it's been torturing enough at times through the years, if I'd of looked for longer or even checked her pulse, then I would've had a breakdown forever.

After banging heavily on the downstairs window, to wake Gary and Lesley, the police were called and they got there quick. We climbed into the back of a police bus and were looked after as we weren't suspects!

We were taken back to the station, and given coffee after coffee in the police restroom. Once I told them it had to be my lodger, and that the only place he would be was at his ex's house, we went to check. I didn't know her address, I just knew exactly where she lived; I'd delivered Chinese to their neighbour and I would often see his van parked on the driveway next door.

We went off in an unmarked police car and Caroline stayed at the station, sure enough, on arrival his van was parked on her drive; we went off and the arrest was made.

After some very painful times and hearing that he'd gone into a pub, where a friend of mine Ernie Turnball was having a pint; he was bragging that he thought he may have just killed a young lady. He had basically just handed himself in; he was sentenced to life, with a minimum of nineteen years; he was thirty-six, she was nearly eighteen and a beautiful hearted person; he'll be fifty-four before he can try and get out. I wish I'd never let him back in my home or my life.

I wasn't allowed in the flat until the following Tuesday, whilst the Forensic team did their stuff, so I moved back into my old bedroom at Mum's and Perry's for a few months. On Tuesday, I arranged for four mates and myself to go in, quickly empty the flat and for different things to go in storage at different destinations, Barry took my drums and martial art stuff, Nick had my entire record and CD collection, Gail and Matt had my furniture and TV.

On arrival to clear the flat, I walked in to find they hadn't removed my old white sofa as promised; I felt sick and couldn't go in, it was very heavily blood-soaked. I made a phone call, and to be honest we didn't wait long; a truck with two ladies turned up and they went in and did the clear up. That was great, so in we went, but I'll never forget the minute I closed the door; to see blood splats all over the back of it. I still get the visions and the occasional nightmare. I hate myself for letting him stay with me. I have to live with that vision for the rest of my life, and I really do feel for Dave, Lynne, Jamie and Josh as they have to live without Kerry.

Work let me have a few weeks off, and I stopped doing the Chinese rounds for a bit, as I was in no place to be facing people. Although, by October, an old Ashcombe Park buddy and best friend Craig Tildesley; who'd moved from Weston and up to Bridgnorth in the early 90's, had got news of what had happened and rang my mum as it's always been the same number.

He came down from Bridgnorth, picking up his mate Mark Bird from Bristol on the way and we went off for a drunken night in Newport, with a bunch of Craig's Newport buddies. Although I wasn't really in the mood for partying, we still had a great night and I was happy that Craig had invited me, I'd not been out of the house much! I slept on a sofa, with six drunk Welsh men, spread all over the place and not one chick! To be honest after seeing a naked dead girl, kind of put me off wanting a female for quite some time, especially a naked one!

Caroline couldn't cope with the aftermath of the murder. We were sat having a coffee in Gardens Restaurant shortly after and I just burst into tears, it got me upset for quite a while, she ended the relationship; I was gutted.

I went to the Long-Fox unit at Weston Hospital, not as an in-patient; they did help as I'd become a wreck and I started having to take stress pills and anti-depressants, they actually made me feel suicidal so I stopped taking them.

Towards the end of October, I went back to work but was put on light duties, that was nice, no pressure, just to be a shadow with new postie's and make sure they were doing the job right!

One early cold morning I was with a newbie cycling up Bridge Road and I spotted Faye. Faye was a young lady, that worked in six ways cafe and lived in the flat above. It was early and cold and she'd not been in there long, she was warming herself up with the heat from the grills, and a fresh cup of coffee; I popped my head around the corner to say hi, and she invited me in for a hot drink; I sent the other postie off and caught up with him a bit later. The cafe still wasn't up and running, so it was nice for us to have a normal chat and not the usual transport cafe banter that took place in there on a normal day. I hadn't been in the cafe since before the murder, so this time was really nice; Faye told me how she'd heard about what had happened through cafe gossip and was lovely about everything. After handing me her number, and offering her shoulder to cry on should I need a chat; I cycled off a happier postie.

I did take her up on her offer, I went round for a coffee, as well as a good cry and chat on many occasions, for a couple of weeks it was purely plutonic.

On the 6ᵗʰ of November, I travelled to Oxford with Cheryl, Drew, Abbie, Ryan, and Adam. We spent an amazing well needed day, with family at my Cousin, Lisa's wedding to David. Once the wedding was over and we'd eaten the meal, I then sat at the bar with my Cousin Steven, and we downed at least fifty bottles of Budweiser between us. I fell into the back of the people carrier and slept all the way home, as did the kids and probably Cheryl!

What had happened two months before, was still playing on my mind as the court proceedings seemed to take forever! Although they actually dealt with it all quite quickly, I was still worried, that the murderer was going to get out of jail and get me. Faye was really there for me, and after a further few weeks and approaching Christmas, we became a couple and I moved from mum's and in with Faye above Six Ways Cafe. It took a while for me to become a lover again, as I really couldn't cope with naked bodies, but we just carried on being a loving couple. I started going swimming three days a week at Hutton Moore, I'd do sixty-two lengths, a mile a day. Faye's flat was great; her spare bedroom had a bed in it, but it was never used, so we arranged for the landlord to come and remove it. Then I got all my bits back from my friends' and had a new Timmy's room for my music system, television, drums, and general boy's toys, the punch bag went up too and I got back on the home weights.

Breezer played at The Winter Gardens mid-December for a talent contest. There was a magician, a couple of solo acts', a couple of stand-up comedians', and then there was Breezer, "BOOM;" the poor little OAP ladies, that had got there early for the front seats, were deafened by

"Parklife" and "The River Boat Song." On a more funny note, we were halfway through a song, and I suddenly dropped a couple of inches and felt a pain right up my rectum. The seat base had only broken, and the centre rod shot straight through the foam, but luckily for me not the leather. I did a quick bodge job and we finished the set.

Barry, Rambo, and the Smurfit bunch, had organized a New Years Eve party; mainly for the Smurfit staff, as having kids always made it awkward to go out and celebrate. Breezer played a great night, and everyone brought their own booze to the Scout hut, the same hut we had our first rehearsal in. I still managed to get through the awesome night with a dodgy drum stool. Everyone had a great time, and soon after the midnight chime's, I went home to Faye and we had a mini New Year toast together!

Breezer with Edwin Starr 2001

Nick,Barry,Me & Steve @ Baz's wedding

CHAPTER 5

A BRAND NEW START

Now we come into the big Millenium! The band had a gig break for a couple of months', as I didn't really feel up to gigging. I still played at home as often as I could and we still had the occasional rehearsal; I bought a new cymbal stand from "Bob's Music Bunker," as my old one had fallen apart, and taxi driver mate Pete, loaned me his keyboard stool to use for my drums.

Dad bought himself a brand new Vauxhall Vectra, with "Day," our sir name on the number plates. By this time, I'd picked up a cheap silver Astra to run around in. Daz had his 10th birthday in March and by now he was having several celebrations'; he'd be with Traci and her family one day, and with my family and I the next. Mum turned sixty in April, so twelve of us went for a lovely Greek meal, at Demetris Taverna and a great night was had.

I turned thirty in July, so Faye and I took a drive to Paignton, and stayed at one of Dads' and Margaret's pub's for a lovely weekend away. We visited Paignton Zoo, and did some general sightseeing. The day we were leaving to come home, was actually the day of my birthday, so we popped to Torquay, to spend the last day there; I decided I'd get my nipple pierced. No problem having it done, I didn't feel a thing! The only trouble was; I had a white T-shirt on and the seat belt kept catching it on our journey home; I had a left nipple blood-stained T-shirt by the time we'd got back. Faye had bought me, a pair of brand new red, white and blue Lambretta bowling shoes, and to this day they've been worn about eight times; and one of those times was for the cover photo!

It was nice to see a sign taped to the lamppost, right outside the flat on our return, with "HAPPY 30ᵗʰ CHEESY" on it; Cheesy was my nickname, used by only Steve, Nick and Rich, as I've always had a big "Cheesy" grin on my face!

Mum had bought me a ticket, for a Helicopter ride for my birthday; I took the trip at Weston's Helicopter Museum mid-August. I loved it, as did Abbie, Ryan and Adam. Cheryl and Mum came along too, to check out the Helicopter Museum; before I climbed aboard, and went for a very enjoyable flight around Weston. The end of the month saw me taking the usual trip to the Isle of Wight Scooter Rally.

Nothing exciting happened for the remainder of the year; I worked, Faye worked and we had our evenings in; catching up with the weekly episode of "Friends." Else I was out delivering food, and gaining a few more points on my licence!

Breezer pulled three gigs out the bag in December, one in O'Malley's, one in the Foresters, and we finished the year off at The Imperial.

2001 had started, and it was time for some changes. A great, long-time bass playing friend of mine Gail, was always telling me that I needed to buy a new drum kit. She was so right; I'd been working myself stupid, so I thought why not!

I got on the phone, and started phoning all the numbers in my Rhythm magazine and asking for booklets, on anything drum related. Before I knew it, there were booklets', magazines' and all sorts of drum info coming through the letter box.

On Saturday the 6ᵗʰ after work; I grabbed my then, ten-year old hi-hat stand, and faded hi-hat Cymbals; I jumped in the car and shot up to CB Drums in Bristol. For two-hundred quid; I got shot of the old skinny rubbish, and bought a brand-new, Tama Iron Cobra hi-hat stand, and a pair of Sabian Pro hi-hat Cymbals, so there it started!

One particular shop that had sent a lot of info, was The Birmingham Drum Centre, they had also sent a leaflet for a January date at the NEC in Birmingham. It was a Pearl Drums open day, selling all Pearl stock at trade prices. As Pearl was my preference, this was my chance to start buying some stuff I needed. The weekend approached and it was my weekend with Daz; Faye was at work, so Gail and her daughter Beth came with us on Sunday the 14th. It was a fantastic day, there were a couple of celebrity drummers' performing on Pearl kits, and we all had a great day. I blew the best part of three hundred quid, but I left happy, with a boom cymbal stand, a fancy snare stand and a couple of pairs of 5AN, Vic Firth sticks. Best of all though, was a Chad Smith signature snare drum, brand-new in a box, worth three hundred and eighty quid; I paid a hundred and forty for it. All my life, I'd played thirty to eighty-quid snare drums, so for those of you who don't know the difference, for me, it felt like I was going from a Robin Reliant, to a Porsche nine eleven!

By the 20th, Breezer had played a gig at The Old Pier Tavern in Burnham; "Oh My God," with my new hi-hats and new snare drum it sounded lovely! A week later, we were playing in the Borough Arms, but now my kit looked sad, ugly and old and it looked like a beginner's kit, now it had a new snare and hi-hats. By the first weekend in February; I'd been to see Keith Bailey at the Drum Store in Bristol, I gave him a two hundred pound deposit, on a thousand pound Pearl SRX kit. Admittedly it was a tough decision, but I had to sell the scooter content's of my garage; I did keep the best scooter though and sold the rest for two hundred quid.

Breezer played a couple more gigs through the rest of February, and the start of March. Mid-March was when things got better, and I struck some deals with Keith; I bought a new, Sabian AAX sixteen-inch stage crash cymbal, a new Tama Iron Cobra bass pedal, to match the hi-hat stand, a straight cymbal stand, and a new teal blue SRX drum kit. He threw in all the necessary cases for seven hundred quid, plus my drum kit, and another drum kit I'd obtained, and was stored at my flat. The kit only came with three tom's, a ten, twelve and fourteen-inch; I wanted a sixteen-inch as well. Unfortunately, the kit had been in the shop for six months, so Pearl no longer made those drums in teal blue; I ordered the nearest colour, dusk blue, so I waved goodbye to another three hundred quid, and it was a four weeks wait before I received it, as it had to be specially made. I now had a new complete kit and a new beginning for me.

The start of March, and Breezer were pulling in happy punters' at O'Malley's. The end of the month, we were playing our first proper support act gig, with none other than the soul legend Edwin Starr, at Club Oasis in Weston. We played an awesome set, followed by Edwin; I'd seen Edwin a couple of times over the years, as had Nick (hacket and his Edwin Starr jacket); Nick and I were really happy that we'd had the pleasure of supporting him, we had been following his music for many years after all.

The night after and we played in The Imperial. On this particular night, a friend of Nicks, Andy Davies, came over and introduced himself, and asked if I could teach him the drums. We exchanged numbers and became great friends; after work on a Saturday, Andy would come to my place for his lesson; he'd always stay for a few hours and he soon picked it up; he also bought himself an electric Yamaha Kit. He was very eager I'll give him that. Before I knew it, we had been off to drum clinics, including Drum-Tech in London for a day out, and Birmingham Drum Centre; I purchased my brand new, "Dennis Chambers" signature snare drum from them; I love this snare and still use it today. I now felt like I'd gone, from a nine-eleven Porsche to a Ferrari; I soon swapped my Chad Smith signature snare, for a brand new Sabian twenty-inch Stage Ride cymbal, with Keith at The Drum Store.

April was a quiet month for Breezer, so I spent all my spare time with Faye and Daz on the weekends. I would swim a mile a day in sixty-two lengths at Hutton Moore three days a week; I had weights and a punchbag at home, my drums were always set up, so I would often have a CD play along, as well as teaching Andy on the weekends, and going off to drum events. Life was good.

On May the 9th, Breezer played a "Battle of the Bands" event at Sands nightclub. We didn't win, which was a bit of a let down but hey ho. Three days later and we were playing the very busy Foresters Arms, biker Big Mac ran this pub, and a great night was always had; I could drink for free all night long and leave my gear in the pub over night, then stumble home in the early hours. Of course, I do have a confession or two, as during many years with Breezer, I found it hard to be a one woman man; Faye was an awesome girlfriend and to be fair we were the perfect couple, she was really good to me and I was unfaithful more than once! I know it's years' later, but I really am sorry Faye. After the gig, I left the pub with a lady who was at least ten years older than me, she lived in town, so we went back to her place and had some fun. After waking naked, in a room over looking Dolphin Square at five AM; I grabbed my things, and got dressed as I made a dash for it; I didn't even know her name!

Our last gig of the month was in O'Malley's, to a nice busy and happy audience.

June was spent with Faye, Daz and teaching Andy; Breezer only played one pub gig that month, again in O'Malley's, as we'd pulled in such a great crowd four weeks previous. We also played at a 21st birthday bash at the Conservative Club, loads of mates were there, and Miles Dolphin and his wife Mel, had brought Caroline with them; I dated Caroline in the late 80's (remember the Iceland's window?) Well, by the time Breezer finished playing and we'd packed up the gear, most of the guests were leaving, it was then I made my move on Caroline. We ended up canoodling, under a pool table in another room for quite some time. By the time we came out from under the table, everybody was gone and the doors were locked; Barry had taken my drums and all of the other band gear, so we both opened the back door and left! We got a taxi back to Caroline's for some more fun, and then I went home to Faye. Andy and I did some more drives to various drum clinics, and drum superstores in Wales, no satnav was fun, as we got lost on more than one occasion. Breezer had a busy July, as we played and packed out the Borough Arms in the first week, got drunk for my birthday the next week, then we were back in the Imperial the following week, and we ended the month at The Old Pier Tavern in Burnham, to another awesome crowd. By now I'd also scrapped the silver Astra, and bought a lovely white, two litre Ford Granada from Mike Lewis.

August was a gig free month, spent working, spending time with Faye, Daz and our families. Faye and I took a trip to Dartmouth on Regatta week, to see Mum and Perry on their boat, we took in some lovely sights and had the break we needed.

I was a hard-working postie, delivering Chinese food at night and playing drums most weekends. A fellow postie friend Keith, had booked Breezer to play a gig, at a tattoo convention he was organising at The Winter Gardens in September. It was a Sunday afternoon gig and what a gig it was! It was a very busy day, with tattooed people everywhere. A great skinhead mate Steve Gready, was having his head drilled too, well, that's what it looked like when I went over to say goodbye. We got a good report in a tattoo magazine, and we were happy with that.

In November, Nick, Barry, Rambo and myself, took a trip up to Birmingham to the NEC, as it was "Music Live." It was a yearly event, that was full of instruments', musicians', a few celebrities' and stalls', selling everything from guitars' to saxophones' and drums' to didgeridoos'. It was whilst I was there, I treated myself to a brand new, Sabian seventeen-inch AAXplosion cymbal for trade price. Whilst watching the great Steve White showing off his drumming skills; Barry decided to record it with his video camera, when Steve finished showing off and stood to speak and answer questions, the first thing he did was point at Barry and say, "could you turn that camera off please!" Barry did as he was told, and we listened to what he had to say for twenty minutes, then after we grabbed a bite to eat, and made our way around more stores, meeting more people; Including Steve White, who made a joke about the camera incident. We watched Ocean Colour Scene bang out a couple of tunes, but their beat master Oscar Harrison wasn't with them for that gig, so Steve White was their drummer instead. They only played a few songs, but it was still an awesome show.

With no gigs in December, I was able to spend the month with Faye getting ready for Christmas. We did various shopping trips, whether in Taunton, Bristol, or Weston; Faye and her mum Brenda went shopping for the food, as we were having Christmas Day with Brenda, and Faye's gran in Tarnock, a couple of miles outside Weston; they certainly knew how to cook a great turkey roast! A great day was had, and Faye and myself also popped in to see Carol and Ian, Faye's sister and bro-in-law, as they lived about two hundred yards away. New Years Eve was spent at Faye's best mate and newly weds, Rachel and Gary at their house on Mead Vale. I chose not to drink until we got home later, so I drove and made up for it when we got home, and a great New Year was had.

The start of 2002 was the normal, until Breezer's first gig of the year, at the Borough Arms in the middle of February, and two more in March, one at the Nut Tree in Worle and back in the Borough Arms again mid-month. We played in the Imperial at the end of May.

At this time, Faye's landlord Docker had informed us that he was selling the place, and we'd need to move out as soon as possible. Luckily for us, Auntie Val's husband Graham being a property owner, was able to offer us a lovely two bed flat for a great price, above a laundrette in Clifton Road. It was a lovely flat and we moved in quickly, and this was our first proper flat together, it was semi furnished so we brought Faye's furniture with us.

Life was again good; I also had a storage space behind the laundrette, so I was able to get my scooter from Mum's back yard, store it at mine and do the work that needed doing, like a re-spray and make over.

June was a busier month for Breezer, we were once again back in the Nut Tree on the 3rd, but this time, a Sunday afternoon for a celebration of the Queens Jubilee. It was a lovely busy afternoon, an outside gig under a gazebo.

Mid-month, Steve Wilkinson, Nick Cavill, Rich Southcombe and I, made our way to the Bristol Academy, we were off to see awesome 80's mod favourite's "Secret Affair." I don't think they'd been back together long at that point, well, only front man Ian Page and great guitarist Dave Cairns from the original line-up, but still a great show and night was had!

The month later, for my 32nd birthday; Faye and I jumped in my white Granada and took a drive, to spend three days in Newquay. A lovely time was had, the weather was great, we spent plenty of time checking out Cornwall. A day on the beach one day, The Eden Project the next, and Lands End before a long drive home with our Fat Willy's Surf Shack T-shirts'. Breezer played the month out, once again at The Borough Arms, another satisfied landlord, by now I'd stopped drinking at gigs, as I didn't like leaving my kit in pubs; I'd worked hard to buy what I had, and didn't like the idea of leaving it anywhere over night. Instead, I dedicated my time to Faye.

August and Breezer played another gig at the Imperial, this time we hired a recording outfit to come and record us live. Another great fun packed night was had by many; Smurfit Corrugated were our biggest audience, both Barry and Rambo worked at Smurfit, we also used their canteen for rehearsal's on many Sundays'.

Gigs were scarce for the rest of the year, with only a couple, one in November at The Borough Arms and a week after, the Breezer boys spent their yearly day out, at the NEC, for "Music Live." It was another great day, and this time I bought myself a Sabian AAX ten-inch Rock Splash. Soon after the purchase, we bumped into Zoro, an independent drummer, who has toured and recorded with many artists, including Lenny Kravitz, Bobby Brown, Frankie Valli and many more. I was honoured when he signed my cymbal for me. By the end of the month, we played a Christmas gig at The Borough Arms once more.

Faye and I spent Christmas together for the first time in our new flat.

A mate I went to school with, Jonny Drinkwater, lived two doors away from me in an upstairs flat, he'd come with me on occasion when I was out delivering food at night. Well, he owned a spray shop, and offered to spray my scooter for a good price, as long as I got it prepared. As I finished work by twelve every day, and was home early after swimming; I'd put myself to work and I dismantled my black Vespa. I sanded it down; I sprayed it with primer; I cut it back, then I coated it again with more primer. Within a week, the frame was ready for spraying, so, I took it to Jonny and spent, what seemed like forever picking the colour; I made the final decision and left him to it.

Once I left him, I headed for Banwell to see another great mate Nick Taylor; Nick has worked for many years, since I've known him for his family business in the chroming world, he has been mentioned before, as he's always been in charge of anything I've had chromed in the past. Anyhoo, I took him a set of forks, a couple of sets of wheel rims, and a few other small bits; I left him in charge and off I went!

Very few gigs took place through 2003, so I concentrated on getting my scooter done. At this time, I was being hit hard by the CSA for Child Support payments, and I was feeling the burn. My drum's were set up in our spare room; Faye went shopping with her mum every Wednesday, and we also had our veg delivered. By this time, Faye had left her job at Six Ways Cafe, as it had closed down after it was sold. She went on to work serving breakfast's in the mornings, and coffee all day to the Asda customers, a new job and a new venture.

In March, Jonny Drinkwater drove Andy Davies and myself, over the Severn Bridge and made our way to the Marriott Hotel. We spent the night watching Steve White and friends, as he showed off his new Premier Steve White signature drum kit. It sounded awesome, first there was a young lad, Dewy Young; he was only about fifteen and put me to shame; I was ready to go home and hang my sticks up for good! Al Murray the Pub Landlord, was hosting the show and we got to chat with them all during the break; Damon Minchella, Ocean Colour Scene's bass player, jammed along with Steve, as they finished the night off with a spot of Drum and Bass.

I got all my scooter bits back, and paid the bills. I spent the summer after work, building my newly sprayed Vespa, it was great. As our flat had a lovely outside patio, overlooking the rows of back yards; I could sit outside on a nice hot day, and rebuild the engine and the smaller bits, ready to take down and put with the frame; I got any other necessary parts from a great mate, Ian Harvey, who at that time owned Eddie Bullet, an LML supplier in Nailsea. I'd also taken it to another long-time friend, Steve Page, he did bike repairs and MoT test's, so by the end of August, it was on the road and I was able to take it for it's first ride. It was now a shiny blue, with pearl violet flicks and loads of chrome, off I went to the Isle of Wight, to spend another drunk weekend with my mates; I was one happy mod!

Once a week, I'd make a Friday visit to Santander to bank my bags of change; I'd always see a good mate and bass player Ian Simpson, stood outside his family furniture shop underneath an old nightclub. Every time I'd stop, we'd have a short chat and he'd always ask, "when am I joining Breezer then!" We'd have a giggle and I'd be on my way.

Earlier in the year, Micks mum had passed away. Once things had calmed down for him, he treated himself to Pilots courses which he passed, he then bought Sarah and himself a Micro Lite. He was happy and he was off, if the sun was out then he and Sarah were out flying, what an awesome way to be closer to his mum. They both became members of the Weston Zoyland Flying Club near Bridgwater. On one occasion, Breezer played at the club as Mick had organised a party. It was a fun night with plenty of food and booze, we all crammed into a Transit van I'd borrowed from Drew, we got drunk and all slept in the van like it was an 80's scooter rally all over again.

On one sunny Sunday evening, Barry, Nick and I had turned up at Smurfit for our weekly rehearsal. We had a chat with the cleaner Andy, but after a while, Mick still hadn't arrived. We tried ringing him but no answer, so in the end, we put the stuff back in our cars and we went home. Later, I received a call from Barry, to say that Mick was out flying when we were at practice. Breezer were always working and practice was important, it was at this point, we all decided to let Mick go and I put a smile on Ians face! I rang Ian to tell him that he was finally able to join Breezer, he was well chuffed and was at rehearsals the week after.

Soon after and I wasn't so happy; Faye turned to me one day and said, "I don't love you anymore, I want to call it a day!" That was different and unexpected, perhaps she knew that I'd been unfaithful in the past, even though I'd not cheated for a long time.

I popped to Jonny two doors down, and soon after, I was cramming all my belongings onto his landing and sleeping in his spare bedroom; Faye and I talked, but no it was over, three years of love switched off, just like that.

To be honest, it was only a week or so later and I was delivering mail in the town centre; I'd delivered that round a lot over the years, so I made acquaintance with a few regular faces. One particular young lady, worked in F Hinds the jewellers and I took a shine to her, now I was single, I made the move and asked her out for a drink; I left a happy postie with her name and number.

Lisa only lived around the corner from me, so I picked her up that night, and we went for a drink in Bleadon, at the Queens Arms. We had a lovely evening and I took her home, as her mum was looking after her young lad, we kissed and said goodnight and from then on it was pretty much full on.

During this time, I'd also applied for a taxi licence, so I would be self-employed and not be hit so hard with the CSA; by the 14th of September, I received my first taxi badge.

Jonny came home one night, and mentioned that there was a house around the corner, it was being renovated, but we could have it cheap to rent when it's ready. We went and looked at it; wow, it was massive, three bedrooms, the usual layout downstairs, and a nice back yard to work on my scoot when necessary. We were in there the next week; I had Sky installed as we never had it before, and we were sorted; I'd also been round to see a taxi driver Dave, to sort renting a car for my next venture, that was sorted, so I handed my notice in with Royal Mail. After six years it was sad to leave to be honest, but I felt it needed to be done.

So, by the start of October, I had a new woman, a new job and a new house. My Granada gained a bad radiator leak, but I did drive it hard, especially when I was delivering Chinese food; I'd also stopped that by then and the car was knackered. I took it to Dale Burrison's recycling and scrapped it. It didn't matter, as I now drove a taxi, but only from seven AM til five PM every day, as it was a shared rental.

Jonny often got cars in for sale, and he did me a deal on an older Renault; I didn't have it long to be fair, but I still had a car for the evenings. Lisa didn't have a car and I didn't need it when I worked, as we only lived about two-hundred yards apart, it was easy for her to pick up should she need it.

Mid-October and Breezer played our last gig for Big Mac at The Foresters, he was moving on and the pub soon changed hands; Lisa was there, and me playing the drums was a great aphrodisiac.

We played at the Imperial for our Christmas gig, and that was another great night. Lisa and I hadn't been together long, so we spent Christmas apart, but we made up for it on the New Years Eve. Great friends, Lynne and Dan Hodgetts, had invited us to their New Years Eve party; Lisa's lad was staying with his grandparents for the night, so Lisa drove us out to Worle and a great night was had.

Into 2004 and not having many gigs booked, I was able to spend plenty of time having fun with Lisa, and our boys got on too.

Early April; I took the boys to Vue Cinema at Cribbs Causway near Bristol; Lisa had to work on the Sunday, so I took them to see Scooby Doo 2, an entertaining film, and we laughed all the way through it, and a McDonalds before travelling home.

Whilst out on a day at work, and being the flirt I often was in those days; I'd become friendly with a regular fare Trudy; I got talking one day and before we knew it, we were taking a drive up to Roman Road and enjoying some car park fun. This went on more than once, and she started buying me gifts, that was great but it was clothing, and Lisa would get suspicious; I wasn't making enough money to be buying loads of Ben Sherman clothing. Lisa and I, had plenty of fun in nearly a year, but she soon got fed up with my lies and we split.

Breezer, played an hour gig in a Weston nightclub, Europa one Thursday night, it was a great night with a great audience. The end of the night however was not so nice, Barry informed the band, that he, Rachel and the kids were moving to Australia within the next year. Breezer were about to be no more!

By now, my house mate Jonny, had met and was about to settle down with his new girlfriend Sarah; he gave his notice and was gone! I however, now had to make sure I didn't lose the house, and had to look for a new house mate.

I still had fun with Trudy when I could, as well as the twelve-years older Julie, who lived in the house opposite me, and after bumping into Faye, we shared a few bedroom moments, so it wasn't all doom and gloom. I was working a nightshift when I got a radio message; I was informed that a lady, who I did know, had phoned and left her number and asked if I'd ring her. I got the number and made the call, then spent about two weeks dating Sarah. My family went to The Viceroy, in Whitecross Road for a curry night one Friday night, it was only around the corner from my house; Dad and Mel were already going there for Dads birthday treat, so they got me on the way and we walked round together. We met Cheryl and Drew when we got there, and the five of us celebrated my 34th birthday, and dad's 60th. We ate, and we drank plenty of Cobra, a lovely night was had; I went home and enjoyed the comfort of my bed on my own. Of course, exactly ten-years before, I was on remand and Sis and Dad took me to our surprise birthday party; for me that night meant a lot!

The end of the month and Breezer were playing in the Back Bar. We were setting up after six-thirty and two girls walked in; they got a drink and sat to watch us set up. One I knew, and was a girl I'd not seen for a very long time, Chelle; she was with a sexy blonde girl who I immediately took a shine to; so after a quick hello and hug with Chelle, I was introduced to her friend Sarah. From that moment I was happy, we exchanged numbers and she stayed for the gig. Within a couple of days, I was introduced to her children.

I was still renting taxis at this time, when I noticed a photo in the Apple cabs office, it was a white Mondeo; a plated taxi and for only four hundred quid. I couldn't buy it quick enough! It didn't take long to sort the paperwork and expensive insurance; but now I had a car again. The Renault was soon sold, as I needed money to go to the Isle of Wight, for the scooter rally at the end of August.

The beginning of August was just the best. Great friend and sound engineer, Mark Bolam, was the owner of the New Hobbits in Weston, the old Charlie Browns; it was a new great music venue, where many great acts had taken the stage. Well, this particular night was Bad Manners, with support from Breezer; how chuffed were we, when Mark asked if we'd like to do it. Loads of long-time friends were there for a great night of entertainment, there was another ska band that played too. Buster made it a night to remember! As the rest of the Breezer boys had all gone home due to work commitments, I however thought, "Sod that, I'm having a day off!" I had the best night ever, as I sank pint after pint with Buster and the rest of Bad Manners.

The morning however was a different story. As I'd not left Buster and Hobbits, until three thirty and wobbled home by four; I chose to stay in bed as late as possible. To my horror, my next-door neighbour Sally, was having a fire place removed in her bedroom. Well, her bedroom was the other side of mine, at about eight-thirty in the morning; it sounded like a hammer drill was coming through my wall. I leapt up, whilst spinning out of control, I was in a bad way; I'd only been home for about four and a half hours.

I finally revived myself and after a nice long shower, I decided to leave my house late afternoon, and go and visit Dan and Lynne; they too were there the night before, and I had a surprise for them from Buster. It was their anniversary, the night of the Bad Manners gig, as I'd spent a further few hours with Buster after they'd gone; I'd given Buster a flyer from the gig and he wrote on it, "Happy Anniversary Lynne and Dan, Love Buster X." Even though they too were absolutely hanging, they were thrilled to bits when I handed them the flyer, as a lovely gesture, Danny then handed me a new chrome front rack for my Vespa.

The following week, we were gigging back at The Borough Arms; it was now approaching the end of a good band life! We were soon playing in Hobbits again, but this time supporting "London's Calling," they'd not been together long at this point, but it was still an honour to be supporting a great act. Nearing the end of the month, it was time for the last night live with Breezer. We packed the Back Bar, as everyone came to see us perform for one last time; it was a very emotional night for many, including me.

I rode my Vespa to the Isle of Wight at the end of the month, but now with a new front rack and I'd also added four mirrors' and three spotlights'; I know it's not every ones taste, but I loved it.

This particular year, the journey to Southampton was most memorable. We were riding in the usual six plus scooter convoy, and we were probably only twenty miles away from the ferry port; there were a couple of scooters in front, and a few behind. Travelling at about fifty; suddenly, the rear end of my loaded up with luggage scoot, just dropped; it felt like a blow out, but it was making a scraping noise, and felt lower than a flat tyre. It was a wobbly maneuver to pull over, but after inspection, I realised my back wheel had indeed come off. Rear scooter wheel nuts are a castellated nut; with a hole through the drive shaft and a split pin keeps this safe. Well you see, Timmy "Quick engine re-build" Day, forgot to put a split pin back in and the nut had worked loose and shot off somewhere. We were stopped in the only drive way for a few hundred yards; it was then that we noticed a big long shed; we knocked on the door of the joining house and a frail little old lady answered. We asked if there was any small chance, that she might have something in the shed we could use as a split pin and a nut. Well, would you believe it; she opened the shed, for us to find about ten tractors; some old and rusty, and a couple of newer ones', and hundreds of dirty tubs full of nuts, bolts, washers, split pins and rusty sockets; it looked like something out of "Shed and Buried" on Sky TV! We found what we needed, and also Danny Hodgetts found a Lambretta wheel nut spacer, I know that's of irrelevance but Dan was quite excited about it. We got there Friday and we got drunk all weekend, I got my patch and T-shirt, and we came home Sunday.

Mike Corran, whom I'd known for years, had recently split with his wife Julie; so he moved into one of the spare bedrooms. As I had another spare room, Colin Smith took that one; so we could keep each others costs down.

With Breezer now over, I was able to work hard and do nights as well; I could spend more time with my new family unit and Daz on weekends. By November, Andy Davies and I were over the Severn Bridge, to see the Mod God Paul Weller at the then CIA; it was another awesome gig, with a quick run to the train station not to miss the last train home; but it did mean we missed Town Called Malice; gutted.

Sarah, her kids and I, had Christmas together, and Boxing Day with my family and Daz. I worked the New Years Eve, as it was the best night for a cabbie, once midnight had passed, I drove back to Sarah's and as the kids were fast asleep, we did our own celebrating.

Into 2005 and no longer in a band; I worked hard as a taxi driver and was there for Sarah when I wasn't busy. I did spend a lot of time at friend's Mike and Trina's house; they'd had one of my kittens from me a few years previous and by March the 8th, their now big cat, gave birth to six kittens. As I was as good as living with Sarah and she already had two bigger cats; I decided I'd have the tiny black fluffer; she was so cute, and looked like she'd had an electric shock; I named her Sparky. The end of the six weeks came, and I was ready to take Sparky home; I was told that someone had let them down, and were unable to take the last little grey fluffer. As I lifted Sparky from her sister, I watched as their tiny little squeaks' left me in tears! I couldn't resist it, so I left their house with both kittens; with her tiny thin face, she looked like the Mogwi from the Gremlins Movies, so I named her Gizmo and I now had the grand-fluffers of Max, my last cat.

The week later, I was asked by Nick Cavill, if I'd like to join him and Steve, at the Winter Gardens for "DJ Mike Reads Pop Quiz;" he'd also asked if I could bring a friend, preferably someone with plenty of pop knowledge; I asked my friend Karleigh and she was happy to join us. The team was complete; mid-March the night took place; a Beach Boys tribute act also played a set, and they looked and sounded spot on. Mike Read had organised a great entertaining night; we didn't win, but we didn't lose either! House mate Colin, had a spare ticket for the first T4 Party on the Beach on Weston seafront and asked me if I'd like to go; I had nothing planned and went along. I was glad I did, as I managed to see Madness right at the start. We had a great day; as Colin and his mate Kevin, had brought an orange juice container full of vodka. The sun was shining all day; my little sun hat wasn't enough protection, so I purchased a union jack umbrella hat and from that moment I've bought several more.

Barry and Co, were ready to leave for Australia, and a farewell party was organised; Breezer turned up, and Rambo once again played with us; Ian came along to say his goodbyes and a great night was had. Barry got to play some final tunes with us for one last time, and when the party was over we all went home. They left in August to enjoy life in the sun.

Early July was Exmouth Scooter Rally weekend, this time, Sarah came with me as the kids went to stay with their dad for the weekend; we had a great time, with plenty of cider and live music. Sarah enjoyed herself, and we had a safe journey both ways, well, accept the Cruciform was dodgy on my scooter. For those of you who aren't aware of what the cruciform is; it's a cross-shaped piece, that runs through the centre of the gear spindle; if this said piece is damaged, it will jump between gears; usually 1st and 2nd a lot; 3rd a few times, and 4th gear is occasional. So as you can imagine, Sarah did quite a few star jumps there and back, it was very entertaining!

What wasn't entertaining, was when we were on our return journey home. We were all riding in a pack, three solo riders and I was two up; Mike Corran was riding solo in front of us, when a Land Rover in front of him; with no indication, braked hard to turn right. Mike at this point, went crashing into the rear of the vehicle, folding his Vespa in half and him eating tarmac. I stopped immediately, as did everyone else and thankfully Mike was ok, just a bit shaken; his scooter wasn't going anywhere; so we pushed it down a lane and camouflaged it, and he jumped on the back of Darren Brown. Mike, Adam Dermody and myself, went back a few days later and picked it up in Adams class two truck.

During July, I fitted a new cruciform to my Vespa, I corrected that problem and I also had a spare Vespa frame. So, after work every day; I sanded down the spare frame, and sprayed it with grey primer; then I sanded it down again, and then sprayed it yellow. Whilst I was getting the frame ready, Mike was stripping down his now damaged scooter; once the spray job was finished, I rebuilt Mike another scooter with his help; he was now able to come to the Isle of Wight. Sarah was coming to the Isle of Wight with me too in August, no star jumps this time, but instead, we had a very argumentative weekend; mainly about the fact, that we had to take a king size duvet, and her whole make up box; it was two days camping at the Isle of Wight Scooter Rally, yet you'd think we were going for a week in Malibu, with our clothes as well; all loaded on a Vespa! It wasn't long after being home, our relationship was over; Sarah had started working for H Samuel the jewellers, and had become friendly with a male co-worker; I begged her back and sent her twenty poems, but to no avail. She also told me that she was pregnant!

I was working hard one day and I was on my way to my next pick up; I'd travelled over a bridge and was indicating right to turn into the Bournville estate; there was a lot of traffic coming the other way so I waited patiently. After checking my rear view mirror, I could see a red car approaching and still at speed; there was still no gap so I couldn't turn, there were cars to my left; I couldn't go anywhere! I gripped the wheel tight, and with my foot on the brake I watched; as the red car plunged in to the back of my car; it went silent for a second, before I realised I couldn't move and the panic set in. People came running from the pub opposite and the ambulance was quick to arrive; my back was in agony, I couldn't move, I was lifted from the car and spent a couple of hours in hospital for an X-ray; I spent a couple of weeks suffering, but was soon able to work again. A great taxi mate, Huw Phillips, rented me a Renault estate, and I eventually got a couple of grand in compensation.

Before the Isle of Wight rally, and whilst working one day in July; I was sat in my taxi minding my own business and doing the crosswords in "Take a Break;" waiting for my next job. A lady walked past walking her dog, wearing a red dress and looking stunning; she was wearing the dress by the way, not the dog! I said hello and she stopped for a chat; after finding out her name was Louise, we even shared the same birthday, month, day and year; I took her number; I did also mention that I was in a relationship.

Literally, as soon as I'd split with Sarah, and took my cats and other belongings, I gave Louise a ring; she only lived round the corner from me, so we met for a coffee and we became a couple.

Now with a new woman and no band, we were able to spend all of our spare time together; I could work all day, come home and have tea, walk to Louise, then spend all night at hers, with her and her dog

Mutley. I'd leave early in the morning and walk home. House mate Colin, was booking to see The Fun Loving Criminals mid-September, at the then Bristol Academy, he asked if I'd like to go along; what another great band and an awesome night was had. The end of November, saw me and Andy Davies, watching The Mod God Paul Weller; once again giving us his best at The Colston Hall in Bristol. The support act that night was a band we'd not heard of, The Ordinary Boys; I thought they were brilliant. As Louise was from Bude in Cornwall; she'd always spend Christmas with her family down that way for a week or so; I was gutted, so I spent Christmas with my family instead.

Breezer support Bad Manners

With Buster after a great gig

CHAPTER 6

ORDINARY BOYS AND CHEEKY GIRLS

I'd received a phone call from Louise, whilst I was out working on a cold morning at the start of 2006; I soon forgot about the cold, when she informed me that she had ordered two tickets to see Goldie Looking Chain at the 02 Academy in Bristol. Maggot, from GLC had recently been in The Big Brother house, he made me laugh all the way through it; during his time in the BB house, Lou and myself had gone out and bought GLC's albums'; so funny and a great entertaining band.

At the end of February we were at the 02 in Bristol to watch them live; they had a Beat Box guy for support who was very impressive, they were as awesome live as they were on CD, so we went home happy.

Orange Wednesdays, were a popular night out at the Odeon; we'd usually go every other week. We saw Ice Age 2 at Weston Cinema one week; then Lou and I took Sam and Emma (Lou's niece and nephew), to the iMax cinema in Bristol the week after; I don't remember what we saw. At the end of the month another great night was planned; the lead singer Preston from The Ordinary Boys, was also in the Big Brother house, I'd also seen them supporting Paul Weller the year before. Louise booked us two tickets, so on the 29th another awesome night was had at the 02 Academy. From Mod to Rocker, as a few weeks later we were on a Bakers coach, heading for the Birmingham NEC, but this time to see The Darkness; we got up there in good time as the motorway was clear, we handed over our tickets and made our way to the bar. We stood waiting for the support act to finish, they weren't bad but not really my thing; we finished our bottles of drink and we made our way to the bar for another; the bar was so busy, it was a long wait until we got served; so we got two bottles each to see us through the gig.

Back in the stadium and the support act had finished; there were people stood everywhere waiting for The Darkness, when suddenly, it went dark and a guitar started playing, the rest of the band started playing too and then the stage lit up. Whilst the band were there playing the sounds, we were all looking around, desperate to see the singer Justin Hawkins; we could now hear him, but we couldn't see him! Up above; there was a spot-light shining; we all looked up to see Justin singing, whilst in a massive pair of boobs! it was quite an introduction, he soon joined the rest of the band on stage; for a great show. Once it was over, everybody made there way out to their vehicles, we got back on the Bakers coach and made our way home.

Nick Cavill gave me a ring one day! We hadn't been in touch much due to Breezer coming to an end; he informed me that a friend of ours Stuart Davies, needed a bass player, a guitarist, and a drummer; that was great as we hadn't done anything together for nearly a year. At that time, Stuart had a gym in Sunnyside Road, not too far from my house and a rehearsal was arranged. Nick, Ian, and myself got there, and we met with Stuart, Rachel, and another Ian. It was for a one-off gig in June, on The Grand Pier on Weston seafront. Rachel handed us all a list, and said "These are the ten songs we'll be doing live in five weeks!" No problem, but did I have some work to do; we had a short practice and it didn't sound bad to be fair. We were now a six-piece, with Stuart Davies and Rachel Milverton on vocals, Nick Cavill on guitar, Ian Simpson on bass, Ian Hewitt from 80's favourite's Racey, on the keyboards, and of course, there was me making a racket behind them all!

The first week of June and Louise had sorted a cheap flight and accommodation to Rhodes for a weeks holiday; having never really been abroad before, made me very happy. The week was spent really enjoying ourselves, it was like I'd won the lottery; Karaoke on the holiday site we stayed in; we travelled daily on a coach and during the week, had spent time in every destination on Rhodes Island; I had never had so much fun; as well as laying on beaches, listening through my headphones to the songs I was playing on the pier, the week after our return.

Once home, I was back to work and band rehearsals continued. The weekend came and the gig on The Grand Pier took place, along with a couple of other bands, including Devious Phat and headlined by The Orphans; another great night and we pulled it off really well. It was only meant to be a one-off gig, but before we knew it, people were coming over and asking for our details; we were being booked all over the place. "Off the Record" was born. We were covering Pink, the Scissor Sisters, Mika, and a couple of 70's and 80's anthems for the first ten songs on the Pier.

As June came to a close, I was with Lou again heading for Bristol, but this time to see my all-time favourite band, The Who. Sadly, John Entwistle had passed on by then, I believe Simon Townsend played bass instead, they had great support from the Zutons, other friends were there and we left with our memorabilia and a T-shirt each, happy birthday to us.

The week after; Off the Record played our first pub gig at Neptune's Nook, on Weston's seafront; we were now known and out there, but we needed to build our set; so we didn't play any more gigs for the year.

Wayne from Apple Taxis, was selling his red Mondeo plated taxi; I bought that and was happy that I no longer needed to rent a cab.

Orange Wednesday saw Lou and I, going to see Pirates of the Caribbean at the Odeon on the 2nd of August. On the Bank Holiday weekend, Lou and I took a drive to Dartmouth and we stayed on the boat with Mum and Perry. It was the Regatta weekend; we saw some live music and we ate plenty of ice creams; but the best part of the weekend, was when the Red Arrows did their display; they flew so low over the River Dart and Louise was able to get some great pictures; she'd not long purchased a digital camera and we were on the boat as they flew over. It was awesome to see and a lovely weekend was had.

At the end of November, we were travelling over the Severn Bridge to see The Scissor Sisters; this was helpful at the time, as Off the Record were now covering all sorts of songs, Scissor Sisters included. We stood and watched the stage, as a working lift slowly started making its way down, with a huge pair of scissors on the doors; the music started and the band began to play; the doors opened, then Jake Shears and Ana Matronic stepped out and sprang into song and dance. What another awesome night and a smashing performance from the band, and some handy drum tips for me thanks to Paddy Broom.

The following month, I worked every day right up to Christmas Eve, Louise had gone to her parents in Bude for the usual period. I didn't have a good start to Christmas Eve though. I was working hard as it had been quite busy; I was driving near my house whilst travelling at about twenty mph, when a cat came from nowhere! I hit it and immediately stopped in panic; I knocked on a few doors, but nobody knew whose cat it was, so I asked for a towel and scooped it up; I put it on my passenger seat and shot to the nearest vet. I was in tears being a cat lover myself; I got to the vets in good time, but unfortunately he didn't survive. I left very sad, but I had to carry on my day and earn some money; it was a long sad day after that and I finished at four. After a shower and a bite to eat; I then made my way at six, to Bude, to spend Christmas with Louise and her family. It took me about two hours to get there, and a great time was had. It was a sad day to hear that soul legend James Brown, had passed away Christmas morning. After breakfast we made our way to Bude seafront, to watch a hundred plus crazy people doing their annual Christmas swim; I was tempted but way too cold for that! I left early Boxing morning, and had a lovely two-hour drive home; I was able to listen to all the CDs Lou had given me; Seal, The B52's, Booker T and the MG's, and The Monkees. I got home in plenty of time and picked Daz up at twelve, and spent the day at my mums with the rest of the family; a great Christmas and New Year was had.

With a quiet start to 2007; the preparations started for Cheryl's 40th Birthday celebration's. She turned forty near the end of February and in March she organised a massive party, at the Royal Hotel; Off the Record played and we smashed it. To everyone's surprise, Cheryl and her dancer friends had arranged and prepared a dance. After we did our sets and I read a poem out, in front of all for Cheryl, Thriller by Michael Jackson came from the speakers, then suddenly people were getting up and doing the dance from the Thriller video; it was surreal but lovely to see and another great party was had.

The week after; I took Daz to see Chitty Chitty Bang Bang at The Bristol Hippodrome; it was a lovely gift from Cheryl for us, for Daz's birthday; Cheryl and Lou came too. Off the Record, were asked back to Neptune's Nook mid-month, and by April, Lou and myself were enjoying an Orange Wednesday once again at the Odeon, to watch Mr Bean's Holiday.

It was a sad day for some in May. Mr Slaney was a regular taxi fare and he always did a wait and return; one morning, I picked him up about eleven-thirty, I drove him into town and I waited whilst he did his banking. He was an elderly, very tall chap, but he was always very pleasant, he returned from the bank, climbed in my car and the journey home commenced. We were talking as we always did, when he just stopped in mid-conversation, I thought it was a bit weird so I took a quick look at him, to see he was in fact motionless; I grabbed his arm and shouted, "Mr Slaney are you ok, talk to me please." Then without warning he went rigid, completely rock-solid; his feet were deep in the foot-well, his back had lifted from the seat and by now his eyes were rolled back, showing only white. I was really worried and put a call through to Joy in the Apple Taxi office; she spoke as she normally did; we usually had a great bit of banter, but instead this time I shouted, "I think Mr Slaney is having a heart attack!" I then turned into an ambulance and rushed to the hospital. I was still talking to Mr Slaney, when suddenly, he went from rigid to flumped and still silent; I was now racing safely along Devonshire Road, calling his name as I drove; then he did it again and went rigid; nearly giving me a heart attack!

The hospital was nearby, so it was minutes before I got him there; I parked in the ambulance bay and ran in shouting for assistance; two nurses and an orderly came rushing out with a wheelchair; I told them his name and they whisked him away. I did call the hospital later to see if he'd improved; but unfortunately, he'd passed away twenty minutes after I dropped him off. Rest in Peace Mr Slaney!

Mid-May; Nick, Steve, and I, made our way to see From the Jam, at the 02 Academy in Bristol. Both Bruce Foxton and Rick Buckler were in FTJ at the time; we stood outside after an awesome show and I got a selfie with Rick Buckler. Lou and I took a drive to the Plymouth Pavilion, on a Saturday in June to see Jimmy Carr do a very funny and entertaining stand up show. July the 11th saw us at The Playhouse in Weston, watching "Songs from the Shows" with Weston Operatic's; Cheryl was in that show and she delivered a great performance; as did the rest of the cast.

The day after our birthday Off the Record played a blinder of a gig; only for half an hour and DJ Downsy, from the local radio station "Star Radio" was very upset, when we extended our play by three minutes. The Mid Summer Buzz was always a great event; 10CC had played the night before, as had Racey, with our keyboard player Ian. Daz came with Cheryl and Drew; the Cheeky Girls played straight after us, and we had a laugh with them too; they were followed by Southwest's favourites The Wurzels, it was another great memorable day.

Nearing the end of the month I had a problem with my taxi! It was pouring down with rain, it was a cold day and my car was overheating. I went to Sainsbury's fuel station to check my water; the rain was so heavy and I didn't want to get too wet. I popped the bonnet, immediately removing the cap from the now hot radiator; "BOOM," boiling hot water over my right arm. At first I thought it had missed me, but no; it literally took about thirty seconds; the pain kicked in, after the boiling hot water had seeped through the cuff of my week-old Harrington. Now screaming in pain; I still topped up my water, then jumped back in the car, I then drove as fast and as safely as I could. It was still hoofing it down with rain, and I drove from one side of Weston to the other, with my drivers window down, and my now burning arm out the window to stop the pain with the rain. The pain was unbearable, especially when I stopped at traffic lights, and the rain just wasn't enough; but I had to get to the hospital, so once again I parked in the ambulance bay and ran in; they quickly had an orderly come out and put a cooling substance on my arm, it really didn't help much to be honest; I only sat for another ten minutes and jumped the queue as I was clearly in agony. I soon left the hospital and made my way home with a new injury.

At the end of the month, Off the Record played a friendly gig at the Liquid Lounge, (ex-Hobbits). During that gig, my now-massive blister on my bandaged wrist popped, it was very messy I can tell you; it was about a month until it just became a scar.

During the last few months of the year, Louise and I did our Orange Wednesday visits and saw Run fat boy Run and The Heartbreak at the

Odeon. During November we played a Thursday gig in Seven, (ex-Stars), a nightclub on Weston seafront. Thursdays were always quiet, but a gig was a gig; we always gave it our best and we were back there every other Thursday for a couple of months. The week later and we travelled to Newbury, for our last gig of the year. This became a yearly gig for us, as we played to the Honda Motocross Race team, always a great night with a great audience.

The end of December and soon after Christmas, is Rich Southcombe's birthday; on his birthday night, Rich, was hosting an 80's fancy dress party at his house. I wasn't sure at first if I was gonna be able to make it, as I had parental duties; luckily for me and at the last minute, I found out I could go; but what do I dress as? On my way to dropping Daz home, we nipped into a charity shop; I rummaged through bag after bag, I dragged hanger after hanger across the rails', finally, and only for a few quid; I left with a cream mac, a kipper tie and a berry. I dropped Daz home and went home to get ready; I sorted the appropriate shirt and left my house looking like Frank Spencer, from "Some Mothers Do 'Ave 'Em," I even had a poo bag with a bit of cat litter in it. Rich dressed as Vyvyan from the Young Ones, Rich Lewis came as Wurzel Gummage and Steve Wilkinson wore a great big paper-mache head and came as Frank Sidebottom; plenty of music, cider and fun was had. I saw the year out with Louise when she returned from Bude.

Nothing much happened at the start of 2008, well, not until March when my closest family, Mum, Perry, Cheryl, Drew, Abbie, Louise, and myself, took Daz for a lovely Chinese meal at The Sea Palace; it was a very popular restaurant, owned by the Mu family. The best part about the night, was when I handed Daz his 18th Birthday present and he opened it; to find a Sugababes CD; he was very very happy as he had recently found the Sugababes and fell in love with them. After asking him to open the disc cover; he soon found three tickets, to see them at the then CIA in Cardiff. Lou, Daz, and I saw them in April and Daz was over the moon. I won't lie, I have two of their albums.

Through May, I went with Andy Davies to see Paul Weller in Bristol at The Colston Hall; I was also searching the internet daily, as I was now desperate to get out of driving a taxi all day. It was around this time, that Cheryl and Drew separated and they later divorced.

The August bank holiday weekend was spent with my mates, on our yearly visit to the Isle of Wight; it was at this rally I had the pleasure of meeting Gary "Nutty" Newton. A few of us had ridden over early, the friends I'd travelled with had all booked hotels; it was the campsite for me, so off I went; to find the campsite on my own, on my shiny blue and chrome steed, packed up with a tent, sleeping bag, and my holdall full of my weekend belongings; (it's not the 80's anymore you know). After pulling over to a short skinhead who was waving me down; he informed me, that he had a garden which could be used to set up camp; it was a lovely cheap option, but I was meeting other friends the next day and I prefer being where everything is. So after the helpful chap had pointed me in the right direction, I started to make my pull off; I noticed a black Vespa pulling up behind me and waving for me to stop; he pulled up alongside me, and asked if he was in the right direction for the site; "Follow me" I said, and then we were off!

After finding a suitable spot, we dismounted our scooters' and began the procedure's; The first thing is to find a loo. Then remove the tents from the scoots and erect them, fill the tents with all the other stuff from the scoot; once that was done, we went to the night do on the site where the discs were spinning; we downed a couple of pints, then went back to our tents for a laugh; before zipping up and getting the sleep we deserved.

On Saturday morning, the phone rang and I was informed that the others will soon be arriving; Dan Hodgetts and Darren O'Callaghan eventually turned up and we helped them set up their tents'. Once that job was done, we all had a good look around the site stalls to buy our patches and T-shirts; then we jumped on our trusty steeds' and made our way to the local Tesco Superstore. It was like a weekly shop, we'd buy crates of beer or cider, cartons of orange juice, crisps', chocolates', milk, and alka-seltzer; we took it back to our tents to drop it all off, then we rode into the centre of Ryde. There were scooters' everywhere, pubs full of skinheads', mods', and general scooter fanatics'. After parking our scooters' with thousands of others; whilst a DJ span the discs on the seafront, we found a (not too busy) breakfast bar to feast ourselves, we ate our full English breakfast and went back to the site.

Later in the afternoon, we were back on the site, and "Nutty" pulled out a bottle of Peach Schnapps from his bag; "Holy Shit;" that was a powerful drink; about 60% or higher. You see, Gary was in the Army and was based in Germany; he came back the week before to Sheffield, stay with his wife and kids; he'd then ride to the island for the rally; then he'd travel back to Sheffield, see his family, then go back to be a soldier in Germany. He'd brought this bottle with him from Germany, as well as the cider and any other drink we consumed, we were not in good health; but still we made it to the evening do at the ice rink, to see the awesome Secret Affair; followed by a night of scooter tunes span by some top scooter rally DJ's; so another fantastic night was had on the dance floor. What a weekend, and now I was in touch with Nutty who really was a top bloke, we stayed in touch by text quite often, but more so as we approached the Isle of Wight weekend, and we always arranged to meet.

I received a phone call one day in September, from one of my longest known best mates, Craig Tildesley; he asked if I'd like to work for him, he'd had a few businesses over the years involving debt management. I was interested; I was looking to leave the taxis for good anyway, so we made a date. On the 8th I was on a train, dressed nice and smart and off to Wolverhampton; on arrival, I met Craig at the station, we had a coffee and a sandwich in the cafe; we talked about life in general, as we've always been best mates; we'd not seen each other since he took me to Newport in 99. Once we'd eaten and drunk, Craig drove us in his silver Merc, to his lovely rural bungalow in a quaint town Bridgnorth, near Telford. We spent the day looking through paperwork, and I listened intently as he told me the procedures, I also listened as he answered phone calls', so I knew what I was looking at doing. After a long day he took me on another trip, to the outskirts of Birmingham to meet Joy; she was another work colleague of Craig's. It was at Joy's house that I was presented with a laptop, a mobile phone, a box of the necessary paperwork, and a satnav. Best of all was a brand-new Seat Leon with a fuel card, and the registration number, NH08 VBM it felt personalised, (Never Home 08 Very Busy Man). It was about nine-thirty PM by this time, so I set the new satnav and made my way back home. After a safe trip, I went straight to bed; as six hours later I was up and showered and out the door by seven; for another long drive back up to Aldrington in

Manchester, as I was meeting the main boss Giles at Invocas; Craig had sold his company, Netchwood Networks to Giles.

The job was great; I travelled all over the place on a daily basis, I could be in Poole Dorset one day, Kent the next day, Walsall for a meeting, or London the day after. As the job was helping people get out of debt, I only saw clients in the night times; I didn't see a great deal of Louise, having Daz and band rehearsals on Monday nights, also started putting a strain on the job. Cheryl had started a relationship with Bernard, a fellow dancer and performer, and during November they moved into their first flat in Portishead.

October, and Off the Record were again gigging; on the 11th we played our first gig at The Salthouse in Clevedon, and at the end of the month we travelled to Oxford to play a wedding evening do. It was good when we did that gig, my cousin Lisa, her husband David and their kids live in Oxford; so after setting the gear up, I gave her a ring; she came and got me and we went for a drink which was nice.

November saw us playing in Newbury for the Honda lots Christmas do again.

I took a drive to Swansea one Thursday afternoon, as I had to see a client at six. After a trip over the Severn Bridge, to a very nice house and a lovely but heavily in debt couple; I sat for two hours, going through piles and piles of organised paperwork. I had my calculator working overtime and over heating, as I typed figure after figure; I gave them their final fee, had a quick wee and said my goodbyes; leaving satisfied that they were happy. I put my stuff in the boot of my Seat at eight-thirty, and then took a long drive, to arrive in Stanstead by midnight.

On arrival, I checked into a Premier Hotel; the next morning I was on a flight to Belfast from Stanstead Airport. I woke up late and made a dash for the airport; I had very little cash on me and no cards, as Louise was sorting my finances for me; I lived on what I had in my pockets and asked her if I was desperate. As I was late getting up, I hadn't had time for a breakfast at the hotel, so I grabbed a sarnie from the airport shop. Big mistake as it cost a small fortune, what with the Cappuccino too; I was hungry so it really didn't matter. I didn't wait long, then I boarded the plane and was soon in Belfast. Once we landed and I'd set my satnav to where I was heading; I left the airport and made my way on foot for the six mile hike. I was getting hot, as I was wearing a suit and tie, and nice (not made for distance) shoes! After walking for sometime my feet had started bleeding; I spotted a closed nightclub, with a hundred taxi numbers stuck to several phones; I was now happy and made the call. The taxi soon arrived and he took me to the house, but now I was very early; so he dropped me at a cafe at the end of the road, leaving his card, and me twelve-quid shorter in my wallet!

I sat and enjoyed a couple of coffees, and was able to let my sore feet free; the Irish lass in the cafe was lovely; she made me a bacon sarnie, a lovely big cup of coffee with a refill, and she also got me a bowl of water to soak my sore feet. I mean how nice was that! Oh, and she charged me nothing, as well as giving me a couple of plasters for my new blisters.

I finally made my way down to the house, to meet my client and he was there when I arrived; so we sat after he made a drink to discuss his finances. It was after I asked him for ALL his paperwork, he then said, in a very strong Irish accent, "Oive got no paperwork at all, and this is my daughters house." To which I responded, "Well sir, without ANY paperwork at all, I can't see what you owe or what you earn," check mate! I got on the phone to Craig to tell him of my dilemma, to which his reply was, "Come on home then mate!" Well, I wasn't expecting that, so with my last fifteen quid in my pocket I rang the taxi number, and he came and got me; but this time he took me further than when he first got me, sixteen bloody quid the other way, I handed him the fifteen quid and the sixty pence I had in my pocket; he was happy and off we both went. I got on the plane and flew back to Stanstead. Then I got stuck on the M25, for too many hours to remember and finally got home at midnight; I'd left my house at four the day before, that was my longest day ever!

Due to parental commitments and me having to ask for too many days off; after a long drive to Aldrington on the 5th of December, Giles handed me my notice, as he had to let me go. I really did enjoy the job and my time there was educational, Craig is a best mate so that was good; I made some great friends on that journey too, including Vicky Hovland and Jo Pinckard from Northampton, whom I stayed friends with thanks to Facebook and after sorting their debt's. Towards the end of December, Off the Record played their last gig of the year at The Imperial. Christmas was spent with family, until Louise came home from Bude, then I was back driving my taxi with a great ending to 2008.

Enjoying the Cheeky Girls' company

With The Jam's beat master Rick Buckler

C H A P T E R   7

FROM ONE TO ANOTHER

W hat a busy year 2009 was; within a couple of days of January, Off the Record were banging out all the favourite Bee Gees, 70's anthem's, and up to date chart sounds in The Back Bar. We saw the packed pub enjoy the night as we entertained.

During the week; I was sat with many other taxi drivers, upstairs at the Borough Arms and not earning any money. The week was spent listening, reading books, watching videos and doing tests; it was a so-called must have for every cabbie; it was paid for by Apple Taxis, but we still lost money not being able to work anyway! A week later I received an NVQ, and BTEC certificate; "Yipee," I'm now a qualified cabbie!

The mid-month was awesome; Off the Record travelled to Silverstone; to play for F1's Force India at their after Christmas party. What a place that is; there was a huge double Marquee set up on the side of the track, we changed in the F1 drivers changing rooms, it was pretty cool, seeing Fisichella, and Sutils locker's. My uncle and auntie, Stuart and Cherie did our sound for us; as what we had just wasn't powerful enough; their 10K rig sounded great. It was a great, but tough gig for me. As we were leaving the changing area to head to the stage; I stood awkwardly and twisted my ankle, it went crack and I was soon rolling around on the floor gripping my ankle; the pain was excruciating! I got up, and carried on with the gig anyway as the adrenaline soon kicked in; I soon forgot about the pain. We played to a happy audience, and we ended after an awesome two hour set; by this time my ankle had swollen to twice it's size. I hobbled and packed my drums away, and I also helped Stuart and Cherie put their amps and equipment away too, I hopped into Ian Hewitt's van and we made our way back home, me with my shoe off and my leg raised on the vans dash board.

We arrived at Ian's place by about three AM; my ankle was too painful for me to be unloading my drums at my house on my own, so I left the drums at Ians; my car was already there as I'd driven to him earlier; I went home and climbed into bed. That morning, I was meant to be leaving for Walsall at seven AM, to return the car to Craig; even though I no longer worked for him, I still had the car, laptop and other bits. So instead, I got up and made my way to the nearby casualty department, to get my ankle X-rayed. After inspection, it turned out that I did in fact have a hair line fracture; they wrapped it up and I was on my way home. Joy arrived from Birmingham later in the day and picked up the Seat Leon.

Early February, and Louise and I put the Orange Wednesday to use; this time we made our way to Burnham on Sea, to one of the oldest still operational Cinemas. This time we saw Slumdog Millionaire; there were only about ten people in the audience with us, and what a great film and lovely cosy little Odeon. Through the rest of the month we played a couple more gigs; ending the month blasting out our sounds in a very busy Nut Tree in Worle.

In March, the band were booked for a wedding do at Rookery Manor; we did have a small problem that was fixed quickly. Stuart, as well as being our essential male voice; was also the organiser and owner of the local Kick Boxing Fight Nights, that were held in Weston; he'd realised he was double booked only the night before; a last minute call was made. Ian our keyboard player, sorted it for Phil Fursdon from 80's favourites Racey, to come and sing for us for the night, he did an awesome job and we all sounded great. The week after; Louise and I took Daz to Bristol to see the TV series "Brainiac Live," at the Colston Hall in Bristol. What a very exciting show; they blew up a microwave on stage, as well as anything else they could blow up; it was a great treat and we all enjoyed ourselves; Daz enjoyed it a lot more and that's all that mattered.

Mid-April, was the celebration of Auntie Hilary's 60th birthday;

it was held on a Sunday afternoon at The Batch Country Manor in Lympsham. It was a fantastic afternoon and a lot of the family were there. Dennis my uncle, had organised a helicopter to land on the grass at the back of the hotel, and take Auntie Hil's for a ride and back again; Uncle Maurice got up and sang; he is a professional singer so it wasn't just a drunken karaoke.

Just before the first weekend in May; was a sad time for the old Ashcombe Park boys and girls and many others; ex-Ashcombe Park buddy Dave Payne, had passed away, Rest in Peace Dave! It was a sad occasion, but all his friends old and new had turned up to say their farewells; after the funeral at the Crem, and a few drinks in the Ebdon Arms for the wake; a couple of us went back to Justin Pangs house. Justin, Dean Cooke and I, then spent the rest of our day in his back garden, drowning our sorrows and reminiscing about our times with Dave and the rest of the Ashcombe park gang. It was whilst we were having our chat; Justin had mentioned to me that his little brother Ben, who was knee high to a grasshopper the last time I seen him, was a singer and guitarist; I gave Justin my address and told him to tell Ben to get in touch, it turned out that he only lived just around the corner from me.

Off the Record, were playing Karen and Sean Browns joint 40th birthday party the day after, Sean being an ex-Weston skinhead, meant that there were plenty of old-school skinheads' and other friends' there; to think we were all fighting together twenty years before was rather amusing. There was a massive pig roast and loads to drink; we all drove so drinking was out the question for us anyway. Karen is also Daz's God mother, and her dad Dave, lived in the flat above Louise, so it was easy for Karen to get hold of me.

Unfortunately for me, housemate Colin had finally been given a council flat he was waiting for and soon moved out; luckily, Martin, who was a radio operator for Apple Taxis, was looking for somewhere and he moved straight in.

I'd also bumped into my ex-Sarah, she was just leaving Tesco Express as I'd pulled in to get lunch; we had a quick chat and she introduced me to her very young child; it made my mind tick, after she jokingly said, "he could be yours you know!"

Still early in May and we hired Stuart and Cherie to do our sound again; this time at The Winter Gardens for the Mayor of Weston's Ball; it was another fantastic and very posh night. Then the last weekend, we finished the month off playing in the Imperial to another great crowd. Of course, Stuart and Ian the bass player, both being high-up in the Kick Boxing world, meant that there was always one hell of a hard audience and I don't mean hard to please, I mean hard as nails.

We decided as a band, that Off the Record needed a booking package. First we paid a fee to allow us to record cover version's on to CD, then we spent every evening for a week; recording six songs, at Brian Monks Horizon Studio. It was a great time had, laying down Maroon Five's "This Love," The Jam's "Town called Malice," Kim Wilde's "Kids' in America," Katrina and the Waves "Walking on Sunshine," Manic Street Preachers "Design for Life" and The Scissor Sisters' "I Don't feel like Dancing." As well as an info page, we now had what we needed to advertise Off the Record.

In the 70's, Stuart and Cherie were in a Folk band called Folkal Point, they did make one vinyl album; there were only a limited amount of this record made. Of course, the parents all got their copies; as well as any they may of given to their friends'. The rest of these albums were stored in the basement, of my great auntie Eileen and uncle Stan's (Stuarts mum and dad), fruit and veg shop in Bedminster Bristol. Well, after a very bad rain storm, many streets were water logged, the fruit and veg shop took a big brunt of it; "Oh Shit," the records were ruined, as well as half of Bedminster. They later went on to form a rock outfit called Touch, they'd play in Dubai for six months a year which was pretty cool. After a few years with Touch, they went on to join Les Grays Mud, yes, that's right, that's right, that's right, that's right, the real Les Gray and Mud, (check them out on YouTube). Now they're sound engineers, for a long time they always supplied the sound, for the main stage at The Ashton Gate Festival in Bristol. Cherie is also a singer in a folk band once more.

During this time, I'd had another bump in my car; but this time it wasn't actually my fault. I'd turned into a left-hand bend and started to accelerate; as I approached a group of parked cars on my left, a door opened in front of me; it was too late and, "Wallop." The door folded and creased, as my headlight smashed, along with the wing, bonnet and bumper. After jumping out to ask what she was thinking, I checked to see if she was ok, she was fine but her door wouldn't close as it was crumpled. I was now pissed off, as once again I was going to lose money. I made my way to see Dale and Pete Burrison, as they were in charge of keeping me a supply of Mondeo parts should I have a bump. I unbolted a green wing, I grabbed a front bumper and a headlight too. I popped over to Halfords, bought some primer and the necessary red aerosol cans, then went straight home to do a job that needed doing (again). Over the years I did a few rear enders and probably changed four sets of headlamps, between three different cars as well as the occasional mirror, wing and front grill; all was good, within three hours I was back out earning money.

June, and Off the Record played another busy night at the Back Bar, and the evening after, Lou and myself were watching a Ben Spiller classic, Night at the Museum, great film and a great night. Nothing much else happened in June, except jogging for five-miles most nights with Lou and Mutley. There was a knock on my door one evening; after answering it, I was greeted by a six feet tall Ben Pang, I invited him in for a coffee and we caught up. It had been at least twenty years since I'd last seen him in the late 80's, when he was just a tiny boy. It was only a matter of days, and we were in Brian Monks Studio, rehearsing Bens original written songs'; there I met with fellow musicians, William Allen on the guitar, and James Byron on the bass; we got together every week for rehearsals and we sounded great.

Louise had sorted tickets' for the two of us and Daz; so the start of July; saw us once again heading over the Severn Bridge, to the then CIA, to see "Britain's Got Talent." It was a great performance from all the runners up, including Stavros and his son, Helen Coyle and many more; of course, the real stars were Infinity, as they showed us their skills at the end. We waited around after the show to get some autographs, we were only able to get Stavros to sign our tickets, but still we left happy; until we got stuck on the motorway coming home.

For our birthday we spent the day in Bristol at the Banksy exhibition, at the University in Whiteladies Road, what an amazing artist and display; a lovely birthday was had. We did our usual visit to the Odeon, to watch The Proposal near the end of the month, and two days later, it was "The Ben Pang Experience" gig, at The Princess Victoria Rooms in Burnham on Sea. We pulled off an awesome show, it was headlined by Two Choices; a great original band, managed by Doug Clarke; we also met a group of older ladies known as the Wrinkley Rappers; very entertaining they were too! We played this fantastic one off gig, and I carried on with Off the Record.

Off the Record started the month playing at The Imperial, this time Rachel's sister Alex, joined the stage to sing Town Called Malice with us; she also sang with Nick and Gavin Cox, in their acoustic trio called "Three."

Louise and myself did our frequent Orange Wednesdays; we saw Ice Age 3 and The Ugly Truth. Lou had many certificates' in literacy, and we used to have a small separate night college for Literacy courses in the Boulevard, in Weston town centre. I enrolled for the first course and Lou enrolled for the third; she had already passed one and two; we went along together and we worked hard. By the start of September, I'd gained a City & Guilds in Adult Literacy, Level 3, so I was happy with that and Lou also passed her course. Off the Record didn't have many bookings at this time; we did play in the Back Bar at the end of the month, and Lou and I saw The Time Traveller's wife on the Wednesday at the Odeon.

As well as the two of us jogging, or taking long walks with Mutley, Lou and I did take Daz and my mum to the Playhouse, to see "The Abba Story Live;" it was a great performance all round, they did look and sound exactly like the real thing. The rest of the month was keep fit and films, we saw the Invention of Lying, Couples Retreat and UP2D.

Off the Record, kicked started November off with a gig in The Back Bar; it went down hill for me the very next day. It was a Saturday, and I had an early drop off in Clifton Bristol, the roads were clear and we made it up there with no problems. I've driven this particular route many times in my life, and I started my journey home. No sooner was I leaving Clifton, and travelling at no more than 20 mph; a car appeared, as if from nowhere, right in front of me! I hit the brakes hard, but it was too late! "CRUNCH;" I drove straight into the drivers side of the little Fiat. I reversed back a few feet and jumped out; she was a young lady, who was fine but very shaken; her door was stoved right in, so I turned into Superman; I literally tore the door open; I helped her out and sat her on a wall. After she had calmed down and stopped crying, we exchanged details and I drove off gutted; no more earnings for me that day.

She admitted it was her fault, before I'd even got home my phone had rang; it was her insurance company, and a brand-new courtesy Skoda Superb was with me the next day, unfortunately for me, my red W reg Mondeo with three hundred and thirty-three thousand miles on the clock, was now a write off.

I only received eight hundred quid in insurance money; due to the age of the car, now I had to buy a new car and get it plated for a taxi. Within the last year, a new plating law had come in for taxis'. Any car of any age that was already plated, could stay on the road as a taxi, but now the Town Council had brought in a new scheme; it meant that any new taxis being plated for the first time; cannot be any older than eight years old. This caused me a problem, as there was no way in this world I could buy an eight-year-old car, or younger, and plate it with only eight hundred quid in my pocket and a bad credit record. Thanks to Louise, Mum and Perry, I was able to start looking, I soon found a lovely green 02 plate Mondeo; with seventy-two thousand miles on the clock; it was an immaculate automatic petrol, I got on the phone and the seller was only a mile away; the purchase was made, within a week it was plated and on the road.

I was able to use my new car, for Off the Records last appearance at The Salthouse in Clevedon, it was a very busy night, as they always were, my cousin Jonny who's also a drummer, came to the gig with my niece Abbie and many other friends. Cheryl, Bernard and the Elkins kids', moved to a nice big house in Weston around this time, so it was easier to pop and see them from then on.

As the year came to a close; Louise and I were having some tough times together and we soon split up. Suddenly, I had to come up with a few hundred quid that I still owed her for my car, she went to Bude to be upset and be with her family.

Off the Record played their last gig of the year at The Imperial, it was a busy pub and a fun night for me. Sarah, who was a taxi office operator at that time, was out to see our band. She looked stunning whilst stood watching me all night; when the night was over, we went back to mine and enjoyed the night some more. We did see each other from time to time; usually we'd take a drive through Bleadon, park in the lanes near The Webbington Hotel to enjoy some car park fun. I remember on one occasion, it was a really hot night and I was stood outside the car doing the business; a bunch of stinging nettles got me, right on the bum cheek, it was stinging for ages. We didn't tell a lot of people, as she was nineteen and I was nearly forty, but we did have a lot of fun.

I also started dating Tanya, she was a regular taxi fare and we'd become friends over the years, I asked her out and we became a couple. The 19th of December and only six days before christmas. "BOOM," my nice eight year old low mileage car, had decided to blow a piston. I called a mechanic mate Shaun, and he came to inspect it to inform me it was pooped; he towed it off and I waited; I was told two days later, that the engine was indeed a write off.

I spent that Christmas with Tanya, her daughter Jade and her boyfriend. We had a lovely dinner and after the turkey roast; Tanya and I got the pudding ready, I opened the side of the box, of what I can only remember was a nice sized strawberry delight, with jelly and the full works. Well, as I slowly slid it from the box and not on the sideboard by the way; "SPLOOSH," it fell straight out the box and it spread everywhere. "Oops!" We didn't have pudding in the end!

Boxing Day was spent with Mum, Perry and Daz; Perry had recently retired and told me he'd lend me the money to get a new engine. A new engine was sourced, but as it was Christmas they couldn't get it too me for a few weeks, so instead I enjoyed my free time with Tanya; when she wasn't working hard looking after the elderly.

Now into 2010 and awaiting delivery on my new engine; there were no taxis available to rent so I wasn't earning any money; and I still owed Mum and Perry money for the car and engine. Tanya really looked after me though, and made sure I ate and could get through it ok. The new engine arrived, and I had it delivered to Mark at Motormend, he had a workshop and all the tools I needed; we had my car towed over from Shaun's garage, Norside Motor Services, which wasn't too far away. Every day for three days, I'd walk in the snow to Motormend and work on the car all day: Mark helped with the forklift, to lift the pooped engine out and drop the new engine in, I did everything else and asked for assistance if required. Every day, when it just got too cold to carry on; I'd walk back to Tanya's where she'd have a bath run, followed by a beautiful tea. I may not have been working or earning but she made sure I didn't suffer, I'd come home to find new jeans one day and a new shirt the next; life was good.

The end of the month was the first gig for Off the Record, as we graced the stage of The Back Bar once more.

After driving the new engine car for two days; it started to blow out bellows of black smoke. I rang the bloke I bought it from and he arranged for another engine to be delivered; this time I thought differently, so a great taxi driving buddy Paul Johnstone offered his services, his brother John, also a taxi driver, offered us the use of his drive-way and tools. I popped to a hire company and gained an engine crane for two days, by February the 13th the second engine was fitted. We wrapped the knackered engine, and arranged for its collection; I returned the crane and carried on my way.

Tanya was still buying me gifts', mainly Ben Sherman and Fred Perry shirt's from The Sole Room, my mate Dave's shop; there were many Saturdays' I'd spend in there; with other mates playing table footie, whilst listening to sounds on Dave's jukebox.

I was still working as often as I could; I had so many people to pay money to; as well as the run of the mill stuff, like house rent, bills, car insurance and cost's in general; it was tough as I hadn't been earning properly for ages, but I did my best. The start of March, Off the Record played a wedding reception at Rookery Manor. By this time, and doing anything up to a hundred and fifty miles a day in my taxi; I found I was using far too much oil. I would be popping into Proper job every three days, to buy 5 litres of engine oil, after a couple more weeks; it started to feel like it was costing more in oil per week than fuel, even on a quiet day; I made very little money using minimum fuel, yet I would still be topping up the oil. After another call, the third and final engine was sent the following day; this time I chose to do it myself. I hired the engine crane again, and I nipped to Proper Job, to purchased any tools I didn't have but knew I'd need. I worked the early morning on a Monday, and finished by ten AM; I drove the car down the lane at the back of my house and went in to make a coffee, have a bite to eat and get changed into my now, covered in oil engine changing clothes.

When I was ready, I went out and took the bonnet off, following the same procedures I'd followed twice before; the engine was out by twelve-thirty and in my back yard. By two, the new engine had arrived and I got on with the fitting. During the afternoon, Tanya had popped by en route, to bring me some lunch and make us a coffee or two; after a quick snog she was gone. By six the engine was purring, by seven, I was at Off the Record rehearsal's and after picking Daz up too! By the end of the month, we were playing at The Imperial to the usual satisfied audience. Craig had also phoned me, to ask if I'd like to come and work for him at Netchwood Networks again; same money as last time, but now I was given a blue Mondeo, and a year older than mine. I didn't complain and it was only for a month until he found someone permanent; he needed my help and I was privileged that he'd asked me. Tanya and I had not been getting on; I'll blame myself, as by this time I was still unsure what I wanted in life; she was lovely but deserved better!

It was another sad time in April; we said goodbye to Nick Payne; as his brother had died the year before, Nick couldn't cope without Dave, and he took his own life on the same date; Rest in Peace Nick! I finished working for Craig after a few weeks, and went back to driving my taxi. I was sat at home one morning after I'd worked a few hours, having a coffee break; whilst I was sat with my drink, I turned on the computer and scrolled the internet to search for a new job. After all the engine trouble's I'd had and not earning enough money to cover the bills, as well as pay what I'd borrowed, I really needed a new job. I found that Hunt's, a food delivery service, were looking for summer, seven and a half tonne drivers; well, my licence entitles me to drive that size vehicle, so I got on the phone immediately. A guy called Martin answered, he told me what the job involved and asked how quick I could get a CV to him; well, as we were talking, I was tapping the buttons on my computer keyboard, I printed a copy of my CV, I said goodbye, switched off the computer and jumped in the car with the CV in my hand. It was literally a five minute drive and I was walking into Martins office to see him. We shook hands and we sat down, he scanned my CV and said, "When can you start," The following day I was sat in a cab with Dave, travelling off to Woolacombe to deliver ice creams and other frozen foods.

The 1st of May, Nick, Steve and myself, took the train to Bristol; we got off at Temple Meads, downed a quick pint or two in The Wreckless Engineer, opposite the station; then spent the rest of the night at The Tunnels, watching "From The Jam." What a venue and what a gig, it's actually under the road you drive up to get to Temple Meads, for those of you that didn't know! It was a fantastic gig and we left after purchasing our T-shirt's. It was funny outside mind you; we were hovering around hoping to see the guys come out, when Steve started getting excited, "Look, there's Gareth Chilcott" he was saying. Now, I'm not at all a sporting man, so my reply was, "Who the hell is Gareth Chilcott?" After finding out he's a rugby legend and the owner of The Tunnels, I had to have a selfie. Great mate Paul Flint was happy to take our money, and drove up in his taxi to take us home, three happy and slightly tipsy old boy mods. Of course, I got home to find the T-shirt I'd bought was in fact a small; I never got to wear it so I gave it to Daz.

A few days later and Mum treated me to a show at The Playhouse; we saw Albert Lee, and this time with both Mum and Perry. The end of May saw Off the Record filling the Back Bar with happy drunk punters' once more.

Thanks to the joys of Facebook, I was now back in touch with a lot of my ex-school mates, ok, so a few of us had always stayed in touch, but unless you bumped into anyone, you wouldn't even know if they still existed. My best school mate Sean Thomas, was turning forty in 2010, along with many other school friends and myself.

Seans mum and dad, Jayne and David, hosted a great party for Sean and his friends from old and new. It was held at the Weston-super-Mare Golf Club, that was great, as it's only a fifteen minute walk from my house. It was an awesome nostalgic night, as was the meal we had at Hussain's Indian Cuisine; when we celebrated Tony Fords 40th, with other ex-school mates', Tony Coram, Richard Johnston, Sean Thomas, Jo Malik and a couple more.

Louise and I had been in touch and we decided to give our relationship another go.

During the early days in Charlie Browns, I made many new mod, ex-mod, skinhead, psychobilly, scooterist and other friends. One great ex-mod mate, Mark Latchford, who was also a postie when I was, asked if I'd like to join him at The Thunderbolt in Bristol, as 80's mod greats

The Purple Hearts, were playing together again after their twenty year plus split. We were there and I'm so glad I said yes, we were outside in the smoking area with the whole band, we had a right laugh. Gary Sparks, their drummer, had been a friend on my Facebook for some time, after I posted pictures of them live, in The London Hippodrome in 1986; we became mates and stayed in contact. We chatted and we laughed, we took some pictures and went back in the pub to enjoy The Purple Hearts, sure I have their records but to see them live again after twenty-four years was the best.

As I was now driving trucks all day, I decided to rent my taxi out for a bit of spare change; a night driver borrowed it and he would return it to me every morning, ready for me to drive to work. He returned one morning, I jumped in and made my way to work; but the car wasn't driving the same and didn't have the usual kick it had, I got to work and went about my day. When I'd finished my deliveries, and handed over my cash or returns, I got to my car but it wouldn't start. I called Glynn Smith who had a garage around the corner from my work, he came to have a look, but we still had no success. I rang the night driver, to tell him I had no car and to ask if he put the right fuel in, he said he did, so we were now all baffled.

The 3rd of August, and we were back to the Orange Wednesdays, with a visit to the Odeon to see K9; I think I must of slept through that one, I don't remember it at all; the week later and Off the Record were back at The Imperial.

An Ashcombe park friend, who none of us had seen for many years, Julie Williams, had moved to Australia many years before. She came back to the UK for a few months to visit family; thanks again to the wonders of Facebook, a few of us were able to meet at The Summerhouse in Weston, for a great nostalgic night out. Dave Hawkins came from Winscombe, Craig came down from Telford, Miles, Dean, James, Traci (Daz's mum), and myself, didn't live too far away so it was easy for us. It was lovely to see her after all those years.

The week after and I was off with my mates, on my still shiny trusty steed; for what has now become my last Isle of Wight rally, and Paul Flint's first, on his recently purchased Vespa PX125. As well as a puncture on my scoot in Churchill, only ten miles out of Weston;

constant downpour and having to take a detour due to road works! We were finally able to dry out a bit at Southampton Ferry Port, whilst we waited for the three AM ferry. Another awesome weekend was had, and I also did my yearly meet up with Nutty; as well as spending a great weekend with other mates' Danny and Lynne Hodgitts, Craig Tildesley and Mark Bird from Bristol. I had to rush back on the Sunday though, as Steve, Nick and I had tickets, to go and see The Chords, another awesome 80's mod band; they'd reformed for one year and did a tour. The irony was, they did actually play at the Isle of Wight rally, but I didn't see them, as I was falling asleep (stood up) at the Bad Manners gig instead; they probably passed me on the way home!

I arrived home at five thirty, and Steve was picking me up at seven, all my best shirts had been on the rally with me and needed washing; I rummaged through my wardrobe and finally decided that it was going to be a brown night; that was the only coloured shirt that didn't need ironing. I had a quick shower and shave, slid down my Bat pole and came out dressed and ready to go. I was absolutely knackered, but what a night. After a loud and very powerful gig, we got to have a good chat with the band, and get the usual selfie's and autograph's. Derek "Daleboy" Shepherd was there too, so we spent the night watching the gig with him; he's the guy who used to write, "In the Crowd" modzine in the 80's. Drummer Brett "Buddy" Ascott was gone after our meet; I asked the bouncer if he minded if I got behind Buddy's kit for a quick picture, his response was, "Ok, but don't try and play it as it's still miked up," "yeah ok, of course I wont play it," was my reply. No sooner had Steve finished taking the pics, I put my foot on the pedal and gave a quick few bass beats and a quick roll round the kit. Before the bouncer even had time to get on the stage, I was off, straight over the other side and into the crowd, we got some great pics. We soon left and I slept all the way home.

The start of September; I was told by Martin that my summer drive work would soon be over; he let me keep my car there for a short while, until I could get it moved. But now I had no working car and I was once again desperate for work, no one had a taxi I could rent and Christmas was on it's way; I was just covering bills and I was still borrowing money to survive. As I'd been in touch with Ben Pang again over the last year, and played a gig with him, he would come to my house once a week and we'd play Tiger Woods Golf on the Playstation 2. It was always a great night; well, he came round one night for his game, and informed me, that there was a job going where he worked at Smart Systems in Yatton. I made the call the next day; went straight for an interview and I started the following week. The money wasn't great but it wasn't a bad job; my time was spent working with Ricky England, he was also a drummer and as crazy as me; we actually made the days bearable and fun, even the bosses were entertained by our constant stupidity. Not having a car on the road, I used my Vespa to get to work and back every day; this was great until the end of September, when the engine seized on the way home from work one day, the engine turned out to be knackered; from that day, the scoot came off the road and I started catching the train to work.

October, Louise and myself were back at the Odeon to see Grown Ups; the week after, we were both on a train heading to the NEC in Birmingham, this time to see Rock Legends, Guns and Roses. We decided not to go with Bakers this time, so we got a train instead; we booked a hotel right next to the arena and had ourselves a very memorable night of Cider, Love and Rock and Roll.

December was upon us, the first weekend was spent at the scooter do, at the Weston, Rugby Club house in Sunnyside Road; the week after, Off the Record played their final gig of the year in the Back Bar; it was also to be our last gig! Louise came back from her Christmas in Bude earlier than usual, so for our New Years Eve, we went to the Odeon to watch Little Focker's, we enjoyed the great film and we finished the night with a drink in Bonds after the cinema. During the holiday season, I gained tennis elbow in my right arm, that hurt I can tell you; I could barely lift my arm, so it was pain killers for me and the end to another year.

Now in to 2011; Off the Record had a meeting early January. We all met at the Summerhouse and we discussed the bands future. We made the decision that we would call it a day, we'd had a good run in four and a half years and made a load of new friends' on the way. Rachel carried on singing solo on weekends, Ian had already joined Reoffender by this time and still plays with them now, Nick went on to join Majitos, Ian Hewitt carried on his keyboard skills with Racey, Stuart was already a very busy business man, I was now on the look out for my next drumming adventure, either way, Off the Record was no more!

By the end of the month, Louise and myself decided to go our separate ways again. We did give it another go but it just wasn't working, we stayed great friends.

Now single again, I was out when I could be as well as having Daz on the weekends. I went to a scooter night out in Hollywood's, a club that wasn't about for long to be fare, but all the same it was a great night. This club and restaurant was run by guitarist, singer and great friend Steve Mitchell, a very popular local guy, and Neil Urch, who also owns HouseFox, a local estate agent. DJ Dave span the discs all night and a great night was had by many.

The 24th of February, I got up early and travelled to Bristol by train and spent a very long day at the BBC's Casualty set, as I was an extra. I spent all day standing around, until eventually, laying in a bed for about ten minutes, that was all I did all day, then I travelled home. When I watched the episode on TV a few months later, and I'd also put a big Facebook post, to tell everyone to watch for my big scene; I was a dot for about point six of a second, so I decided not to do it again. Both Cheryl and Abbie did it for many years, they appeared in many episodes of Casualty and Teachers, as well as the occasional advert and speaking part.

During March, housemate Mike and myself had to find another housemate, as Martin had decided he was moving out, he did leave within a week, but luckily I'd met a friend's brother Josh, who was looking for somewhere to live; bargain we had a new house mate pretty soon.

I went out one night, to Sole Room Dave's 50th Birthday Bash, and his son Jordan was performing; he sang in a band called The Stanley's, I'd heard a CD Dave had played for me once, but I'd never seen them live. So I was stood watching them and thinking, "Yeah they're really good, but not sure about the drummer;" I couldn't help but think, "Every song has the same beat, even their cover versions!" I was out having a fag after the gig, when Jordan approached me. Of course, I'd known him as long as I'd known Dave so we had a good chat. The first thing he said to me was "Please be our drummer!" It couldn't have come at a better time. With Off the Record being over, I needed something to do in my spare time, I was also single, even though I did spend the occasional night, with the now twenty-year old Apple taxi blonde Sarah, and I also met Cheryl in the local Post Office, she lived nearby and we shared fun on more than one occasion.

By April, I'd had enough of rushing to catch the train to Yatton every morning, so I gave Hunt's a ring; sure enough I was to start there in May, so I handed my notice in with Smart Systems, happy knowing I no longer had to rely on catching trains to work.

I rehearsed with The Stanley's every Wednesday; we nailed it within a couple of weeks I was still suffering with pain from my tennis elbow too. By early August, we were playing a multi-band charity night, at the Football Club in Sunnyside Road, a great first gig for me as their new drummer; a couple of days later and we were playing another local pub, The George and the Dragon, the week after in the Kameleon. We ended the month playing a big event in Clarence Park, Jordan played the gig wearing a Scooby Doo outfit.

The end of August, during the bank holiday weekend, we had the pleasure of playing the main stage at the Watchet Festival. I'd borrowed a Hunt's van on the Sunday, picked up Jordan and we got there about eleven, we were on at twelve. We set up and it was booming, with a great sound, but unfortunately, as we were the first band of the day there wasn't a massive audience.

Literally, a couple of days later I was being let go by Hunt's; I was only there as a temp driver during the busy summer period. It wasn't long until I was back driving taxi's again.

I hadn't been back on the cab's long, when I got a fare one late morning. I arrived at the house, a pretty, dark young lady got in; it turned out she was a pole dancer in a Weston Men's Club. We ended up going everywhere for a few hours. After driving down Whitecross Road, she spotted a shop called Joy, then asked what that shop was, as the windows were covered; after telling her it was a sex shop, she yelled for me to stop and then went shopping. After forty minutes in the shop, she finally came out with a couple of carrier bags crammed. She got back in the passenger seat of my car and I proceeded to drive her home;

she then asked if I'd mind if she tried the stuff on in the car; of course I didn't mind, I even offered to pull over to give her some privacy; she told me to carry on driving and then stripped her jeans off followed by her knickers. She put on a sexy new pair of panties and asked how they looked. Well, once I told her they looked gorgeous, we were off up to the Roman Road car park for some (safe) pole dancing of our own, I gave her some discount and dropped her off home. I have no clue of her name and I don't do pole dancing clubs!

Around this time I received a call from Steve Wilkinson, to ask if I wanted to join a singer friend of his, as they needed a drummer. I went along and met Paul Hatton, Andy Evans and Tony Slattery at Paul's house. He had a handy room to rehearse in, with an electric drum kit, a couple of guitars, a keyboard and a computer set up.

We did the introductions; Paul showed me a small list of songs they were working on, and we went for it; it was great, something different for me; we were playing Tom Petty, Fleetwood Mac, The Beatles and many more, The Curve were born.

The Stanley's had nothing planned until October. Early September and Off the Record were asked to play a one off gig at The Rookery Manor in Lympsham, it was for Rachel's sister Alex. She was getting married and had pre-booked the band before we'd split, it was actually nice to do it as a one off and get together again; as neither of us had really seen each other since we went our separate ways. By now Rachel and bass player Ian had become a couple too.

A couple of weeks later and Pauls daughter Beth, married Carl Bowen, and they asked if The Curve would play. It was an honour for me, as Carl is Steve's (car crash in 88) brother, and he's always been like a brother to me. It was a lovely do, held at Coombe Lodge near Blagdon, and plenty of people were there. With The Curve playing softly behind, Beth got up and sang a song for Carl, then Carl did the same.

Rehearsing hard now, with The Curve on a Monday night and with The Stanley's on a Wednesday, life was again good. By mid-November, The Stanley's played a gig at The Imperial on Carnival night; one of the only years I didn't take Daz. It was a great gig with a packed pub, we started playing to a big audience; by the time the carnival floats passed us, everyone ran outside to see the bright bulbs and loud music; we played to the end anyway, then had to wait ages for the carnival and people to clear, before I could get my car and load my kit. The end of November, The Stanley's played their last gig of 2011. We had nothing until January, so rehearsal's stopped for us; I still practiced with The Curve on a Monday and we built our set.

Christmas was spent with the parents, Boxing Day with Daz and New Year was spent working in my cab until two AM, then I went home and downed some cider, 2011 was over.

Mark Latchford and Me with The Purple Hearts

Off the Record

CHAPTER 8

WASN'T IT SUCH A FINE TIME!

A week into 2012 and The Stanley's played for Neil Buchanan's 40th birthday bash, at Carnaby's, a great establishment managed by a great mate, Fergus Jack, who also sang with a known popular local covers band Reoffender.

It was a great night, packed with a lot of familiar faces, one particular face, was that of Carrie (Neil's sister), Well, I'd known Carrie for many years, but I'd not seen her for a while. We soon got chatting; Lily Pink took a picture of us both and it was posted on Facebook; before we knew it, everyone had been saying how good we looked together, to be honest the picture did do us justice; before the night was over, I had asked Carrie if she'd like to meet up, before we knew it we were a couple.

I was still driving taxis for Apple, Carrie had a horse and was always busy at work too; so I was gutted, as we never had a lot of spare time and didn't see a lot of each other. We drifted apart a few times, as I was always moaning that I didn't see her enough. We stayed as close as we could, but I was busy too, as I'd not long been rehearsing with Paul Hatton and The Curve on a Monday night, then practice with The Stanley's on a Wednesday.

February the 18th I played with The Curve, for a private do at The Mooseheart in Winscombe. We arrived and set up; a taxi driver buddy Dave Knight, turned up with a great light display for us to use and the sound and venue were great too. When I was relaxing before the gig my phone rang; it was a number I didn't recognise, I answered it; to hear the voice of a young sad sounding girl, who introduced herself as Abbi, then through tears, explained that her dad, Gary "Nutty" Newton, had passed away. They lived miles away in Sheffield; I was heartbroken, so we chatted for a bit and said goodbye. We stayed in touch thanks to Facebook and I proceeded to play the gig. It was probably the one and only time; I've been behind a kit for an entire gig and not smiled!

As I enjoy writing poetry, and more so when my heart strings are pulled; I wrote a nice poem about "Nutty" and sent it to Abbi on Facebook messenger. I couldn't be at the funeral, but I was honoured to hear that the poem was read at the service.

March and April were quiet months and The Stanley's had a problem during this time, I don't know the details; all I did know is that Jordan, Chris, and Gareth had a fallout! At first I put that on the back burners; I carried on driving my cab and tried to work out my relationship with Carrie. I remembered, that we had a gig booked in July at the Weston Scooter Rally campsite; I wasn't going to let Stuart Lanning down, a mate I'd known for thirty plus years; the co-organiser of the Southwest Scooter events' and a top bloke too!

Jordan went on a mission, and sourced a young guitarist Stell, and a Bass player Eddy, playing at a jam night. Jordan got chatting, to find they were both students at College, studying music and were both very good; we all met and clicked and they were happy young men, to be in a band that already had gigs' booked; we got together every week and carried on.

Fergus Jack had been in touch, Reoffender needed a drummer for an upcoming gig in Yatton; their drummer John Hutchins, was double booked and wasn't available so I was happy to help. I've been mates with all the guys in the band for years; the lead guitarist Geraint, is the brother to the original bass player Gareth, from the Stanley's, the bass player was Ian from Off the Record, front-man Danny Murphy, I'd know since the clubbing days in the late 80's early 90's and obviously Fergus, a very well-known Weston man, club owner and generally a great mate. On the 24th of April, after being handed a set-list of twenty plus songs, the rehearsal took place at Studio21 in Weston, which was run by a friend Aaron and it sounded great, but boy, am I glad I wore my ear plugs!

Hunt's had contacted me as they required me back on their trucks; I was happy with that, as it was hard trying to keep on top of everything. I gave a week's notice on my taxi radio and worked hard until my start date. A nice start to the month, as I was out for a few drinks in the Brit Bar, watching my best mate Nick, but this time playing the bass guitar for the new band he'd joined, Mojito. What a great band; their drummer was Mark, who now plays for Bad Manners, their guitarist was Keith, who is Ian Simpsons brother. The other band members, Dale and Jo I didn't know.

Mid-April; Abbie came and picked Daz and myself up, she'd brought Mum too, we went for a brunch at the Uphill Boat Yard Cafe and a lovely family time was had.

The week after, The Curve all jumped into Paul's car and we made our way to the Cotswolds; Paul was formally in a band called The Accelerators, so this trip was to meet Ian, an ex-band member of the Accelerators. It was great when we got there; he had a lovely house, with a good-sized studio in the back garden; there was a drum kit set up and a couple of guitars; we had a jam together and had a great day, it was also a pleasure to meet a great guitarist, Ian Hounsley.

On the 2nd of May I was back at Hunt's, but this time I was handed a contract; I was now a full-time driver and not just for the summer. By the 4th I was at Reoffender Rehearsals, in a very small, very loud studio; this particular night I forgot to bring my earplugs, by the next morning my right ear was mute, but my left ear was fine.

I just had to get on with it and adjust my listening technique. On the 7th, the Reoffender gig took place at The Bridge Inn, in Yatton; what a great gig it was. A great long-time friend and ex-Sea Cadet Andy Smith, was there as their Roadie, Dan Patterson was in charge of the sound. Even though it was a small audience for this band, it was great and I was happy all the same; Cheryl came with Bernard, their landlords and good friends, Carol and Paul came along too. By the following Monday, my right ear had really started hurting, so the doctors were sorted and antibiotics were prescribed; as well as having my ear syringed, the pain did go but I was still mute!

The 11th was a very sad day! It was the funeral, of ex-Breezer bass player and great friend, Mick "Rambo" Evans, he'd sadly passed away at forty-eight. My boss wouldn't give me time off, so I didn't go to the funeral, but I made it to the Cricket Club for late afternoon, and was able to give my condolences, to Mick's wife and lovely friend Sarah, and other of Micks family members. Nick was also there; we left together, went back to mine for a coffee, and for Nick to sit and play the drums; whilst we sat and reminisced; playing Breezer tunes on the stereo, listening to Rambo sing. Rest in Peace Mick!

On the 19th, The Stanley's played The Brit Bar with the new line up, and it went brilliantly; of course, I just felt like an old man; I was forty-two, Jordan was in his twenties, Stell and Eddy were only eighteen, and they'd brought all their college friends with them.

Things were good, but by this time Carrie and I had come to a complete end; don't get me wrong, we'd had some great nights out and I met some new people, some of her friends I knew, so that was nice.

Now and again, I did pop to have a coffee with Claire; she was a great friend and didn't live far from me, well, one night we did share some bedroom fun!

I did a lot of car boot sales over the years, I was asked by Hannah, who lived in Highbridge, if I'd like to join her on Sunday the 27th of May, to do a car boot sale. "Hell yeah," was my response, I had loads to get rid of. So, I loaded my dad's car and made my way to Highbridge. I spent a fun night with Hannah and we were in a field by seven the next morning, the sun was bright all day, and finally my arm colours started matching; drivers arm's a nightmare you know. We had a great day and I left for home by two, with some change in my pocket and a load more crap gone.

On June the 3rd, The Stanley's were playing at The Live lounge in Weston, (now Vinnies), but the day after on Sunday the 4th, I was travelling to the Cotswolds with The Curve, to play an outside event in the pouring rain, it was a bank holiday weekend, of course it was going to rain!

It rained so hard that they had to pull the plug in the end; it could've become dangerous, and the field was looking like a bad Glastonbury

Festival; people didn't care, they were still dancing in wellie's and rain mac's, drinking and having fun.

Good news though, they moved the venue to a nearby pub, and we were still able to play. Hannah came with me as she had brought my gear; Ian who lived in the Cotswolds, played with us that night too; we played a very entertaining gig until late, finishing the set with The Curve's rendition of 500 Miles by The Proclaimers. The entire pub joined in with their drunken vocals; we left after midnight and I was home by two. I was at work by six AM; I only had a few deliveries, but guess what? back to the Cotswolds, but this time in a truck that stuck at 52 mph. So I was back up the very quiet, bank holiday Monday M4 on cruise control. I did my deliveries, one being literally next door to the pub I'd just played in, and I ended up with three points on my licence and a ninety quid fine, for doing fifty-two on the M4; it was a fifty at the time and very empty, I was gutted.

The Stanley's played a gig at The Imperial on the 10th of June; it was after we'd set up the drums and amps, that we went outside to have a pre-gig chat; a fit woman walked past and said hi to Stell, straight away, I was all, "who was that?" It was Stell's mum Sharon, out with her sister; I spent the night chatting to her when I could. The gig sounded great as always and in a very busy pub.

Hannah from Highbridge, would pop round for a coffee and chat on occasion. The Stanley's had a gig in Bleadon on the 23rd; Hannah drove so I could get my kit there. There was free food and free booze, thanks to Miles Orme and his Bleadon Party; the only bummer was, it poured it down all night and we played in a big marquee, so it was very wet and very muddy; but still we went down a treat and we were followed by The Fallen Apples, another great local Weston band. There were plenty of friends there, like ex-boy racer buddies', Kade Penfold, Ryan Hunt, Gary Watts, and Beaumont Thorne, and ex-Hunt's driver, Chris Pearce. After an awesome, but wet and muddy night, Hannah drove a very drunk me home, we cleaned off the mud and had a nightcap.

On Saturday the 7th of July, The Stanley's rehearsed in my lounge, I had an electric kit that I'd bought from my Nephew Ryan. It was good in the lounge, and my neighbour Sally enjoyed it too; she'd mute her TV and listened to us rehearse.

Carrie had been in touch again, we gave it another go but still didn't see a great deal of each other; as we were both busy; we always made it a memorable night when we did get time together, whether it was walking her dogs, a night out or just a quiet night in. I'd booked a week off work, as my birthday was approaching; on my first day off and hoping for a layin, I forgot I said I'd run my dad and Mel to Bristol Airport, at five-thirty AM, I would've cried but he did let me have the car for the week.

However, it wasn't really a holiday week, as I drove Mum and Perry to Bristol every day until Thursday. Mum's brother Nick, was in Crown Court for paedophile offences, involving my cousin Karyn years before, when she was a lot younger. It was a very traumatic week for everybody; I was there for support, for Mum and Karyn; I also got to meet Emma, who is one of Karyn's best friends, she was also there for support. He was finally sentenced so we all left happy, it was a great result and the end to a long week. On my birthday, I was being taken out by Carrie, so we had a lovely curry at Hussain's; my good friends Wayne and Cath Flemming were sat at the next table, so that was nice. I'd been given some lovely presents' before we went out, so we stayed out and got extremely drunk at The London Inn with other friends, Rachel and Brian, then we went home. By the time we'd got home, I was moaning about something and I got stupid and angry, the taxi had already gone and I told her to just leave; that was the end of that relationship! I'm happy to say we eventually became friends again!

On the 21st, The Stanley's played a charity gig at The Boro Sports Club in Weston; there was a kit there for me to use, so I didn't have to lug mine about. We played the gig and it went great, to be fair it was only a thirty-minute set. I spent the next week driving my truck; delivering frozen food and ice cream all over Bristol and Wales.

The Weston Scooter Rally started on Friday 27th; on the 28th, The Stanley's had the pleasure of playing a gig to lots of drunk scooterists'; it was an awesome outside gig. The sun was shining and Stell's mum was also there. During our sets, I had a chat with Sharon, to find she'd recently split with her boyfriend, and was temporarily moving, with her six-year-old son Keanu, and Stell to Kits. Kit was her step-mum, and Sharon's half-sister Liz, lived there too; with her husband Dan and their two children. I had a spare room at the time so I offered my services, for

Stell to come and stay at mine; it was also the same day I asked if she'd like to go out for a drink that night. We did go for a drink and it was lovely. I was just looking out for them all and wasn't expecting anything else, I was only thinking that it might go somewhere one day.

The following week, I had Daz for a few days, so he came with me on my frozen food deliveries; he loved it, it was great having someone to help and to have my top lad with me was the best!

Dixstock was a small festival held in Brean near Weston; The Stanley's were asked, if we'd like to play for half an hour on a Saturday afternoon. It was nice and Sharon came with her mate Ali, it was a short gig with a small audience but worth it; Steve Fitch whom I worked with at Hunt's was also there. After a great gig, Sharon dropped Ali home and we spent a cosy night together, but still as friends.

I was driving my truck on the 8th of August, and I was doing a regular early delivery in Portbury. It was a small garage, with an old Jaguar parked outside, and a transit van with a fridge inside. I would deliver to this place about three times a week, the orders were always very similar and fairly big. As I always still had at least twenty-four deliveries to do after this one, I had to be quick, which was difficult with a Jag in the way. So, picture if you will, a set of yellow sack truck's, which I then loaded with five, ten-kilogram boxes of frozen chips; I then whilst walking backwards, had to first open the small normal sized door, then lift the heavy trucks over a small lip and then continue; between a parked van and a sidewall; with only about a four to five feet wide aisle. Once at the other end of the garage, I had to then spin right by forty-five degrees, and lift the heavy trucks by the top angled handle, up a foot high step. I'd done this manoeuvre at least fifty times before; I took a step back and I lifted, but then I lost my footing and fell. The fifty-kilogram plus trucks had nowhere else to go, and gravity sent it crashing down on top of me; my hand was still gripping the angled handle and I couldn't move it quick enough. Before I knew it, "Crack," and I was screaming like an injured baby! The fall had caused me to break my wrist. After putting the boxes in the nearby freezer one-handed, quick thinking saw me jump in the back of my freezer; rip open a box of frozen peas, then I sat in the cab and made some calls'. First I phoned my office and waited to be picked up, then I phoned Sharon and sobbed down the phone for comfort. A few hours later after another hospital visit, I was sat with Sharon and Keanu with a blue plaster on my arm.

Although it was a nightmare having a broken wrist, it did turn out to be a godsend. I had no car on the road and the school summer holidays were here; even though my wrist was in plaster and I had to get other drummers' to play my gigs for six weeks; I was now able to spend twenty-four hours a day with Sharon. We went for our first proper night out on the 19th and by then we were a couple. It was about this time, that Sharon's long-time friend offered her a house to rent in the Maltlands Weston, Sharon jumped to the chance and the move took place, fair play to her; she'd left her ex with nothing but the clothes on her back and all the kid's clothes. Luckily the new house was furnished, so there were only essentials like more clothes to buy. I was getting full pay from my job, so I had money in my bank and we had the best six weeks.

We'd often spend a Saturday morning, drinking a cappuccino or cups' of tea whilst watching Keanu swimming; he'd been having lessons for a short while.

The 13th of September was the date my wrist was free again, it was the best feeling ever having that plaster removed. By the 18th, we were watching Stell do his solo act in The Red Admiral, he was great and Sharon was one happy proud mum; she was also proud at the end of September when I taught Keanu to ride a bike. He was happy and free with the stabilisers gone! Seeing his little face light up gave me great satisfaction, he was a new boy, so our seafront walks became more regular and K dude could ride like a free man. We also checked out BrightHouse where Sharon made a purchase on a new sofa.

Keanu, had started as a Beaver at the 2nd Worle Scout group; some of his school friends went too so he knew other kids there; he was an Invested Beaver on the 1st of October, another proud moment especially for Mummy, and many nights were spent sewing patches on his light blue jumper, or building a robot out of cereal boxes with a happy Keanu.

After two years with my Mondeo being static, I finally got it going; it turned out, that it did in fact have the wrong fuel put in it when it was last used. So after draining the tank of fuel and cleaning out the system, I was finally able to get the car for it's MoT; unfortunately, it had been sat still for so long, the two front shocker springs had snapped, so it failed.

By the 14th, I was able to put some new shockers on the car, thanks to Spartan Parts and their good discount, and my good mate Glynn Smith at his garage, as he put the springs on the shockers' for me.

I played my first gig after my break, on the 20th of October with The Stanley's, playing at The Imperial once more; Sharon and her mates Ali and Anna came along, we all had a great night.

Master K had his school disco near the end of the month, so we walked him there and dropped him off; went back to Sharon's for some lovely alone time, then later went back to walk master K home, whilst listening to the tales of his energetic night.

By the 30th, the Mondeo finally had an MoT and we were back on the road!

A venue I'd never played a gig in before, was at The Cove, at Marine Lake in Weston. On the 3rd of November; The Curve played a charity night for the Heart Foundation, it was a great night; Sharon was there to support me, Cheryl and Bernard were there too, Mum and Perry enjoyed the night, as did many others and it was a very charitable night. The week later; I was back with The Stanley's playing the Brit Bar once more; Sharon was there, along with my sister, my niece, and both nephew's, it was a great gig and a busy fantastic night.

For a week mid-month I was CPC training in Yeovil, it was another necessary licence for all LGV and HGV driver's. It was boring, but four modules done in a week was good enough for me, just one left to get!

Keanu was still swimming every Saturday, Daz came along to watch on occasion too. Housemate Josh, had handed his notice in on the house, and was moving in with his brother. It was at this time; I decided I'd not have anybody else move in, but now have that room for Daz as he was growing fast!

Sharon, Keanu, and I, took a walk up to Milton School one evening, we proudly watched Keanu perform in his Christmas play; that was a tear-jerker at times for all the parents, but especially for us I can tell you!

We only had one gig booked in December, at the live lounge to end our band year. Sharon and I did the Scooter Christmas Bash, at The Market House on the 23rd; then I was able to concentrate on Sharon, Keanu and Stell having a great Christmas. It was lovely having our first Christmas together, as a new couple and a proper little family unit. We ate a proper big meal that we'd both made and we had a very enjoyable time. Boxing day was spent with Daz and all the family, a great New Year was celebrated together too.

January 2013 was a quiet month for the band, the 5th was Perry's birthday get together at his and Mum's house, lots of the family were there, I took Daz, Sharon, and Keanu. The rest of the month, I just carried on working hard delivering food. I did have one tough week; Sparky went missing for five days, I was out with a torch all night, I'd printed posters and posted them through all the doors; my neighbour Aimee was out with me looking too; after five days of worry she came back, looking at me like she'd not even been away. I was very happy, then could get back to be with my new family; by this time, Sharon had also bought a new double bed, that was a fun job, getting that to fit in her tight bedroom.

February the 3rd; The Stanley's were playing in Burnham at The Old Pier Tavern, it was quite a quiet night, but still a great gig was had.

Work was quiet as it always was at the start of the year, although there was still plenty to deliver! I was delivering ice creams, drinks, and frozen food to the SS Great Britain, Bristol Fruit Market, and many restaurants, cafe's and Premier shops around Bristol. By mid-February, The Stanley's were playing at Weston Rugby Club, for another charity night with a couple of other bands, it was a great short gig and the last of the month for us.

Hunt's had informed all the drivers, that any driver without a class two licence will need to have one; well, you see my licence is old school, so I was able to drive a seven and a half tonne, so I needed a class two; it was all good as the company offered to pay for it. The rest of the month was spent revising, and on the 25th I had passed my theory test in Bristol; for a couple of days after I was off to Yeovil, with a fellow driver and mate Chris Pearce, for our first aid course, that was a blast. He's Welsh and I'm not shy, so we kept those few days very entertaining!

Secret Affair were playing at The Fleece on the 2nd of March; Steve, Nick and myself were not missing that! Another great night was had; we also had the pleasure of meeting Tracey Dawn Wilmot, Secret Affairs Personal Assistant; now we never miss a gig when they're this way, thanks to the joys of Facebook.

The next day; The Stanley's had another charity afternoon gig at the Boro Sports Club, in aid of The British Legion; Sharon attended and we later got very drunk in the Market House, at the pre-rally scooter do. We soaked it up the next day at Pizza Hut, as I took Sharon, Daz, and Keanu, for Daz's birthday treat. The rest of the month was reasonably quiet, Sharon's mum was down from Wigan and she stayed in Bristol; at the end of the month, we were treated to a Frankie and Bennys before she went home.

The Kings Head in Weston, had booked us for an afternoon gig at the end of the month; Sharon was able to come to that with Keanu, as it was a family pub; other friends attended and it was a fantastic end to the month.

Sharon's Birthday was on April the 1st; Keanu wasn't with his dad, so we all had a nice stay in celebration. A few days later and The Stanley's were back, playing in The Back Bar on a Saturday night, on the Sunday, Sharon, Keanu and I took a trip to The Sea Life Centre, on Weston sea front and a lovely day was had; Keanu really enjoyed himself and afterwards, he could whizz around on his scooter.

The next weekend; The Stanley's were once again gracing the stage at The Brit, and by the 27th, we were gigging in The Golden Lion in Worle to see the month out.

At the start of May; I took Sharon out for a month late birthday drink. The Stanley's played a gig mid-month, for a friendly private do at the Hand Stadium in Clevedon.

There were no more gigs booked for the rest of the month, so I was able to concentrate on my class two and spending more time with Sharon and Keanu, and Daz on my weekends.

The last day was nice; Sharon, Keanu and I made our way up to Bristol and spent the day in @ Bristol, what a very educational place that is, where kids, like Keanu and I could have a real fun day.

Six months after The Stanley's had played at The Old Pier Tavern in Burnham; we were back there again, to grace the stage in early June; this time was much busier, and a great gig was had.

Every morning for a week, I'd have to go to my work place early; help finish loading the trucks for their deliveries, then I'd get in a faster work van and drive to Yeovil. Once there, I'd get in a class two lorry; drive to Taunton with an instructor, then spend the best part of five hours driving around Taunton and Wellington; then I'd drive back to Yeovil, get in the Hunt's van and drive home. My reward at the weekend, was going to Pizza Hut with Sharon, Daz and Keanu; by the 11th I'd passed my Class two. I won't lie, it was my second attempt in two weeks, but I passed so who cares!

Gutted for me though, as over the weekend I'd got Gastroenteritis and ended up with all sorts going on! As I worked with food, it was two weeks off no questions asked; I stayed at my house, Sharon would come and look after me when necessary. To be honest it only really lasted a week, but I couldn't go back for food hygiene reasons.

Nearing the end of the month; The Stanley's played another Bleadon party for Miles Orme; this time it was a Jungle theme, so we all dressed up, and Sharon came for her first Bleadon Party experience. They were really well organised nights out, usually in a big barn, with statues and decorations set up; they'd always pull off a fantastic party. A few hundred people would each pay a fee, then have a night of free food, free drinks, free everything. Eastertown legend Mark Ely, would do a solo act with his guitar and vocals; The Stanley's would take the main stage, followed by a DJ.

July was quiet on the gig front; on my birthday, Sharon and I spent the afternoon, at Grove Parks "Party in the Park," we saw a couple of bands, including The Communicators and we stayed until late. It was a really hot day and plenty of our friends were there too. At the end of the month; Sharon came out with me on my deliveries, it was a fun day with plenty of ice creams on tap: the night after, I took her for a Bottelino's Italian Restaurant to say thank you. The Stanley's had played another blinding gig at The Kings Head, as the last gig four months earlier went so well, they booked us again.

On the 3rd of August, I drove Sharon, Stell and Keanu to Bournmouth, as Sharon's half brother was getting married. It was a clear drive down, we made it there in a good time. We met with Sharon's family, then made our way to the church. After a lovely service and a finger buffet reception, a great day was had. We danced and had fun; K dude had his face painted, along with his cousin, Sharon drove us home the same day. We couldn't afford hotels, especially for four of us.

The week after, Keanu was with his dad, so Sharon and I spent the day in Bristol. We had a lovely meal on the water front at The Stable's; then we went Gromit spotting until parking time ran out, then home for drinks at mine.

The Curve had fizzled out, but we'd had a fun couple of years. Paul Hatton needed some drum beats putting down for a project he was doing; on the 12th I was at his place laying down the tracks, I was happy to help a great friend and privileged that he asked me.

Back in band land, The Stanley's had played a couple of local gigs mid-month, one in the Back Bar, and the other in The Tavern on the town.

On the 19th, I woke up and said to Sharon, "Get some things together we're off on a road trip!" We jumped in the car and I drove us to Torquay for a short break. Once we arrived, I popped into a couple of Bed and Breakfast's to find they were full, we eventually found one; The Belgravia Guest House and they had an available room. We had a great three days, a fun fare was on the sea front so Keanu could go on all the rides, we ate candy floss and ice creams; we had meals in the evening at Amicis, a great Italian Restaurant. We bought K dude a new jacket; me a trilby hat and we rode the big wheel, a fun and relaxing time was had!

The bank holiday weekend was approaching, The Stanley's were once again playing at The Watchet Festival on the Sunday afternoon. We decided we'd go on the Saturday and set up camp for the night. We did a great job loading the Mondeo; we managed to squeeze my complete kit in, Stell's amp and guitar, a tent, Sharon, Stell and myself, and a king size duvet. As we'd stayed, we saw some great acts, The Hoosiers were on the main stage, we watched them play "Goodbye Mr A," and a couple more tunes. The Rocker Cover's were playing "The Udder Stage," in a colourful marquee, so we went to check them out. They were awesome, and we had a drink with them afterwards In the "Something Else Tea Tent," which is run by a longtime known great friend Gail.

Lunch time Sunday; The Stanley's were live, also on The Udder Stage. We pulled off an awesome gig to a satisfied audience; it was also great to see Melissa Hudson-Bond and her other half Jamie, I'd not seen them for a long time. Ex-housemate Colin Smith, is always a steward for the weekend, it's always good to see him too.

Into September, Sharon was busy at work; I was busy at work and the band played a couple of local gigs, one particular was The Live Lounge, Eddy couldn't play it, so Leo Parsons played that one for us and he was always great to work with. Daz came to that gig; Abbie and her friends came along too.

On the 28th; Sharon and I went for a night out, after entering the Brit Bar we bumped into a bunch of mates. Great long-time buddy Paul Coles, had taken a year out in Australia, after retiring from his very long service as a fireman, he was out celebrating with other long-time scooter buddies, Steve Parker, Tim Briar, Neil Dancey and Pauls brother Andy. They were downing jagerbombs and we joined them, as Sharon and I weren't used to this, we only did a couple and went to see a band in the Back Bar instead. The morning came, boy did we regret drinking those shots; we spent a very rough day together on the Sunday!

October was a very busy month for the band. We played a few local gigs early month; then Bridgwater mid-month, but that gig didn't end well for me! The landlord of the pub we played in, said I could leave my car in Lidl car park, whilst the gig took place; that was handy, but I still ended up with a sixty-quid parking fine. At the end of the month, we played another afternoon charity gig, for Children in Need at St John's on the Bournville. Sole Room Dave span his discs', Sharon and lots of other friends attended, so it was a great day.

The Bear Inn is a local pub, it's only just up the road from my house; The Stanley's had a gig there on a Saturday night in November, it was quite a busy night for our first visit to this establishment, lots of our fans came along too.

The next day, I read some worrying statuses on a Facebook page. A friend Paul, who was an ex-taxi driver mate, had moved away a few years before; I'd read that he'd been having troubles and he was on a real low. As he had no real friends where he was in Derby, I was worried; a fellow taxi driver mate Kevin Wood, had contacted me as he too was worried about our friend, so we made plans. Kev paid for Paul to travel on the train from Derby, and I put him up in my spare room. We met him at the train station, after a hug and hand shake, I took him to my place; made him a hot drink and caught up. After a couple of days to get himself back on track, I took him to the Apple taxi office and got him back driving taxis.

It wasn't long before he met a lady friend and moved out. He's now doing really well, and has since gained his PSV (Passenger Service Vehicle) licence, for that I'm very proud. I once saw him at his lowest, but happy to have pulled him out, well-done Paul Haughey.

The 8th was carnival night, I took them all to this one, Sharon, Daz and Keanu.

Sunday the 10th; Keanu was marching with the Beavers for the remembrance Sunday parade, Sharon and I marched proudly, with all the other Beavers and their parents.

Unfortunately, the following week saw me unemployed, Hunt's had to let go of four drivers and right before Christmas!

Now, once again jobless, the band, Sharon, Daz and Keanu, were all I had to concentrate on, as well as finding another job. We played a gig in Street, that was a very quiet night, with only a few old people watching and complaining it was too loud. My uncle Maurice was there, he lives in Street and he enjoyed it!

By the 25th, the Mondeo had started to become poorly again; it was time to wave goodbye, to a car that ended up costing me a small fortune! I dropped it at Burrison's scrap yard and took my hundred and fifty quid.

Christmas Eve; there was a knock on my front door, my dad had come round to give me the keys and documents for his car. He lived nine doors away from me, as I had no car on the road at this time, I would often use his car when needed. It was an old car, but with only seventy-six thousand miles on the clock, it had been re-sprayed a few years before, it was in great shape for a sixteen-years-old Vauxhall Vectra. As he'd now retired and after being a long time lorry driver, he decided he no longer wanted to drive. Christmas Day was our second Christmas together; a great day it was too! On New Years Eve, The Stanley's played a gig at The Ebdon Arms in Worle, it was a packed pub with happy drunk punters; Leo stood in again on bass guitar as Eddy wasn't available. Sheridan, a great friend of Sharon's also came along, to keep her company whilst I played, we went home and said goodbye to another year.

During our busy Christmas, Sharon and I had discussed, that going back on the taxi's might be the way forward; also, as The Stanley's were so busy, it was time for me to take a step back. I sourced a taxi to rent from a mate Mark, at Motormend.

I also handed my notice in with The Stanley's, we played a gig in the Back Bar mid-January on a Friday night; Sharon came with the car during the night to finish watching the band, and then helped me to take the gear home. After we'd dropped the stuff home, we went for a late night McDonalds until three in the morning, then we went back to mine and enjoyed the early morning some more.

Saturday the 19th, and Jason Ferdinando was hosting a leaving do; he was off to work in Dubai and what a great night we all had. Sharon went to school with Jason and I'd known him for years too. Steve Mitchell and Matt Wilkins, entertained us for most of the night with their fantastic duet skills. Mandi was there, she's Jason's ex-wife, and the mother to their kids; other long-time friends Debbie Danvers and Daz Cassidy, Debbie's daughter Paris, and many more were also there and we all got very drunk.

February the 2nd saw me play my final Stanley's gig. It was very memorable, everyone was there to say their goodbyes; Sharon came for the whole gig and drove, so I could have a drink. After we had dropped the drums home, we went for another early morning McDonalds, for a multi-box of chicken nuggets and a coffee each.

Now it was time for me to concentrate, on a fuller happy life, with Sharon and her boys and Daz on the weekends. Wednesday the 5th was Keanus 8th birthday, so we took the little dude for a pizza at Pizza Hut.

The next night, we took him to cricket; he'd not long been going to Sam Tregos cricket school, he loved it and got really good at it. The week after, there was a party for Nick Cavill's daughter Paige; as she was leaving for a new life in Australia, I was doing nights on the taxis, so I only popped along to say my goodbye's.

The 5th was a long day, as Sharon, Stell and myself went on another long road trip, this time to Falmouth. It was their college open day and Stell wanted to check it out, we dropped Stell at the college and went on a romantic adventure for an hour or so; then picked him up later and drove home, he liked it, so they made the plans for him to go there.

We took Daz for his usual birthday pizza, at Pizza Hut on the 10th; the week later and I was back at The Fleece, with Steve, Nick, Rich and Reeves, to see Secret Affair and the crew again. Although by this time, my ear had kept me up all night in pain; I made another visit to the doctors and got a prescription sorted.

A couple of days later, Sharon, Stell and I, were once more off on a college road trip, but this time to Bath Spa Uni. I think he nearly took this one but preferred Falmouth!

The next weekend and we were now in May; the Stanley's were playing and as Keanu was at his dads, Sharon and I went to see the band. It was weird watching a band I'd played in for so long, but as a fan on the other side, they were brilliant; Thomas Fear played for them that night as their stand in, until they found a permanent replacement drummer. I went to school and did Ninjutsu with Thomas's dad, Aaron.

Then it was just a normal week of work for me, college for Sharon and cricket for Keanu.

One Sunday afternoon, I made my way to The Brit Bar, as Sole Room Dave was spinning the discs. I bumped into a great mate Vespa Marcus; I've known him for years and we worked together at Hunt's too. He was laid off at the same time as me; he told me what he was now doing and gave me an agency number to ring. So I made the call, and by the 19th I was handing the taxi back and starting a new job!

I didn't have a good start mind. I remember it so well, I was wearing my brand new bright orange uniform, ready to drive the recycling trucks. It was a Monday and I headed to Nailsea, with Skippy and Shaun; we had a successful day and no one got hurt. When we returned to the depot in Weston later in the day, I had to drive, the now full of rubbish truck onto a weighbridge; I was lining it up, left a bit, right a bit and still moving forward, I made contact with the ramps and accelerated. Then "BANG," the front left tyre had hit the weighbridge causing it to pop; the boss was stood right in front of me and saw it all. I shit myself, being my first day as well, and the loaders had both jumped out the cab and ran off! The boss dealt with it and I got the rollocking I deserved; it turned out I'd also knocked the bridge out of calibration, I didn't lose my job, but my small mishap cost the company a lot of money, so that was Strike one!

The end of the month and the Stanley's were playing another gig, at The Nut Tree in Worle; this time they had their new drummer, Dave Burbidge from The Leylines. Sharon and I made it a date night and we went to see them, they played a great gig, Sharon stood proud, as Stell sang and played really well through the night as always. We left, and went back to my place to make a great night even better.

At the start of the month; the Stanley's drummer wasn't available for a gig, at The Old Pier Tavern in Burnham, I happily stood in and really enjoyed it. The night after I was at a cards night, with Rich Southcombe, Steve Wilkinson, Nick Cavill and Reeves Cooke at Rich's house, and his nice little man cave in the back garden. The sun was shining, the thatchers were flowing and I lost the contents of my Darth Vader money box, once again to Nicko.

Andy Davies's birthday was approaching, and some months earlier his good wife Aly, had messaged me to ask if I'd like to escort Andy, to a Paul Weller concert in Cardiff. Aly isn't a fan, and Andy and I, had been to see the Mod God many times together before. She offered to pay for the tickets, if I didn't mind paying for us to get there, I was happy with that! But then I got a message a few days later, I was informed, that the Cardiff tickets had in fact sold out! But, there were tickets for Sherwood Forest in June, I said yes, and I drove us there in three and a half hours! We watched an awesome gig, in awesome sunlight with a very happy and drunk audience. Not me of course, as I drove us back in three hours.

I was rewarded the following day, when Sharon and Keanu had prepared me a lovely Fathers day meal.

Saturday night, and I was playing once again for the Stanley's; this time for Miles Orme's Bleadon party, the last one we were ever to play! Sharon came along but not alone; I'd sorted a ticket and she took her mate Ali. Everybody got smashed and it was a Hollywood theme night, so most people were wearing fancy dress, I wore a suit and Sharon wore a dress. Ali disappeared with someone she knew; Sharon and I went home in a cab, and the next day I went back with Daz, to pick up my car and drums'.

I'd been looking forward to July for a short while; I was taking Sharon to see Bad Manners at the Winter Gardens on the 4th, there were plenty of people there and loads of mates. After another energetic show,

I took Sharon back stage to meet Buster and the gang, after some selfies together, he then asked if we'd like to join him, as he was off for a few pints in Scally's, a known pub not too far down the road. Of course, I wasn't going to miss out on that, so I grabbed Sharon and a couple of mates, including Steven Griffiths; John Cruse and his wife and a great night was had. I'd also taken a few photos' with me, from the last time we had the pleasure, so I had the picture of Nick and Buster signed and the one of Buster with Breezer signed. Nick was happy after I framed it, and gave it to him as a gift as he's a big fan; thankfully I woke ok; no hangover after another night with Buster.

An unlucky day at work awaited! I was reversing my huge domestic bin truck down a driveway to three blocks of flats; I was in every mirror, looking left, looking right, I couldn't see the loaders! I was still travelling backwards, and only at five mph, then "BANG," I reversed straight into a row of garages, but it was the highest section; it was out of my sight range; then, a four foot square block of heavy stone, just came thudding down, "DOOF," was the loud sound it made as it cracked the tarmac below. So after a phone call and another accident report form to fill out, I soon got a rollocking and that was Striiike Two!!

Keanu was at his dad's the following week, so we were able to go out and celebrate. It was a lovely night, with a few of the lads Sharon went to school with, Andy Davies my Paul Weller pal, Steve Griffiths, Steve Williams and Nick Davenport. I already knew Andy and Steve Griffiths, and a great night was had, with a taxi home, and feeling a bit wobbly when we both woke! Still, we managed a nice Chinese which we had delivered that night, then went back out, to paint the town red and watch the Stanley's once more.

With the Weston Scooter Rally starting on the 25th, the Stanley's had some work to do. I was playing with them for this gig and what an awesome day; the sun was shining so we played outside. The Tavern on the town was packed, outside the pub was packed, there were scooters' parked around; skinheads' and scooterists' stood everywhere enjoying the sun, cider and sounds, it was a great feeling and an awesome gig! That night master K was at his dad's, so Sharon came with me to the night do at The Winter Gardens. It started well, but within an hour of turning up we started arguing, I don't even know what it was about; off she went in a piss! Normally I would of been after her, but I thought, "sod that, I've been waiting ages for this night; I'm not gonna have it ruined and spend more time arguing!" Instead I stayed, got drunk with a shed load of long-time friends and got in the groove to whatever soul classics, the awesome Emma DJ Cox, or great local mate Ian Rossiter were spinning. The night was soon over and the campsite clean took place the next day.

As it was nearing Cheryl and Bernard's wedding, Abbie took Daz to buy a suit, shirt and tie; he looked great as she'd done an awesome job.

The 22nd was the very special day; I was proud to see Cheryl look so pretty, in her long white dress and Bernard look so smart in his suit. Bernard is a Bristol man, so the day was first spent in a hotel in Bristol centre, the service was in a church that was close by. After a wonderful wedding ceremony; we boarded an open top double decker bus, which took us to the Clifton Downs, over looking the Suspension Bridge; where Pimm's and ice cream were waiting for us to enjoy. There was also a lovely reception held at the Clifton Sausage; we all spent the evening and late into the night, at the Squadron getting very drunk. Daz was happily singing and dancing in the down stairs bar, with all the others having fun. When it was late, we all went back to the lovely hotel for a night-cap and comfy sleep, Auntie Hilary treated us to breakfast in the morning; we got in the car and went home.

The next night, Cheryl and Bernard hosted a second evening do, at Worlebury Golf Club in Weston, it was for anyone who couldn't be there on the day. That was another lovely night and most of the family were there too, Sharon drove up and met us later and another drunken night was had by all. Many people got up to do dance routines and Daz didn't leave the dance floor all night.

The following Monday Sharon, Keanu and I made our way for another few days in Torquay, we ate at Amicis again; walked the seafront eating ice creams; Sharon bought me a T-shirt, we rode the big wheel and had the break we needed.

At the end of the month, I had to do an early drive to Newport; I still had a module to do on my CPC. The bin agency paid for it and hell; it was the longest Saturday ever! I left with a new licence and that's all that mattered!

By the second week in September; Sharon, Stell and myself, loaded the car with Stell's belongings and drove to Falmouth for Stell to join their Uni. It was a nice run down with no problems; we stopped at a Happy Eater for a bite to eat in Oakhampton; Sharon and Stell shared some tears for a while, we met with his new friends to be, and then we had a safe journey home; after Sharon waved goodbye to her not so little boy.

Six days later; Sharon and I were off on our travels once more! Back to Falmouth for Stell's return; off we went on our three hundred and sixteen mile round trip; we loaded the car when we got there, and had a safe trip home. Stell was happy now and chose a closer to home Uni.

I took Sharon to see Skacasm, at the Brit Bar on the 21st; they're an awesome ska covers band from Wales and a great act. The rest of the month was just work, work, work; fun with Daz every other weekend and with Sharon and Keanu for the rest.

In October, it was discussed that the old 13th Valley Scooter Club, would rekindle itself after thirty odd years, so by the 5th, a few of the old gang and some new one's were meeting together, at The Kings Head in Worle for our first meeting. Glynn Smith (former garage owner) now ran this establishment, and as a past 13th Valley member, it seemed the appropriate pub.

The weekend after, I decided to take Sharon and Keanu on a mystery road trip; I drove us to Exmouth, where the sun was shining; we strolled the sea front, ate in cafe's and had a really nice day, then I drove home.

Unfortunately for me, on the Monday I slightly nudged a car with my truck, whilst emptying the domestic bins, and once the boss got the news, I got my Strriiike Three!!! I was kicked off the bins. Unemployed again and just before Christmas, hey ho what was I to do now.

The day after, I was painting my hallway as I was already bored, and the wall and ceiling really needed painting.

On the 29th, I was at St Michael's Hospital in Bristol, having my mute ear corrected. Sharon drove me up, and she sat with me for some time; we arrived at the hospital at nine AM; eventually she went to visit her sister and arranged with the nurses to call her when I was ready for collection. I finally had the operation at about four and by five thirty I was being picked up, I was just glad to get home and rest, I never like the feeling after an anaesthetic.

November the 5th; I was back up to Bristol again, to have the padding removed from the ear; they also explained the operation to me. My Tympanic Membrane (eardrum), had burst so badly that it wasn't healing, even after taking medication for it; they'd removed some skin from my Tragus (outer ear), and patched my eardrum. They removed the padding and it felt a bit strange at first, but within a couple of days the ear became totally deaf!

I still wore earplugs when watching bands, as we did on Thursday the 13th, when Nick, Steve, and myself, paid our usual visit to the Fleece, to see Blues legends Nine Below Zero, my favourite blues band ever!

Then a few nights later; Sharon dropped me at Rich Southcombe's house, with my Darth Vader head full of loose change. I was unemployed and hoping for a lucky night playing cards. My money box was half full and I wanted to fill it up, so the next day I could proudly walk into Asda; tip Darth Vader into the change machine, and claim my fourteen-pound cash return. But no, instead I left with a measly four pound fifty, Mr Cavill did it again.

The rest of the month was spent with Sharon, Daz, and Keanu enjoying ourselves as much as we could; I had no job and very little money! No sooner was the end of the month approaching, and I received a phone call from Jeff, a supervisor on the bins. He informed me, that the boss that had let me go, was in fact leaving on the 30th of November; I was offered my job back to start the day after.

So, on the 1st of December I was getting up early, and once again pulling on my bright orange trousers, after my wake me up shower. It was also another happy night on the 2nd when Sharon, Keanu and I had the pleasure of seeing Stell do his magic! It was a Christmas event, organised by the Weston Uni and held at All Saints Church. There were performances from solo singers to guitarists and small bands; what we'd really been waiting for, was Stell to do his outstanding rendition of "Hallelujah." There were tears in Sharon's eyes; Keanu had a proud of his brother smile, I was proud that I was once in a band with him, and he also felt like a son to me. He dedicated the song to his mum, his dad Nick who was also there, his brother, and me; I was flattered.

The following week was another proud parent moment, for the both of us and loads of other parents; it was Keanu's school Christmas play and a great performance was had by all the pupils and we all left happy.

As we had a Keanu free weekend, we were able to go to the scooter do, at Fergus Jacks club Carnaby's, another very drunk night with plenty of familiar faces. The month continued with Keanu swimming, for one last Saturday before Christmas and having Daz on the weekends, Christmas Eve; we went shopping to Toys R Us for the final gifts. We had the usual fun on Christmas Day and Boxing Day was spent in Bristol, with Sharon's family and Daz came too.

For our New Year celebrations and with Keanu at his dad's, Sharon and myself went for a night out in Bonds pub. Stell and Jordan had other projects; Pretty Soul is one of them, two vocals and two guitars, pretty much doing the Stanley's set; with a few extra songs. Well, they happened to be in Bonds that night, so that was where we chose to spend our night; it was also Auntie Val's birthday, so she, my sister, my niece and nephews', were out with us for the night too. Our mate Steve Griffiths was the barman that night; he introduced us to an Espresso Martini Cocktail. Sharon and I were both hooked, and by the time the midnight chimes sounded, we were wasted. I thought it would be a good idea to take a walk to Rich Southcombe's house; he'd had a fancy dress party that night, and we turned up about forty-minutes later, to Rich and Rachel and nobody else! So we went home and crashed out happy as we entered 2015!

Buster with my hat on

Abbie, Mum & Sis before Cheryl's wedding 3 generations

CHAPTER 9

THE GOOD AND SAD!

At the start of 2015, we were busy doing the usual stuff; take the tree and decorations down, check out the Matalan and TK Max sales and visit family we'd not seen over the Christmas period. We wrapped up warm and had cold walks' down the seafront at night, or we'd sit and drink McDonald's coffee, in the warm car on Knightstone Island and chat for ages, whilst Keanu would sit in the back playing games on his phone. Ok, so we were both working, but Sharon was a single mum and I was only just working again and trying to get back on my feet, we did what we could to still have fun. Keanu would go to his dad on occasion, and I'd spend time with Daz too.

I received a phone call one afternoon, to be asked if I'd been hurt in an accident in the last three years. As Hunt's had paid me full pay when I broke my wrist, I chose not to make a claim, but as they'd dumped me just before Christmas, my thought pattern had now changed. "Yes, I have," was my reply and the procedures started.

I came home from work one evening and couldn't find Sparky anywhere! I looked high and low; I live in a big house and the cat flap was closed. After an hour it looked like my house had been burgled, I made a coffee and sat in my lounge sad, and now a little worried. Had she gone up the semi blocked chimney? No, she's been here for years and never even looked at the fireplace before; I was sat looking out the window baffled. At that time, my drums' were set up in the lounge, as I'd

164

recently spent a ton of money on a load of new skins, suddenly, I heard a cat meow, to discover that Sparky; the cat that had made me turn my house upside down, had in fact climbed into the bass drum, through the six-inch microphone hole; the outer drum skin was black as is Sparky, I lifted her up and gave her a big hug. Then I spent an hour putting my house back together!

Happy I'd not lost Sparky, I took Sharon and Keanu to Za Za Bazaar on the Bristol waterfront. Now that's a place I could live; Za Za I mean not Bristol. Eat as much as you like, foods from all different countries' and it's a cheap day on Saturday, two hours to eat all you can for ten quid. That night Keanu was at his dad's and I didn't have Darren, so Sharon and I spent the night, at Paul McCarthey's 50th birthday bash at Carnaby's. All the usual local scooterists' faces were there, another drunken night was had.

At the end of the month, The Stanley's asked me if I'd play a gig for them. It was for a 60th birthday in Tavistock, for Sole Room Daves mate Geoff. Dave is Jordan's dad and a great friend of mine, so of course I said yes. It was only an hour or so drive, plenty of Dr Martens', Ben Shermans' and bald heads' were present; it was an old-school skinhead's birthday. A great night was had, then the hour long drive home.

Back to a days' work. It was Wednesday the 4th and what a horrible day. No one liked Wednesdays' as it was Portishead, it was always heavy with tonnes of waste and disgusting as many people don't recycle properly. It had been a cold day and to be fair it was getting close to the end of our day. My job was a quick job, as a driver, I had to jump out my cab, grab as many green boxes as I could, tip them all in the appropriate holes; jump back in the cab and move the truck forward a few feet. So, this one time, I jumped out, Kirk one of the loaders grabbed a couple of boxes, leaving me just one full of plastic and tins. I'd done this manoeuvre, what felt like a million times before. I aimed for the hole and "Bosh!" Kirk got in the way, and the next thing we knew he was sparked out on the floor motionless. "Oops!" After a couple of slaps to no avail, the other loader and good mate Bubba, helped me scoop Kirk up and sit him against a wall. Passers' by came to the aid and I moved the truck. People brought tea and blankets, by now he'd come round, but was feeling woozy. An ambulance arrived pretty quickly and he was checked out, he was told he was ok and good to go. So Bubba and I finished off the now late day, with Kirk as a sick man warm in the cab.

Then, the week after, I think knocking Kirk out must of been a good thing, as I was handed a contract on the 20th, no more agency rubbish and a happy end to the month.

Some time earlier in the month, Steve, Nick, Reeves, Rich and myself, had got together for a chat, at The Bristol House Pub in Milton. It was that night; we discussed putting Inner City back on the scene, after twenty-six years apart; with four of us from the original line up. Gavin would have loved to of joined us, but he was too busy with his other bands, The Orphans and Eastertown. So after a good nights chat, we booked a rehearsal room and on the 30th we again met up, but this time at eMarty, a recording studio in the centre of Weston; Inner City were re-united! For the first time together it sounded brilliant. It did help, that Nick and I had continued to play together over the years in other bands, we worked well together.

I played another stand in gig for The Stanley's at the start of the month, in Bristol at Colston School, for the rest of April, Inner City rehearsals continued every Monday. I spent a day repairing my now rusting away Vespa, trying to get it back to a bit respectable, I got the car through it's MoT too.

The fun fair was at the Tropicana for the summer, Daz had requested that I take him there and of course I didn't mind. Although, going on the "Mouse Trap ride" was a "BIG" mistake, it ruined my back; Daz really enjoyed himself, that's all that mattered.

Through May, my back had really started suffering, I was having trouble doing anything. We still did the odd walk which helped; Sharon and I went to see Stell perform, with Ffuse in the back bar on the 5th, they were a good band, covering the Foo Fighters and Muse. Stell was the lead guitarist and vocals, and another friend Mark Whitehouse was on the bass. I still went to work and beat the drums on a Monday, but in discomfort! I plodded along all the same, but stayed home bed ridden once I'd finished work.

By June my back was much better, thanks to my Tens' Machine and Lloyds Cream.

The Red Arrows were doing their yearly show on the 21st. I'd made plans to meet Cheryl and her bunch at the Cove on the seafront, but I was getting stressed, not being able to find anywhere to park; before I knew it, I was yelling and we ended up arguing. I still couldn't find a space after ten minutes, but I didn't want Keanu to miss the display. In the end, I dropped them at the best spot and continued to search for a space. I finally found one near where Cheryl was, so I made my way and met up with them all, to watch the end of the display with a pint. When the show was over, my phone rang and it was Sharon to ask where I was, she made her way down and we left.

The next evening I was at an Inner City practice; I put my phone down on top of an amp and continued rehearsing; during that practice, some weird phenomenon had happened and my phone stopped working full-stop. Hey ho, new phone needed, the only real bummer being; I'd now lost my Timmy Day Facebook account, I'd had it on the phone so long; I'd forgotten the password and the Email address was no longer going, so I couldn't get a new password. The good thing was, I'd previously set up a Tim Day account with family members only, so I carried on with that one! It was like 2008 all over again, send friend request, join this, tag them, like that, it went on for weeks! The Monday after, was the last rehearsal for Inner City at Emarty as they were closing down, but we had numbers so the calls were made!

The first weekend of July, I decided I'd strip the engine down on my scoot; give it a good clean and replace the necessary parts and rebuild it.

The first Monday of the month; Inner City were again rehearsing, but now at a new place, Studio 13 in Kewstoke, owned by Ken Lintern; we didn't lose a practice!

The next weekend and Sharon, Keanu and I spent a day in Bristol, eating a McDonald's, then ice creams, and having a photo with as many Gromits' as we could. I worked my birthday and then we were back in Bristol again five days later, for the Bristol Harbour Festival, it was another lovely sunny day.

At the end of the month, I decided we'd go on a road trip to Barry Island, over in Wales. I used to deliver ice creams there with Hunt's. It wasn't a bad drive over and the weather was lovely; it was sad on arrival, to see what was once; a really popular resort, totally empty. Seriously, there were three cars parked in the thousand space car park; you could see the tumbleweeds roll in the quiet wind. Still, we took in the sights, and thought there might be rides for Keanu to go on at the fair, nope, half of it had been sold off, and the rest looked like it had just been put up temporarily. It was sad to see, as we walked around the empty shops; sat and ate in a quiet cafe and watched as a couple of people walked their dogs on the beach. It was the end of July, it was a lovely hot day, and what was once one of the biggest holiday resort's, was empty! We finished our day with ice creams; jumped back in the car and drove home, discussing the doom and dismay of a once beautiful place.

The next day, we took Keanu swimming in Hutton Moore, he loved it splashing about, Sharon sat on the side and watched happily as two of her boys played in the water. On Saturday I actually did some more on my scoot, I got the filler out to make good a hole, that I didn't want to get any worse.

Then on Sunday, we did another road trip, but this time to Torquay for the day. We did the usual walk around and a Subway for lunch; we queued up for a ride on the big wheel, and we had a safe and stress-free journey back home, then put our feet up to relax.

August, and Inner City Rehearsals continued hard and fast. Whilst Sharon was being a great mum to young Keanu and Stell, working, and revising for her college courses', she still made time, to come to Inner Citys' first come back gig in the Back Bar on the 13th. What a crowd, friends had got the news that we were back together, they were travelling to come and see us, including, Derek "Daleboy" Shepherd, from the "In The Crowd" modzine days; all our local mates were there too. Most of my family turned up, and my sister had bought Sharon a T-shirt, with "My Boyfriend's in the Band" printed on the front.

Then the week after, I took Daz for a drive to Dartmouth as Mum and Perry were on their boat, Cheryl, Bernard, and Abbie were also there, a great family day was had; catching crabs off the pontoon and eating lunch on the boat. The sun soon started dropping, so we left and went home!

The first weekend in October, Sharon and I were out on the town, well, Unwined anyway, we spent time catching up with a great mate Craig Barlow, I'd not seen him for years. We also bumped into one of my dad's old mates, Steve Austen, we drank more thatchers and cocktails, with the managers' Andy and Sharon Bridgman; then a nice walk home and a great end to the night.

I don't know how we managed it to be honest, but the next evening we were off to Bristol, to see "Jack and the Beanstalk." This time it was Sharon's sister Rachel who was performing, it was a really great, very humorous show, especially the strongly spoken Bristolian man dressed as a woman; I cried along with everyone else every time he spoke; as it was a Daz weekend, he came too and loved it.

The following week I had a weeks annual leave. It was typical though; I also had a bad back again and things were becoming difficult, the only thing I could enjoy was food, so the Friday night and it being payday, I took Sharon and Keanu for a Hungry Horse meal at The Super Mare, where we enjoyed a lovely meal each, and it was served quickly. But really, it was me getting ready for the 12th, as I was finally having a vasectomy. Sharon and I had discussed this, so she came with me and watched whilst the job took place. The doc did his work on the Monday, so I'd booked the week off; there was no way I could do my job after that! Well, five days later, and it looked like I had a pair of mangos' hanging down, it bloody hurt; I had to have another week off, and by then they were back to walnuts!

A couple of weeks before the end of the month; Sharon was having a very proud mummy moment, as Keanu was doing his first big stage show at Westons Playhouse, with The Jacqueline Fox's School of Dance. She was also back stage helping with change overs, when the show was over, we were able to walk next door and watch Stell, performing in the Brit Bar with Ffuse, Stell's a massive fan of Muse, he'd also bought, a Matt Belamy signature guitar with his birthday money.

The end of the month, and it was time for me to be a proud brother and uncle; my sister, bro-in-law and neice were appearing in "Crazy for You," also at The Playhouse, Sharon, Daz and I really enjoyed it, I was very proud.

We had fun on the bins at the beginning of November, as everyone was throwing out their no longer needed pumpkins', we made our own entertainment; well I certainly did anyway. I picked up a pumpkin with a standard face carving, I pulled my faded orange jumper over my head and with the pumpkin under my arm; I came out from behind the truck, I had the loaders and a few house owners rolling around with laughter, they were great times! By the end of the day we must of stunk of pumpkins as well as everything else we got covered in.

After hundreds of phone calls, and tons of paperwork to sign over the past eleven months, I finally received a cheque for my broken wrist on the 15th, it wasn't massive by the time they took their forty-four percent; there wasn't a great deal left. I paid off a couple of larger debts, as the Bailiffs had been harassing me; it was hard to let go of as it really didn't leave me a lot! I did still manage to purchase an electric drum kit from Andy, whom I'd taught originally; now he had a family the kit was gathering dust in the corner of his spare room. I also bought some new, Sabian fourteen-inch AAX Frequent hi-hats, as my old ones had been split for years, but I could never afford a new set. I also ordered a big flat packed wardrobe, a king size bed and a new carpet for my bedroom; at the end of the month when it all arrived, I got to it and spent a Sunday giving my room a sixty-minute makeover (in a day). Chuffed with the result, my bedroom now looked like a new bedroom, and a love nest for Sharon and I on the occasional weekend; after having the snip as well, ooh what fun! I also had a bit of lose change left in the bank for emergencies. I know I should of given Mum and Perry some money as I'm always in their debt, but my bed was fifteen years old and I didn't have a wardrobe; some changes needed to be made.

On December 11th, Inner City played another memorable gig in the Back Bar, Gavin Cox came to see us; at this time, Gav was a front man for The Orphans and sang alongside Mark Ely in Eastertown. As he was in Inner City during the early days, he got up and sang a song with us for old times sake, he then asked, if we'd like to play a gig supporting the Orphans, on Weston Pier on December the 27th. We couldn't wait, as it was a great venue with great sound, and supporting a great band. A great night was had, many friends were there, but most memorable was seeing Lucy Headington-Horton, she'd moved to Hong Kong many years before, and was back visiting family.

Christmas went with no problems, and my sister had given Daz and I tickets, to see a show at the Hippodrome in Bristol the following week.

Now into 2016, Daz and I saw Warwick Davies at his best, in Snow White and the Seven Dwarfs; I was still driving the bin lorries Monday to Friday. As I'd been having the occasional back twinges, and it started to get really bad, before I knew it I was off work sick for five weeks. The excruciating pain meant I couldn't do a thing, I hardly saw Sharon, accept on Saturday the 9th, when we had a fun but uncomfortable night, after a night in the Market House with the scooter lot. Unfortunately, after our bedroom fun and in the early hours whilst fast asleep, my drunk house mate Mike, who's also a scooterist had entered our bedroom, as he was looking for the loo; he'd only been living there for thirteen years for gods sake! Suddenly I was woken by a loud scream from Sharon, after sitting upright, to hear her telling me what had happened, I ran out the room but it was too late, so I shut and locked the door and from that point Sharon never wanted to stay at my house again, and I didn't blame her! Of course, I had a go at Mike in the morning, as it wasn't the first time after a night out but now it was affecting my relationship.

I'd ordered a new lounge carpet the month before, that ex-bin driver Mike Hanslip fitted for me on Sunday the 10th, I'd also treated myself to a new forty-inch Hitachi TV on Black Friday for the lounge. I was scanning Facebook one day as I couldn't do anything else, I came across an advert for Showaddywaddy playing live in Bristol. Over the years, Daz had found Showaddywaddy and fell in love with their songs; as his birthday was approaching, I got on the internet and bought a ticket for us each.

On the afternoon of January the 20th, I was laid up on my lounge floor watching TV upside down, when my phone rang. It was Sharon, upset and telling me she'd had a bump in the car. Obviously I was worried about her, she was able to drive to me so I could give her a cuddle and check out the damage; she wasn't going fast so the damage wasn't looking that bad. It was only a front end nudge; usually I would've been on it and starting the repair procedures, but my back wouldn't allow that, instead, I made a phone call to the insurance company and Sharon went off to the hospital in a taxi, to get herself checked out. A short while later, she called to let me know she was ok, just a bit shaken; she got another taxi from the hospital back to her place, then sorted picking K dude up from school.

A couple of days later, I crawled my way out to the car, so I could park it round the back of my house and have a proper look at the damage.

Gutted, it was damaged a bit more than I first thought; it needed to go to a garage to have the front pulled out, luckily, there was a great body shop right opposite the bin warehouse, where Colin Venn and Barry worked their magic. I bought a very cheap, similar car from one of my workmate's Ricky Ford, Colin then had all the panels', headlights' and the radiator he needed.

Before the car was fixed, I needed another car; thankfully, a good mate Andy Day was selling his older Renault for a few hundred quid, I was able to pay him fifty quid a week.

It was another sad day on the 28th, a great friend of ours and to many others, Matt Jack passed away. Rest in Peace Matt!

Friday February the 26th, I took Daz to see Showaddywaddy. I turned up at his house and he came to the door, he was dressed all smart, totally unaware of where he was going, or who he was going to see! We arrived at The Fleece and parked right outside in the disabled space (don't worry we had a badge), we showed our tickets and walked in, to the busiest, most crammed pub I'd been in for a long time. The band came on, looking like the Showaddywaddy I remember, colourful suits and beatle crusher shoes, boot lace ties the whole caboodle. I was so happy to see Daz getting excited, his face lit up brighter than the stage when the music played, they sounded awesome and as good as the CD; Daz was ecstatic that he'd got to see one of his favourite bands, after a nostalgic performance, we stood outside for twenty minutes and met each member as they left the building later. Daz was in his element; he'd got to meet them all and have his picture taken with each one individually.

Two weeks later and I was back at The Fleece, but this time with Steve and Nick, we watched as awesome mod greats Secret Affair graced the stage once more, another great night, and Tracey their PA made sure we had a selfie with Ian Page, the original front man so that was great. I went to the Sharks Scooter Club do on the 19th with many scooter buddie's, Inner City had also played another packed gig in the Back Bar at the end of March.

By now, I'd gone back to work but my back was still suffering, the guys I worked with were great, Pinball, little Rob Allen and many more, they all did their best to give me a more comfortable day. My mate Lee

Harvey is a Chiropractor and a very good one too, I spent plenty of time and money with him to get my back better.

Mid-April and driving the bin lorry I had a bump, so it was another goodbye from them!

A couple of ex-school Facebook friends, had arranged for a school leavers of Wyvern 86 reunion on the 4th of June; a few of us got together for a good old knees up, thirty years after leaving school. It was a great night, held in the good old Back Bar of Cheers, Rosie and Matt Stevenson who also left Wyvern in 86 ran the establishment, an awesome night was had.

After our gig with The Orphans, on Westons Pier the previous December, I'd posted two pictures on Facebook; one was of Inner City on the Old Birnbeck Pier in 1986, the other, was Inner City on the Grand Pier, but this time twenty-nine and a half years later and the same line up. The Birnbeck Regeneration Trust saw this and we all got together, before we knew it, we'd all started organising a charity night to gain pier funds. It was a great success and on June the 18th the night took place, (eight days short of thirty years to the day since we played on Birnbeck Pier). Thank's to Shane Burnley, we had "Good Times," as Justin Lee Collins spent the night with us, and he kept it lively, we had a Manchester DJ, Jonnie Love Buttons also giving us support, From the Jam sent us a copy of their live DVD signed, we auctioned that off and got over a hundred quid, I think Jonnie won that one. A local painter D-NEK, did a great painting of Birnbeck Pier, and that went for a whopping four-hundred quid, to a local and long time friend Alfie. Our sound man was Mark Whitehouse, a well know music man in Weston, we also auctioned off two tickets, for his up and coming event Hazy Days in July, Rich and Rachael Southcombe won those.

We also had entertainment from "Ellie and Nikon," an awesome duet, and Ellie is also the daughter of a great mate David Smart. Local 80's favourites March of Time, with Mike Headington and Steve Kearns, played a thirty minute set, I don't remember who their drum and bass deps' were. Inner City headlined for the last hour of an awesome night and what a memorable night that was too.

I wasn't out of work for long; on the 21st of June I started working for Brakes Frozen Foods. Not a bad job driving their trucks; for most of my time there I was out as a double, it was great as I met and stayed friends with co-worker Ian Leigh, delivering all over Bristol on a daily basis; although, it wasn't doing my back any good! Sharon and I had been invited to an evening wedding do, of Rachel and Ian Simpson from Off the Record, we had a wonderful night; there was live music as Reoffender did a couple of songs, then Who's Next took the stage for the rest of the night, I was in my element being a big Who fan! There was plenty of meat on the pig roast and the cider flowed nicely, Ian Hewitt, also from Off the Record was there with his good wife Jo, Ian and Rachel had organised a great night.

July the 9th and Sharon's sister from Bristol was getting married, it was at a quaint house in the middle of nowhere on the outskirts of Bridgwater. Maunsel House was a lovely place with an old style look, guns' and other ammo hung from the walls' and ceilings'. Of course, I felt a bit out of place all day, as it was all Sharon's family and I only knew a few people; by the end of a lovely day I became snappy, I'd been drinking, so Sharon drove Keanu, Stell, Ella and my drunk miserable self home. But all I did was shout at her all the way, I was rude, and in front of her two poor sons and Stell's girlfriend Ella, who all sat quietly in the back. She dropped me at my house and they all went off home.

The next morning and feeling like shit; I crawled out of bed as I had a gig to play at midday, with Inner City at the Hazy Days festival at the Tropicana. It was only about five minutes away from my house, so Steve came and got me; it was an hour long gig; but being noon and the first act of the day, there weren't many people there to be honest. But still, it was a lovely sunny day and the sound was amazing; as well as Traci and Rob bringing Daz along to see his dad play, we met some great new fans; especially Mick Nurse who you'll hear more about as the book goes on!

The last weekend of the month; I jumped in my car and took a drive to Exmouth for the day on my own, it was the scooter rally and most of the mates were already down there. I found them in The Merchant, so I grabbed a pint and some food, then sat outside, with Kerry Stark, Gary Watts, Tim Briar, Mike Corran, Pete Hudson, Andy Bridgman, Darran and Anita Wheatley and Wayne and Cath Flemming. After I'd eaten, Gary and I took a walk around the stalls for my patch, then we both left, him on his scoot and me in my car.

It was a sad time at the beginning of August, as I went to the funeral of an old school friend Simon Bidwell. Rest in Peace Simon!

Sharon bought herself a car, it was a nice little black Vauxhall Corsa, cheap on fuel and insurance, she sorted all that and I got my car back.

September the 5th, saw Inner City headlining The Hobphin Festival, at The Dolphin Inn, in Uphill Weston on a Friday night, another great gig was smashed, as was the Back Bar on the 9th.

By mid-September, my back got so bad again I was laid off from Brakes, so this time I put my taxi badge to use, and got myself a job with Arrow Taxis at Bristol Airport. The beginning of October, I was able to get a ticket to see "All or Nothing," "The Small Faces" story, at the Playhouse in Weston, another show I'm glad I didn't miss. Plenty of mates were also there, and one long time mate Gary was leaving when I did but he wasn't a happy man, he was upset, so I told him to ring me if he needed a friend. On the 16th, Steve, Nick, Reeves and myself had booked tickets to see Nine Below Zero at the Bierkeller in Bristol, we enjoyed a great gig and we met with Dennis Greaves after the show. Inner City played another gig in the Back Bar in November, this time, awesome friend and March of Time front man Mike Headington, got up on stage and sang with us for an Inner City number, Mr Mystery Man; whilst his proud missus, Andrea, danced happily in the crowded audience.

Gary had been in touch, through the last few months his long term relationship had ended and she'd left him for someone else, he needed a friend.

By the 15th of December, I was back at Bristol Royal Infirmary for my second operation; this time they were replacing my Auditory Ossicles, (Malleus, Incus and Stapes) with a Titanium bar to get the hearing back in my right ear. Gary dropped me at the BRI and taxi driver mate Steve came and took me home later. The operation was a success; I was able to hear again five days later when they removed the padding.

By now my relationship with Sharon was looking ropey, but still we got on with stuff and enjoyed ourselves, the best we could through Christmas and New Year.

Into 2017; on the 7th of January a big party had been organised, at Worlebury Golf Club to celebrate Auntie Vals' 70th birthday; most of the family were there and a great night was had. My neice Abbie and a few of her friends, got up and did a professional and entertaining dance routine, a couple of people got up to sing and everyone had a great night. Inner City were asked if we'd like to play a multi-band night, we jumped at the chance as it was at The Fleece, the place we'd seen so many bands play before and we finally had our chance. It was a strange night, a few other bands played too, but they were all so young! It wasn't about who was the best band, but about future support slots. We got a great response, but the best thing about it was the comments we got from the parents of the other bands, they were our age and older you see, and a couple of them had come over to give us their awesome views.

We had the usual Pizza Hut for Keanu on his birthday at the start of February, and a couple of weeks later my sister turned fifty; a party was held at The Imperial, another great night was had with the family and loads of friends.

Through March nothing much went on, Sharon and I did nothing but argue and we started to become very distant.

On Sunday March the 10th and on Daz's birthday, I decided Daz and I would take a drive to Dartmouth, to see Mum and Perry on their boat, Cheryl and Bernard were also there, the weather was great, we caught crabs and ate food; it was a lovely day, then I drove us back and got Daz home.

The 25th of March, and The Stanley's played a one off gig at The Brit Bar; everybody was there, Sharon watched proudly as her son sang and played his guitar; I'd like to think she was proud of me, but I think that ship had sailed!

At the end of the month, Keanu stopped going to Jacqueline Fox's school of Dance, as by now we were both struggling to make ends meet.

I treated Sharon and K dude to a day in Bristol for her birthday, and on the 4th of April Sharon received her qualifications as she'd passed all her exams to be a Personal Trainer; I was very proud but it was a little too late!

I still made sure to look after Keanu whilst Sharon went to college. On the 16th Sharon was in Hertfordshire, and returned on the 17th with a new car, a nice little x-reg peugeot 306; her best friend had given it to her, after buying herself a new car. She gave the Corsa to Stell, as he had recently passed his test.

Sharon, Keanu and I took a drive to Bristol and spent the day on the SS Great Britain, it had been a long time since I was on it last, ok, so I'd delivered ice creams there in the past but I never went on it. Sharon hadn't been on it for years, and Keanu really enjoyed himself as it was his first time, it's a very interesting and educational ship, so a great day was had. It was a proud uncle moment for me, as Ryan ran the London Marathon on the 23rd of April.

The end of April saw the Weston Scooter Rally weekend, the do was only down the road, so not too far to crawl home from the pub. The Sunday afternoon was my favourite part; Inner City were playing an afternoon gig in the Back Bar, it was packed out with an awesome crowd to entertain.

I still did my upmost to keep Sharon and K dude in my life, so on the 30th of April Sharon and I got our evening hot chocolates', K dude had his milkshake, and we parked up at Knightstone Island, on Weston seafront to enjoy them. It was then I presented her with a nicely wrapped present, it was an Adam Ant CD, book, some pin badges, a printed T-shirt and two tickets' to see him at the Hippodrome in Bristol, it was worth it to see Sharon so happy.

A Facebook friend and ex-original drummer, from 80's mod favourites The Chords, Brett "Buddy" Ascott, was playing a gig in one of his bands, "The Fallen Leaves" at The Thunderbolt in Bristol. Gary Watts and Steve Wilkinson made it a date and on the 4th of May we went to the gig. I think one of the best moments for me, was when a mod drumming legend like Buddy, walks in the pub, looks at me and says "hi Tim," Steve's jaw dropped, he looked at me and said, "Blimey, Buddy just said hello and recognised you!" It won't mean a lot to you but it did to me!

Ten days later on the 14th, I drove a happy Sharon and myself up to Bristol for the Adam Ant concert, their performance was outstanding; as was their support act Glam Skanks. What a great show and it put a massive smile on Sharon's face, she was up dancing and really enjoying herself. It was the first time I'd ever heard her sing in our four and a half years together, she has such a lovely voice too; I thought this might of actually brought us closer, but nope I was wrong, we had a great night; I dropped her home then went back to my empty bed.

Now, remember Mick Nurse from before? Well this is where he comes into the picture. When we played the Hazy Days gig on a Sunday afternoon, Mick was driving past with his missus Bev, and his son Matt, it was a lovely day and the roof was down on his convertible Saab. As he passed the Tropicana, he could suddenly hear The Jam being played somewhere; Mick being a big Jam fan and still right into his Punk and other music, he parked up and they walked into the free outdoor event, to be faced with Inner City; banging out all the best Jam songs'; he was very impressed and introduced himself.

By June the 3rd we were playing a gig organised by Mick, in Cirencester for Punk 77, it was a charity night for a handicap football team; this was also organised by a couple Mandy and Gerry Watkins. What a fantastic night with a few Punk and skinhead bands including "The Extroverts," "Who Killed Nancy Johnson" and "The Feckin Ejets." Inner City finished the night off to a great and happy crowd, I won a "Feckin Ejets" T-shirt in the raffle, and Steve won some beer, the best thing about the day for me, was that Daz came too, and everybody fell in love with him, especially Gerry and Mandy who would've adopted him if they could!

Now back to Sharon, her landlady suddenly, without any real warning, put the house Sharon lived in on the market and it was sold very quickly. With no spare cash and the use of her credit card, she had to move within a few weeks. A flat was sourced and her friends rallied round, as did I; Gary helped with his taxi when we needed the sofa moved, we did it all in one day mid-June, about ten people and five cars, but it was a success.

The next day and Inner City were playing another afternoon gig, again in The Tropicana, but this time it was a pre flight gig; it was Weston Air Days and The Red Arrows were about to do their thing. It was only a short gig and we played a great one as usual, so we packed up and went home.

The rest of June was spent shopping in Ikea, for furniture for Sharons new place; building beds and flat packed furniture. On a good note, she did buy a new bed so I had her three-year old double; that went straight in Daz's room to replace his single bed, he was twenty-seven by this time and not small.

Sharon and I did the pub rounds on the 14th of July, she drove and dropped me home later; on the 22nd, Sharon, Master K and myself took another trip to Bristol, and spent the sunny Sunday checking out the Bristol Harbour Festival; what a lovely warm walk it was too, nice food and big ice creams, it felt so much like a nice family day, I thought there maybe still hope!

The week after, Inner City played another Reaper event in the Tropicana, again with The Orphans as they'd requested us for support. The gig was the best, as we've all been good friends with the Orphans guys and girl for many years and we'd gigged with them before, it was another very memorable night.

The next day, Steve Wilkinson, Daz and myself were off to The Sounds of the Cotswolds in Cirencester; not playing this time; we were invited by Gerry and Mandy Watkins who organize this event, to come up for the day. What Daz didn't know was; Showaddywaddy were headlining and we got to meet them before they played; of course, Daz was once again in his element, he danced and he sang with many others, right in front of the stage, an awesome day was had.

August was a quiet month, on the 5th Inner City played The Old Pier Tavern in Burnham, not too busy which was a shame, where had all the tourists gone? I did have the pleasure of meeting Lisa the Karaoke DJ. Sharon and I were also busy buying Keanus new Worle School uniform, as he was about to leave his Junior days and move up to Secondary School. There was so much to buy, trousers, shirts, blazer, jumper, sports socks, T-shirt, another jumper; it went on and on, but boy did Master K look smart; another proud moment for Sharon and I.

September was a busier month; Inner City played another Sunday afternoon gig at the Hobphin Festival in Uphill, it was an outside stage and it pissed it down with rain all afternoon, the stage was dry, but very few people stood to watch it. All the same Sharon brought Keanu along which was nice; Karen Bond, her husband Keith, and their daughter came from Clevedon too, Karen works at the airport taxis and we became friends. We still played an awesome gig and saw some other great acts.

The 4th of September, K dude, was on his first day at Worle School mission, he was nervous but he loved it; quite a few of his Junior School friends had started there too. It was also Sharons first day at her new job at Priory School, no more lunchtime supervisor and cleaner, but now a full time LSA; I was very proud, but now she had a lot of courses to complete and a lot more to learn. Then that night at Inner City rehearsals, my snare drum skin broke so that was another twenty quid to find, the band signed the old one and we gave it to Mick Nurse for his birthday; along with some signed broken drum sticks.

A few days later and still driving taxis at the airport, I was involved in a bump on the A38; I left that job pretty sharpish, they didn't really want me there anymore to be honest. I was again jobless but only for a few days, I managed to get connected with BCA for a month or so; moving hundreds of cars about ready for delivery in Portbury. There I made some new friends, more so, was the guy who gave us the training when we started, Garth Aldridge; I didn't recognise him, until he reminded me that I'd actually been out on the town with him years before; he too is a good friend of Craig Tildesley, and he came down with some friends a few years previous. I also met and worked with Simon Jones, we all stay in touch. Inner City played another Reaper event at The Tropicana on the 23rd, this time supporting "London's Calling," the UK's top "Clash" tribute act, we all smashed it and went home happy.

The week after and the Inner City boys were off on a road trip; this time to Exeter, to see more 80's mod favourites The Lambrettas and The Chords UK; both bands were brilliant, afterwards we got to spend some time with The Lambrettas, but best of all Doug Sanders the singer and Paul Wincer their drummer, two of the original members so that was awesome.

So after a great month it was going to be hard to top that. But no, on the 1st of October we played our first gig in Aberdare in Wales; there was a two day music event, "Ska and Mod Weekend," in Jacs; it was a long drive, well for Steve and Nick anyway, but a great gig was had. They booked us for future dates, and Skacasm were playing after us so we became friends with the band.

On the 4th I was sat playing with Facebook and my messenger went "Ping," blimey, I fell off my chair, it was only from Doug, the lead singer from the Lambrettas! He stated that he and his good wife Amanda, would be in Weston the next day and asked if we'd like to meet for a drink. So after I picked myself up off the floor, and messaged the other guys to tell them the great news, a meet was arranged; I rushed back from work in Portbury the next day, I got showered and sped to the Cabot on Weston sea front, we'd all arrived at the same time, and there we all were, sat with one of our legends. We only stayed for an hour as he had to meet someone else on a business level, but still we left happy.

It was another sad loss in early October; an ex-school mate Martin Hodge lost his fight with cancer. Rest in Peace Martin!

On the 14th, we played our first gig in a newly started music venue in Weston, The Electric Banana, run by Terry McQuire, it was a great gig with a great crowd. By now I was seeing a lot less of Sharon; she didn't come with us when Daz and I went to see Cheryl and Bernard, doing their awesome performance in "Half a Sixpence," at the Playhouse in Weston on the 26th.

As well as an Inner City photo shoot, and having Master K for a couple of evenings whilst Sharon was at college; the only other good thing to happen in November, was landing an interview with Royal Mail in Weston. I was desperate to go back to a job I once left and really did enjoy, it was also security; so on the 23rd I made my way to the Post Office; I met with the manager, who was there when I left fifteen years previous, Ian Gregory; we sat and chatted and I left a happy man, then I just had to wait for a start date. During this time, I'd also spent every spare hour writing this book, between the 6th and the 12th I'd already written the first twenty years!

By the 20th of December I started back with Royal Mail; Sharon and I were drifting apart, but it didn't make sence, I was in a better job, I finished work by three every day, I had days off here there and everywhere; I could be an even better hands on step dad to Keanu. We did go late night shopping also on the 20th which was nice, but then on the 24th Sharon and K dude took a road trip to Hertfordshire, to stay with friends for the Christmas and New Year. I spent christmas day alone as I had on a few occasions, Boxing Day was Christmas Day for me, as it was Daz's day too. I had however, bought enough food to feed a small army; I cooked the lot, I made a massive meal for me on a huge plate, then two standard sized plates. One I covered in tin foil and put in the fridge, the other I covered in foil, then took a drive just up the road to the seafront. I then gave it; with a knife, fork, spoon and a pudding too, to two homeless guys, I was happy that I'd fed someone and they were happy to of received it.

I took Daz to see Aladdin at the Playhouse on the 30th, and we got to meet the cast after the show too, it was a great and happy ending to 2017.

Daz and Gerry Watkins with Showaddywaddy

Doug from The Lambrettas comes to Weston

CHAPTER 10

SO SAD ABOUT US!

Sharon and Keanu travelled back on the 2nd and on the 3rd we met for coffee. We did stay in touch through Facebook and we still met for the occasional coffee and chat, we'd talk and we'd often argue, either way, we were definitely becoming more distant!

Early January, I worked hard as a postie. I did a week working in Patchway Bristol, which was hard work in an area I'd never worked before, thankfully, I was soon back in Weston.

Inner City rehearsals had been back on since mid-January and near the end of the month, we played our first gig of the year, at The Swiss Chalet in Swindon, organized by Gerry and Mandy Watkins. A Thin Lizzy tribute act played before us, so we didn't have to rush to get there. Our good friend and sound engineer Mark Bolam got there early, he was supplying sound for both bands. We arrived, set up, and smashed an awesome gig in a very busy pub; by the end of the night, even the bar staff were on the bar singing along to The Jam classics' we were belting out.

By the start of March, we'd had some heavy snow, yes, even down here in the Southwest! I waded into work, as my car was covered in snow, to be told by the boss Dan, that there was no work to do, so we spent the day building igloos' and snow people, having snowball fights, cups of coffee, then home after a fun short day.

At the same time, Sharon was again moving to a new house, and her costs were about to go down! I spent my days off and any spare evening helping her move. Besides the move, which would've been stressful enough for Sharon anyway; we'd been having some tough times through the past few months, so I decided to end the relationship!

Daz's birthday evening was spent at Pizza Hut again; Gary joined us to celebrate too. The week after on the 17th was the date Inner City had been waiting for; we were finally being the support act for mod legends Secret Affair. It was the best night I'd had in a long time; spending the evening with Ian Page, Dave Cairns, Russ, Tracey and the rest of Secret Affair; as well as beating the drums behind my best mates, with my number one Daz stood proudly watching the whole night of entertainment! I had no Daz the week after and was now single, so I had a night on the town with mates and what a great night; the awesome Skacasm were in The Brit Bar; it was a very drunk night indeed! I'd become friends with the lead singer Gareth and the sax player Gary, when we played before Skacasm at Jacs in Aberdare, since then I'd also become friends with their bass player Wayne and drummer Scott.

As the end of the month approached, I was asked by Mick Nurse if I'd like to join him at The Fiddler's in Bristol on the 29th; another great night was spent watching 80's Psychobilly favourite's "The Guanabatz." Many years ago, before Pip (the lead singer), moved to the States to live; he used to race motocross bikes with Mick, we got chatting after and what a lovely bloke.

The last day of the month, saw Inner City travelling over the Severn Bridge once more to smash another gig in Jacs Aberdare; another long night, but with a great audience and at an awesome venue.

April the 7th, was The Stanley's 5th final gig ever! They had actually split, but if asked they would play a gig and I was the drummer for those gigs! Daz was there with my sister, nephew, and niece and many other friends turned up, it was a great gig. Then it was just working and home alone until my weekends with Daz, then it was Treats and family. Of course, now I was looking at living life completely different from the last five-plus years; I'd sit in Treats alone when Daz wasn't around, but PJ's ice cream when he was.

I was a reserve postie for the first couple of days in May, so after some small local postal rounds, I was sent to Bridgwater to get a water hose changed on a van. A nice easy drive there to find they didn't have the part, then a quick drive back, I delivered a few more parcels locally and then went home. I tried to keep myself busy the best I could, a postie friend Sarah-Jane had asked me if I could teach her the drums. She'd not played since she left school, some eighteen years before; I was happy with that as I needed something to do. She played really well and left a happy bunny! My time was no longer Sharon's time, until the Thursdays' when her college was back in full swing. I'd take K dude for a McDonald's, then back to mine, to watch as many episodes of Impractical Jokers he could watch! I had a load recorded on my sky box for him; unfortunately, now he'd not been around as much, there were at least fifty-two unwatched episodes to go through!

Inner City had an article printed in a local paper The Weston Mercury, by the next weekend we were playing at The Electric Banana! Mandy and Gerry came to the gig, so I blew up a couple of air beds and they had a sleepover at mine. It was another great gig and the Sunday was spent with Daz, Gerry, and Mandy enjoying the sights of Weston, after Treats of course! Daz loves the Go-karts on The Weston Pier, so we spent most of the time there until they had to leave for Cirencester.

The week after I had to work, but was in Bristol one night watching Nine Below Zero on The Thekla. Steve, Rich, and Nick had gone up earlier to watch a big footie game; as I have no interest in football, I didn't plan to join them, as I was working, it would have been a rush. I drove up later and parked in The Thekla car park. I met up with the gang as soon as I arrived, we boarded The Thekla and got a pint. I then went straight over to the merchandise stand, Dennis Greaves the lead singer was stood there, I was well chuffed; we'd met a few times over the years, but he must have met loads of fans! We had a good chat; he sold me a T-shirt; I shoved it in my jacket and went back to the lads. We watched the gig and as per usual it sounded awesome, I drove us all home at the end of the night; listening to the newest disc Steve had bought. Just my luck: when I got home, I found Dennis had sold me a small T-shirt.

The Cricket Club Keanu used to use, was only at the end of my long road, well, at the end of May, The Orphans were playing a charity night there, which was ideal for me as I could walk there and back no problem!

Gutted, the tickets' had sold out! After a quick Facebook begging status, a friend Alex Divianni came up trumps and I was now able to go.

The same evening Holly, my nephew Ryan's girlfriend, was singing right over the other side of Weston, in The Claremont Vaults. I shot up there in my car first, saw Holly, my entire family and a few other friends; then I shot home, parked the car, and made my way to a gig I'm glad I never missed! Other friends were there, including Tony Sparling, Sarah and Dave Horn, Zara Powell, Teresa, Alex and a very drunk night was had; as per usual, The Orphans were fantastic.

On the 7th, I took Mum for lunch at The Olive Branch, a mate, ex-bin driver Mike Hanslip and his wife ran. We ate and talked which was lovely, it really helped, but once I went home I felt low again! A weekend without Daz meant I was going to get drunk, sure enough after eight pints of thatchers I was!

Inner City were off to High Wycombe on Saturday the 23rd. We played a thirty-minute gig at noon; it was a long day but we played a great gig, and we got a chance to meet a lot of great fellow musicians.

I was out delivering mail the next day, with the usual smile on my face at work and whilst working, but once I was at home I was in bits! Yes, we'd been falling apart, but now it had really come to an end and I was starting to regret it; by this time through rumour control, I'd also heard she'd moved on!

I was introduced to a business whilst on my post-round one day; after knocking on a door with a parcel, a lovely lady handed me a business card for Utility Warehouse with her name on it. I took the card and carried on with my day. I later went back to Angie's house, to discuss the business adventure for the whole afternoon and evening. I made a lovely friend and an educational time was had, with a new business on its way, maybe.

I'd ended the relationship and was now single, yet I started feeling sad and lonely. I took a lovely walk up Weston seafront one night; I got a drink from Muddys Bar; which at the time was run by friends' Mark Harp and Sharon. Whilst I walked home, everything was a memory; I'd walked that route a lot with Sharon and Keanu, I was sad by the time I got back home; so more cider and a good night's sleep!

At the end of the month, I was delivering mail to a rural area of

Weston. On Monday, I'd delivered mail by foot to one particular house; the weather was up in the high twenties, and this house had a steep driveway; I moaned as I was all hot and sweaty, but still, I climbed the drive and all for one letter! It was a lovely house, the kind of house I'd dream of living in. Then it was back to my van delivering to the rest of the houses along the way; I was working with Rob that day, he finally returned and we went back to the depot to end our day. The next day I had a parcel, a skybox it was, for the same house, "Sod that" I thought, I'm driving up that drive today! The temperature had been between twenty-six and twenty-eight that whole month so I did the loop by foot, leaving the parcel in the van for the house with the steep driveway. I drove up the drive and got out the van, but this time I was greeted by a cute black dog (Freddie) on the other side of the gate yapping; then a lady appeared from the garden in a blue dress, a bit older than me but Phwiiittt Phwooo! not bad if I did say so myself! We had a chat and a giggle; to be honest, I thought this house was lived in by an elderly retired couple, and this was their daughter. But no, this lady was in-fact single and lived there with her eighteen-year-old son; we chatted for a good five minutes, in that time we found a lot out about each other; well, she knew my name anyway! Even though I had her parcel, I'd not even looked at her name. I left her house, met Rob, went home and that was that.

The following day was my last day on that particular round, I realised I had no mail for Freddie's house and to be honest I was a bit gutted! You see, outside work I was a mess, I was crying myself to sleep most nights and I wasn't eating properly; I needed a friend more than anything and a female friend was even better! Nearly six years with Sharon was a hard thing to forget. My thoughts were, "If she's moved on then so will I!" Ok, I had no mail for the steep drive-way house, but I thought "if I don't do this now I may not be this way again for ages!" So when I'd finished my delivery, I jumped in the van and drove up the drive; gutted, no dog was barking and no one was at home, so quickly thinking, I pulled an Inner City business card from my wallet and left a small note; "Hi, if you fancy a drink sometime then give me a call, postie Tim." I finished my day, went home and I forgot all about the note. I spent my evening drinking cider, scrolling Facebook and feeling sorry for myself. Later in the evening, my phone went ping; it was a message from a number I didn't recognise! I opened it to read, "I'd love to go for a drink, but can we leave it for a month as I've just come out of a relationship, thanks Anita." I was happy with that as I too had recently come out of a relationship and still wasn't over mine; I now knew her name and we soon became Facebook friends.

Now in July, I needed to do something to occupy my mind, and I came up with an idea after a funny mishap a few weeks before. What happened was, I was driving my car one evening and my phone rang, the phone at that time was on my seat between my legs, I won't answer the phone whilst driving, as well as it being illegal. So without looking, I thought I'd switched the call off, but unbeknown to me what I'd actually done is set the video to record! Another 80's mod favourite The Jetset, was playing on the stereo at that time and I was happily singing along. I got home and sat down with a coffee, to find my phone was telling me the memory was full; I looked in dismay to find a very amusing video, and it was about twenty-six minutes long. I edited one song (Wednesday Girl), and posted it on Facebook. Mickey Dias the drummer, Angus Nanaan the keyboard player and Paul Bevoir on vocals are all in this band; they're also friends on my Facebook and after seeing it they all enjoyed it, as did many others!

A new idea was born! I was in the car taking a drive to see a mate Lou in Kewstoke, and I'd put a different disc in the player; the video was recording and I was driving down the Toll Road, singing my rendition of "Straight back down" by "Curiosity Killed the Cat," in Timmys Carpool Karaoke!

Once home I was back to my sad self, I sat with a can of thatchers and uploaded the video. The first like within minutes was Anita, not just a thumb but a heart; ooh, she liked that then! There were still tears at night, and I wasn't really eating; then a couple of days later I got another message from Anita, "Forget what I said about the end of July, let's meet sooner." Happy days, there was a light at the end of the tunnel! Was my singing really that good? We arranged a date, and on the 11th I had a shave; got my glad rags on and made my way to Anita's. We then jumped in her bright-yellow Juke and we went to the very quiet, just reopened Nut Tree Pub in Worle. It was only quiet as an England match was on, and there were no TVs in that pub! I don't do footie, so it was lovely as we had the pub to ourselves! We talked and talked (well, I did anyway!) The landlord eventually came over and asked if we could leave as he wanted to go home, so we went back to Anitas and drank coffee until three in the morning, all we did was talk and joke, I left and went home a happy chap.

As Anita and I had broken the ice, I was invited for a meal on Friday the 13th. Unlucky for some maybe, but certainly not for me as it was my birthday treat! "Wow!" two days into a relationship and boy, what a meal! She picked me up, looking stunning in a dark pink dress, I jumped in totally unaware of where we were going. I was more confused as we entered the motorway Northbound, but only one junction, to Clevedon. My brain started ticking, "I used to deliver to some lovely places here!" We parked up and walked into a Chinese restaurant, "Junior Poon," it was very expensive but what a meal we had, Anita paid the bill and we went back for a drink at hers; then she ran me home later!

For the next week, I carried on with my Carpool Karaoke, with classics like "Yeah Yeah" by Georgie Fame, "Blank Expression" by The Specials, and Will Smith's "Summertime."

I went out on a Saturday night; Sole Room Dave was spinning the discs at The Brit Bar. There were a couple of great mates out, including another big Inner City fan, Christopher Rose and his good wife; mod mate Simon Phillips who was spinning the tunes with Dave and ex-Wyvern School friend Caron Moore; there were also a lot of people I didn't know in there too. A mate walked in and met straight up with me; within three minutes of talking, a drunk guy, came out from the bar, he sneaked up behind my mate, who hadn't even had a chance to get a drink and shoved him; he turned and shoved him back! Then the other guy head-butted him and followed it through with a glass, "SMASH!" straight into the left side of my mates now bleeding head. After things calmed down and he was taken care of by the bar owners, the lout got chucked out and was later arrested. The glass had cut his ear and chipped a tooth, but luckily it just missed his eye!

I went to Taunton one evening, for a Pizza Express pizza Tuesday with Angie and the Utility Warehouse crew, it was lovely to meet new people and find out more about what UW has to offer.

Anita's (nine years older than me) birthday, was on the 26th so we celebrated that too, and I got her some lovely presents; although on her actual birthday I had to work, so she went for a picnic with her bestie instead. The last five days of the month were busy, one day Anita and myself took Anita's granddaughter Sienna, to Bristol for the day spotting a Gromit or two and checking out The Ice Cream Cafe. A couple of days later and I was driving Daz up the M5 for the "Sounds of the Cotswolds." This time Inner City were playing with three other bands, but headlined by "The Sex Pissed Dolls." What a great day as always, organised by Gerry and Mandy, for "The Yellow Bus Project" and we got to meet some amazing musicians and some great new friends'.

The next day, I took Anita for a late birthday treat to Frankie and Benny's. This was all great, but every time we did something I couldn't get the thoughts out of my head, "me and Sharon ate here, or me and Sharon came here a lot!" just like Bristol, as we were up there again that evening. Anita's daughter Ashleigh and her husband Mick, had just had their first baby and they wanted to show Rosie off to their mum and I.

Don't get me wrong, my life had had the lift it needed but I still couldn't shrug off the last nearly six-years. Anita really did help take my mind off things, any day off or at the weekends; she always made sure we did something different and memorable. On the 2nd of August, we took a lovely walk in Uphill; we had a Cappuccino in the boatyard cafe, then took a long walk, taking in the essence of the countryside on a boiling hot day! It was on this walk I had my first attempt at "The Floss Dance," but unbeknown to me, Anita was filming from behind and I soon got a roasting on Facebook!

Mum and Perry were on their boat in Dartmouth for two weeks, as they always were during the Dartmouth Regatta. Anita decided one morning that it would be a good idea to pop down and visit them! I wasn't going to complain, she offered to drive and I could see the family; I'd not been on the boat for a while. It was a lovely smooth drive down, although we did have two satnavs on the go, and we followed the wrong one, ending up on the wrong side of the River Dart! We queued for a bit, as we had to wait for a ferry to take us to the other side; once on the ferry we could get out of the car and breathe in the sea air. We got to the other side and drove for ten minutes until we found a space, once parked we had a lovely scenic walk down to the harbour, then the search was on, for "Out of the Blue," one of a few thousand boats' moored up! First I took Anita to the best ice cream shop in Dartmouth, "The Good Intent" in Lower Street, we both grabbed a huge one each and took a long stroll along the harbour, right to the end but still no sign of Mum! We walked all the way back to the other end again; after asking a few locals but getting nowhere, I finally got on the phone to Mum, it turned out we were on the right side in the first place! So after another ferry trip, but as pedestrians this time, we finally found them. They were both happy and surprised to see us, but Anita really enjoyed herself; what a great introduction to my parents'; a great day was had, followed by a safe and quick journey home.

The next day, we were invited to my uncle Maurice and auntie Josies' Anniversary barbeque in Street. Anita didn't drink and was eager to meet more of my family; she drove, so I could have a few ciders'. It was a fantastic night, Cheryl was there with Bernard, Abbie came with little Esme, my cousins Jonnie and Simon were there with their missus, Uncle Rich and my cousin Alison, the list goes on, it was another great night with plenty of food and cider.

We calmed it down a bit during the next week; it was then that I introduced Anita, to the classic TV series "Friends." I couldn't believe, that a woman nine years older than me, with five kids between eighteen and thirty-one, had never ever seen one episode of Friends. I had the first two seasons and a few other seasons on DVD, so we spent every night when there was nothing else on, watching the discs'. One by one we got through them, every time I'd fall asleep; I'd dribble a bit, and Anita always made sure she got a picture to send to me the next day, I'd wake up and drive home.

I was watching "This Morning" on a day off, and Dr Hilary started talking about lumps on the tongue. I was interested in this as I did actually have a lump on my tongue, low and behold he showed a picture that looked exactly like mine; I started to worry a bit, especially as he said: "If you have this on your tongue, get it checked out immediately." Luckily it was still quite early, I got on the phone and was seeing the doctor straight away. He took a look and put the email through for me to have it looked at by specialists, being a smoker I was a little concerned.

By the 10th I was at the Bristol Dental Hospital, having my tongue looked at. The doctor introduced himself and gave my tongue a tug and check, "yep," he said, "you're going to need a biopsy on that!" To cheer me up Anita took me to Cafe Amore for lunch, another establishment I once delivered food to, we did plenty of charity shops and I bought a few Who, LP's on vinyl; we found some more Friends DVDs to add to the collection, and not forgetting the hour or so spent in Primark! I mean come on: one floor for men and three floors for women; what are we supposed to do once we've checked out the entire bottom floor? she's only just stepped off the escalator on the first floor! It did cheer me up, but I was now worried about my health!

The next day, I was playing a one-off gig with The Stanley's, but this time for my cousin Karyns Graduation Party. It was held In a massive back garden, with a huge self-built stage in Kenn near Clevedon. I took Jordan and all his gear, Daz jumped in with Anita and she took him to the party for a great night. Most of my family came along and there was plenty of food and drink, I was driving so that made no difference. Once the night was over and we were loading the cars, Anita had Daz so I put some of my drums in her car, it was tough earlier in the night, squeezing Jordan's stuff in with my entire kit. We went to mine first so I could get Daz into bed and there would be more people to help with the gear. When we were unloading, I did something to my back and suddenly was in major pain, I was as good as in tears and couldn't move; Jordan carried on emptying the car for me, Daz had gone on in and Anita was trying to be helpful, I was in so much pain; like a fool, I just told her to go and leave me alone! so off she went. Jordan helped me on my feet, and I was able to take him home a short while later. Daz was in bed and fast asleep by the time I'd got back, so at least I knew he'd had a great night. I was moody because my back was painful, as well as the fact that Sharon's son Stell plays in The Stanley's. Seeing him brought things flooding back, and I'd also been having a lot of thoughts over the last few days, "Was this relationship moving too fast," "Was it too soon after Sharon to be moving on?"

I apologized to Anita the following day for my childish outburst, and we were back on track, just as well really; the next day she was off to see "Mama Mia" with Mum, Cheryl, Auntie Val, and a couple of others.

The day after that, she took me to The Sidcot Arms in Sidcot for a massive meal, I had my first Christmas in this establishment in 1970, apart from a taxi pick up in the past, this was my first proper visit. It was funny, I'd posted on Facebook where I was and what I was eating, then "Ping," a notification from another great friend Kim Fountain, "My husband Mark is working in there tonight!" I walked over to the bar and introduced myself; I'd known Kim for years and years but never met her hubby, what a lovely man and a small world!

More eating out, and this time on me, we did have coupons after all! The Hobbs Boat Inn in Bleadon on the A38, another place I'd not been in for a long time; we had a lovely meal and a great afternoon. The day after we were back in Bristol for my biopsy. We went up early, so once the car was parked, Anita and I could have a quick Cappuccino and toastie before we got there. Once in the Dental Hospital, the worry kicked in a bit more, I laid in a dentist chair whilst a young girl tugged on my tongue, stretching it as far right as she could. I couldn't gulp, I couldn't swallow, it was a horrible feeling, then another lady went in with the scalpel, thankfully, the anesthetic had kicked in straight away; there was no pain but it felt weird. The whole time in the hospital was over so quick; we soon left, then it was the waiting game to hear my results. We thought we'd visit Primark whilst we were there, and no sooner had we stepped inside; we bumped into a friend I'd not seen for a while, Trina, (who gave me Gizmo and Sparky) and her daughter Gemma; soon after our chat I started feeling woozy, so we left pretty sharpish, I went home and straight to bed!

I'd heard through the grapevine that Sharon was now single, that was great but she didn't want me anyway! Then I had loads going on in my head again, "Should I leave Anita and try and get Sharon back!" My mind was now mixed up once more. Even though I had in fact stayed at Anita's house on occasion, and she thought the world of me, I still couldn't get sexy with her. I loved everything about her, but I was still holding a candle for Sharon; it felt like I was moving on too fast. My brain said let go, but my heart wouldn't let me. A few days later and I received an Instagram message from Sharon, she'd heard through Facebook that I'd had the biopsy and was worried and checking I was ok! I was happy to hear from her to be honest; we exchanged normal texts and she said that she was also happy to see I'd moved on. Of course, I've always had trouble keeping my mouth shut and by the end of the texts, I'd told her that Anita and I hadn't had any bedroom fun, and I'd leave her tomorrow if she'd have me back! She didn't believe there was no nookie and what did it matter!

Nearing the end of the month, Anita's eldest son Robin, and his girlfriend were celebrating their birthday's with a nice big birthday meal, at the Windmill Inn, in Portishead, I delivered food there too on more than one occasion! Four of Anita's five kids' were there, Sean lived in Brazil so it was a bit too far to come for a snack! All their partners were there, and I took Daz too; a great night was had with an awesome sea view of Wales.

Inner City had been rehearsing hard every Monday, ready for our next gig on the 26th at The Back Bar once more, another loud and very busy night was had.

I'd had a small Tax Rebate, so I treated myself to some new toys, I bought some new loafers, I won a pair of Dr Martens on eBay for less than thirty quid, and I bought a lovely Crombie from Matalan. The best thing was the drum throne I bought, target print leather, just right for a mod drummer, the 30th was the start of my physiotherapy, I'd gained a dodgy right shoulder over the last few months, and needed to get it checked.

Straight into September and we were off to The Catherines Inn, I'd not been there for a couple of years, we had a great meal and enjoyed a massive chocolate pudding for two; it was a lovely afternoon together.

That night I received a message from Sharon on Instagram, it was a nice message to ask if I'd had my biopsy results. After a short while, the text's started getting nicer and I thought to myself, "I wonder if this is going anywhere?" I shouldn't have even been thinking anything; I was with someone who thought the absolute world of me, we'd done so much together in the last six weeks, but still, like a lovesick fool I sent Sharon a pic of my private parts, you know, all happy to see her! She sent me some nice comments back about the picture, and eventually after my begging, she sent an up-to-date picture of herself, not naked or topless but slim and gorgeous looking all the same, I was now excited and asked for more, but it wasn't going to happen!

The next day and a day off for me, Anita and I took another nice walk, but this time along the seafront and to PJ's for ice cream. It was a lovely day and I smiled all the way through it. Only the night before I was having fun texting with Sharon, then I was spending time at our old haunts; what the hell was I doing?

Sharon would text from time to time, to see if I'd had my results and we'd have a brief chat by text and that was it. By the 11th it had been two months since Anita and I first dated, she'd bought me a lovely drum-painted-tumbler and I took her for a meal at The Beefeater; again we had tokens.

I finished work on the 13th and was eager to get home and get ready; Anita and I were off to see a duet with Dennis Greaves and Mark Feltham from Nine Below Zero; they were doing an acoustic set at a pub in Cirencester. I was at my house alone and I received an Instagram message from Sharon, just as I was getting in the shower; we sorted to put Instagram on video for a proper chat. We spoke whilst I showered, and I enjoyed myself a bit too much to be honest! Hey, I was home alone, horny and Sharon was with me! We said goodbye and speak soon; I got ready and Anita picked me up. It was only an hour or so drive and we were there, we met up straight away with Gerry Watkins, we grabbed a drink each and sat to enjoy a great performance. The show was fantastic, a great acoustic life story of Nine Below Zero. After the show we got to chat with both Dennis and Mark, I moaned and he laughed that he'd sold me the wrong size T-shirt on The Thekla, we had a lovely night and one of Anita's favourite nights I believe. She drove us back safely and dropped me back home.

A friend of mine Jo was getting married to Craig, they'd booked Inner City to play at The Tavern on the Town for an evening do. On the 15th we were banging out Jam tunes in a very busy pub, right in the centre of town with plenty of friends. Anita had brought her clan of friends too, although she was in fact suffering from a bad back herself, still, she took the drums and me to the venue.

Any texts' I received from Sharon, were lovely caring texts just to see how I was, and to see if my results had come through. By this time I was getting a little anxious, as I still hadn't heard anything myself; I got on the phone to the hospital to no avail, but they took my number and I waited for a call!

As well as any series of "Friends," there were also a large number of popular classic films that Anita had never seen, films like "Warriors," "The Wanderers," "Back to the Future" and The Who classic "Quadrophenia," but also "The Blues Brothers," I have them all so we were soon watching them. I left The Blues Brothers until last, it was part of my plan you see. "The Chicago Blues Brothers" were doing a show at The Playhouse; I'd bought us both tickets to go and see the show a week after seeing the film. Best night EVER! I rushed home from work, showered, shaved, and got dressed, into my black suit, white shirt, black tie, black shoes, and my black trilby hat, I put the sun-glasses on in the Playhouse. We danced, we sang and we met the cast after the show, we had a terrific night.

An ex-school mate and Coca Cola supplier when I was in hospital many years before, Chris Kitching, lived on a postie route I was doing one week; I'd not seen him or his wife Sarah for a long time, I knocked on their door and we all had a good ten-minute catch up and a coffee; it was great to see them both and then I was on my way.

Saturday the 23rd, I worked in the morning as late afternoon, Inner City took a drive up the motorway once again to High Wycombe, This time we were playing a surprise party for Mick Nurses 60th Birthday, he was very surprised and well chuffed as we had become his favourite live band; the night was full of live punk bands and many punks of all ages. Daz came with Steve and I in Steve's car and Reeves went up with Nick. Other Punk bands' had graced the stage also for Mick's surprise, including "The Xtraverts" and "Nuffin;" we finished the night off, with the great sounds of The Jam, Mick's favourite band full stop. He joined us on stage for a singalong, as we ended a great set with "Going Underground." We made plenty of new friends, including awesome Nuffin frontman, Brian Damage, The Xtraverts frontman, Nigel Martin, and Events organiser Mick Moriarty, and many many more top musicians'. Mick had the night of his life as did Daz and many others. Anita couldn't come as there was no room left in any cars; instead, she spent the night with my family at Unwined celebrating Ryan's graduation, she kept me posted with updates and photos throughout the evening which was nice. However, we had a two and a half-hour drive home, well, Steve and Nick did anyway, fair play to Steve for staying awake, Daz and I drifted off on many occasions.

On the 24th we were back off to Bristol, it was my results day and they needed to look at my tongue again. As Anita was a retired lady of leisure, she offered to take me, so we could spend the day together. We left early and went via The Mall at Cribbs Causeway, and enjoyed nice coffee and cakes. Then we made our way to Westbury on Trim, to check out their charity shops as we still had time, then into Bristol Centre to park up and do the hospital visit. It was a great result, as it was only a swollen gland; as they'd taken a slice, it had gone, phew, that was a relief, now I was happy I didn't mind spending half an hour in Primark! I left with a new belt, shirt, T-shirt and jumper, so it wasn't all bad. On the way home, we stopped at Redwood Farm, "Wow," what a place that is, great carvery, so much food and for such a great price! All in all, considering I woke up worried, it ended up to be a lovely day, I'd also text Sharon to inform her of my results.

Back to work the next morning and I was a spare again. Portishead depot required my services, so I jumped in a van and made my way to Portishead. It was a heavy day and with lots of hills, I met and worked with Harry Cranfield, we made it a good day; the weather was beautiful, and the sea views were awesome. Harry was very helpful and a great laugh was had, the day finally came to an end and I was back in Weston for the rest of the week.

The weekend soon arrived and what a weekend that was! It had been a few years since my dad left Weston, and moved to Seaton with Mel, well, Anita turned to me on a Saturday night and said "would you like to go and surprise your dad in Seaton tomorrow?" Again, "Wow," I was so happy as I'd not seen Dad for what seemed like forever! He lived nine doors away from me for twelve years plus, I used to see him a lot! Anita picked me up in the morning, and we made our way to Seaton! It was only just over an hour and we were there; I knocked on his door and a shocked Mel answered, we went in and had a great chat and laugh. As they'd not long been up, we left them to it and we went off for some lunch and sightseeing. It was a Sunday and the shops were shut; the seafront was dead, but we did park in the cheapest car park in Devon, one-pound-fifty for four hours! We found a nice pub in the centre and enjoyed a lovely pub roast meal, after eating we took a pleasant stroll along the quiet seafront, and eventually sat with a cappuccino in the only open, and very peaceful cafe. Dad had mentioned that he'd probably be in a pub which we'd pass as we left to go home, so after leaving the cheap car park and leaving the Seaton centre, we passed the pub to see Mel stood outside having a fag; we pulled over and went in to join them for a pint or six! After a very enjoyable day and night, it was time to leave my now very happy Dad; I fell asleep in the car for most of the journey home. What a great ending to a busy month!

The first week of October was pretty standard, I worked hard but now the Inner City rehearsals had finished weekly for the year, as we had no dates booked until 2019.

Paul Hatton, whom I used to play in The Curve with, was hosting a charity night at The Royal Hotel. On Friday the 5th, Anita and I got all dressed up, her in a lovely black dress and high heels, I wore a black three-button suit and tie, with my new shiny loafers and we went for a very exquisite night. It was all properly laid out and organised, there were lovely food choices too. The Fabulous Doughboys entertained, with another drummer buddy Tim Price beating the skins. Paul and his gang had pulled off an amazing night and made plenty of money for the Alzheimer's Society; we left happy and Anita dropped me off home.

Once home alone, and scrolling through all the old messages' that Sharon and I had shared, over the last god knows how many years; whether it was Facebook; Instagram, or normal texts. I read hundreds of messages, some good, some awesome, some bad and some horrible. I scrolled loads of pictures, some sexy and some standard; all the same I was in tears. I'd had a few pints anyway that night, but continued drinking when I got home; I was in a right state and spent the next day feeling like shit.

After a nice big mega breakfast in Treats, to soak up the cider on Saturday afternoon; I went home and waited for Daz, as he was being dropped to me at four-thirty by his carer. We had the usual Dad and Son evening and said our goodnights later. The next day was spent with me getting up early and doing the housework. I do share my house, but you wouldn't believe it! We did the usual Treats for lunch, had a quick walk around town, and bought some bargains or a bubble machine for Daz.

The Sunday evening was what we'd both been waiting for; Ryan's girlfriend Holly was singing at The Claremont Vaults from four o'clock, Anita was invited too, so she came and picked us both up. The usual faces were there, my sister, my mum, my auntie Val and Graham, both nephews Ryan and Adam; Abbie and baby Esme, Holly's sister Beth; their mum Sally and her boyfriend Adrain, a mate Justin and a big-bro to me Darren (ex-Charlie Browns). We watched as Holly sang beautifully and we all had a great time chatting. Anita, Daz and I said our goodbyes' and made our way to drop Daz home; once we'd dropped him, Anita and I went back to mine for a chat.

All I'd been thinking about for the last few days, was Sharon and our previous texts'. I'd not wanted any bedroom fun with a woman who cherished me; showed me so many new places, took me to Dartmouth to see Mum and Seaton to visit Dad. But she wasn't Sharon and Sharon was all I wanted, and Keanu of course. I made us a hot drink each; I held Anita's hand and told her anything but the truth! I couldn't tell the woman I'd known for three months, that I was still in love with the ex of six years! She even asked me if it was because of my ex and I said no. I even said, that the only reason I didn't want sex, was because I'd watched so much porn over the last three years, I no longer wanted the real thing and I ended it. She was devastated and started crying, it wasn't fair that I was with her; even though I wasn't, it felt like I was using her; I had to call it a day as that wasn't me. She left upset and I then spent the night worrying, as she went for a long walk on her own late at night, she did text me back and she eventually went home and was safe.

All I could think about was how I could win Sharon back and show her how much she really did mean to me! Then it dawned on me; before she'd deleted me from Facebook, in fact, it was when we were still just together! There was a post on Facebook for everybody to play along with, "The top ten albums you grew up with." Sharon had only got to her 5th album by the time she blocked me. I remembered I'd saved those album covers in my photos on my phone, I've got so many pics that I'd totally forgotten about those. Sure enough, they were still there, so I logged straight on to eBay, I made five purchases, and within a week I had all five albums. I then joined Photobooks and started scrolling hundreds of pictures of Sharon, Keanu and Stell. The first night I sat for an hour picking pictures of Sharon and Keanu only; I got the book made and was really happy.

The following day I was back in Treats with Daz for lunch. When he'd gone to bed, I was on my phone, making the next order from Photobooks, but this time with only pictures of Keanu, from the year I first met him at six-years-old, to wearing his first Worle School uniform after he turned eleven. The book got ordered and I was on a mission! The two books arrived a couple of days later; they were great, but as it was my first and second attempt at Photobooks; I was new to the layouts, so I went back into Photobooks, this time I ordered a book full of memories. I sat for hours and made great collages of all of us together, Sharon, Stell, Keanu and myself. By then I'd also found Phototiles and another order was made. This time I used a lovely picture of Sharon and her two boys, stood in front of the old Birnbeck Pier, it was such a majestic shot; that was the one I chose.

The Saturday night, I was out to see "Supersonic," in the Back Bar with Mick and Steve; we had a great night out; it was Halloween, there were people wearing fancy-dress everywhere we went, and we all got very very drunk. I went home and crashed out ready for the next day. It was a tough time for me, as on the 30th, it had been thirty years since the car crash that took Steve, I'd been up to his grave and I cried and chatted; I really could have done with Sharon at that time.

Whilst I was with Anita, she'd bought tickets' for us both to see a show at the Playhouse, "Suggs, King Cnut," well, as we'd split she'd sold the tickets. I didn't want to miss the show, so I made a purchase and sat as Timmy no mates; I really didn't mind as there were people there I knew, but they were sat elsewhere. What a fantastic show, another great night was had and I strolled home alone. I did text Sharon and we had a brief exchange of words but that was it, when I got home I decided the photobook of Sharon and Keanu wasn't good enough, why didn't I do it of her and both boys, why would I forget Stell? So once again, I scrolled my hundreds of pictures; I even went into Stell's Facebook and got a load of great snaps of him with them both. Suddenly I was smiling from ear to ear and thinking "she is going to love all this," another book was ordered and October was over.

Into November, on Sunday the 4th, I woke, and whilst having a shower I found a large uncomfortable lump, in my scrotum! I had Daz that day as he'd stayed over, so I just got on with the day. Once I took Daz home later, I rushed home to rip my jeans off and let my now swollen sack relax. I text my boss Dan, to inform him I wouldn't be in on Monday as I needed to see the doctor; I was at the Surgery early, where he informed me that it was more than likely to be, an Epididymal Cyst and he gave me a prescription. He also put an email through, for me to have a CT scan just in case. By the Friday I was in the hospital for the scan, although by then the tablets had done their stuff and it was nearly gone! My awesome postie mate Chezney had that day off, she offered to take me and she did. I had the all-clear and Chez dropped me back at work.

Sharon's Christmas present was coming together nicely when it dawned on me! It would be better if I got them all something! I got on to eBay and purchased two small T-shirts for Keanu, "Team Q" and "Team Sal" from Impractical Jokers; I went into Photobooks and had another book made for Stell, with a hundred pictures of him in his many bands and family members, I also gave him the first book I'd had made of Sharon and Keanu. Then I went into eBay and purchased an A4 canvas print of Sharon and Stell at Stell's graduation; I had the same print done on a phototile for Stell too. I had also put together a few cheaper presents! I bought a proper good-sized fluffy red and white stocking, I bought four chocolate and orange Carex soaps, I had to order through Superdrug, two tubs of aqueous cream as that was where she always got it from. From eBay, I bought a little box containing a brand new chrome Peugeot keyring and four Peugeot dust caps; a book about the wits of Gin from The Works, and to complete the stocking was a big bottle of pink Gin.

As I enjoy writing poems especially when emotionally charged; within an hour I'd written three poems, "Missing You" 1, 2, and 3, I had also devised a two to six-line poem for every CD, photobook, phototile, canvas, T-shirts and stocking. I wrapped everything individually and numbered them, so the poems would relate, I then made it all fit perfectly in a shoebox which was also wrapped. I then sat it in my lounge and thought about my next move, like how was I going to make sure Sharon opened it and didn't just throw it away!

At the end of the first week, I started posting the "Missing You" poems on Facebook; people didn't want to read that soppy shit! Some felt sorry for me and some people told me to get over her, nobody really knew how I was feeling, I was starting to lose my mind! Luckily for me, it was carnival night on the Friday, as a great father, I've always made sure Daz went every year as he loves the Weston Carnival! It hoofed it down with rain all night and we got soaked! We stood in it for about an hour, before Darren turned to me and said, "Dad can we go home please?" I've never been so happy to hear those words, so we walked home and dried off. After a nice hot drink each, I took him home to his mum and Rob. Once I got home, I carried on with my sad and miserable Facebook posts, Missing You 3 got posted and I got more comments that I didn't really want to hear!

The Inner City boys made a decision to have only one practice a month, and on the 12th we had our first time together in four weeks. I did my carpool Karaoke as it was a ten-minute drive, but now I was doing sad songs, like "Loving You" by Minnie Ripperton, we had a great practice and I left happy, but was soon miserable once home.

The day after, I decided to take Sharon's present to Stell's house and get him to give it to her, I did emphasize that it's important, that she opens it all and with Stell present, as his and Keanu's gifts were in there too! "No problem," he said, "Leave it with me." I left happy, thinking it was going to make Sharon weak at the knees and cry tears of happiness. How wrong was I; on the 16th a text came through from Stell, "Sorry, mate mum can't take the gift as it's not fair, I did knock and I left it outside." I jumped out of my chair and opened the front door, to find the still nicely wrapped box and stocking worth a couple of hundred quid sat on the doorstep. I shut the front door and cried like a baby; I grabbed my jacket and keys and ran out of the house with the box under my arm, I jumped in the car and sped off, I didn't know where I was going, I didn't even know what I was going to do. Mixed emotions were spinning around in my head, why does she hate me so much? Has she got someone else? Or maybe she was thinking, "If I open this, I'll want to love him again but I can't." I was driving along Milton Road aiming for Sharon's house, when I started thinking, "If I was to go there and cause a commotion, with a pub full of drunk people right opposite her flat, anything could happen." I didn't want to die that way, so I pulled over and phoned my sister, she answered but she was out at a show, she told me to go to her house as Bernard and Ryan were home, I was nearby anyway, so within five minutes, I turned up at their house in tears. They made me a hot drink, and they spent the next couple of hours talking me out of doing anything stupid. I think it was a bit late for that! I was going to destroy the presents, but they were all too nice, so I gave Cheryl the Gin as a Christmas present, and I kept all the soaps. I'd hit rock bottom: If it wasn't going to hurt my son or my entire family, I would have ended it that night!

On the 27th, I woke after hardly sleeping and I was in floods of tears! I was sweating and I was panicking; I threw on some clothes and ran to the doctors, it was only around the corner from my house. I ran into the reception crying like a baby, "I NEED HELP!" I yelled, people were staring but I really didn't care, they booked me straight in and I sat for twenty minutes. Dr Jaan called my name and I burst into his room in bits; he sat me down and soothed me with his caring voice. I told him the stories he needed to hear, he then informed me that I was indeed suffering from mental health issues and will need to see a counsellor! He prescribed me some Citalopram 20mg and sent me on my way with a sick note and a number for Positive Step. I walked back to my house and got in my car still sniffling as I walked, I then drove to work but couldn't believe how much I was crying! I parked outside the office and went straight upstairs to see management. The first person I saw was Ian (my mate from old), he was all, "Timmy Day, how's it going mate," by this time he was aware that I didn't look good, and he guided me into a nearby empty room. He listened to my story of sadness through my sniffles and tears, then he went off to get our boss. Dan then came and had a chat; he comforted me and before I left, he gave me the details for the Royal Mail Mental Health support team. Thirty minutes later I went home to cry some more. From the 27th of November, I was signed off work sick for depression and anxiety. I called Positive Steps, but unfortunately, there was a five to six-month wait, I also phoned the Royal Mail Care number, once linked with them it was arranged to have a fifty-minute chat once a week.

Not a great start to the Christmas month, depressed and now losing money too.

I was in a very bad place and didn't want to see anybody; I didn't want to talk to people, I couldn't sleep, I stopped eating, I was smoking heavily, weed too, and I became a mess. Family and friends were all there for me and helped me through every day, my auntie Val paid for me to see a private therapist, and she took me for a nice lunch at The Premier Hotel on Weston seafront. Royal Mail had given me details for their Mental Health team; they rang me every week; another friend Jack gave me a local counselling number too; I saw them for fifty minutes once a week. I did my best every day, just to make sure I made it to the next one.

Best Gal Pal Caz, was messaging me daily to make sure I was ok or if I needed anything; she is very clued up on Mental Health issues and knew exactly how messed up I was; she really looked out for me! Anita made sure to message me every day too, we may not have made it as a couple, but I definitely made a lovely friend. Mick Nurse would message often, and now and again he would pop round with Bev for a man hug and coffee. I'd often take a walk into town, or Gary would pick me up, and we'd spend some time in Treats. One afternoon there was a girl in the queue in front of me; I fed her some cheesy line about recognising her face and before I knew it, I found out her name was Ellie and we joined each other on Facebook.

Sharon's rejected boxed present sat lonely in my lounge, which I only went into, to draw the curtains at night and pull them open again in the morning. I sat and opened the presents one by one, tearing at them like it was Christmas Day for me, although, I wouldn't have been bawling like a baby if they were. I sat and thought about what to do for a bit; I put Sharon's and Keanu's presents in one box, and Stell's in another box, I printed labels and stuck them on the fronts'. As I was off work sick, I wasn't able to sort the postage myself, so I messaged a mate and it was sorted. I did speak to Sharon to find she hadn't received them, but thankfully Stell received his.

On the 13th I spent a couple of hours in Crown Court, as my mates being glassed court case was up! The defendant pleaded guilty and was ordered to pay a large compensation fee!

I'd already had a Christmas card made for Sharon, about twenty-three days after my first Citalopram, and finding out Sharon was in a relationship, I was ready to end it. I drove to Sharon's flat and posted her card, I then drove to the nearby Toll Road and parked the car. I took a walk along the edge of the steep drop, searching for the highest drop and the roughest landing; I was crying and I was angry, I just wanted to die, I walked up and down crying, thinking and screaming. I was in a mess, I'd dated Anita, but didn't feel the love I should have felt, Sharon had moved on but I couldn't!

I was also thinking about Keanu, was this affecting him? For six years it was only his mum and me, even when we were arguing we were still a family, but in the last six months we'd hardly talked and she was seeing somebody, what was going through K dudes mind? As well as all of that, there were hundreds of other thoughts going through my brain. Watching Steve take his final drive, seeing Kerry, a young friend dead, my constant debt; family members' falling out; the list goes on. You can imagine how I felt at that time, I'd even left a note on the passenger seat of my car, with Sharon's name and number on it, she would have got the call to say I was dead, how sad of me was that! Still, I wanted to jump, my adrenaline was going nuts, I took some deep breath's and was going to take the plunge. I'm so glad I didn't; all I could think was "I can't do this!" what about Mum, what about Daz, what about my whole family. I went back to my car to scream and yell and cry some more, to find my phone had been sat ringing and ringing with twenty missed calls. I eventually answered it and it was Anita, she was really worried, as I'd left a poem on my Facebook basically saying goodbye. Anita was both crying and caring, as she told me to just go home and go to bed! After a while I did calm down; I screwed up the note for Sharon, and I went home; once there, Abbie phoned me and we had a cry together, I said goodnight and opened the fridge, drank some thatchers, I turned my phone off and cried and cried until I finally fell asleep!

If I was ever lucky enough to fall asleep during December, I'd guarantee to be woken always once, sometimes more by horrific nightmares'. At first, they were nightmares' of reliving every catastrophe that had ever happened to me, then they became a lot more intense. I'd be stood at the side of the road, and watch, unable to do anything as the car crash I was in, came flying out the woods; I'd wake as soon as the impact was made. I'd be stood on the corner of another road, and I'd watch as a speeding car drove into me on my pushbike, but again I could do nothing! The worst was the murder, even though I wasn't there when it happened, but had seen Kerry's battered body and the aftermath; in the nightmare, I was stood behind the murderer but couldn't reach him to stop him; I'd wake as the hammer made contact and I'd be screaming his name. This went on for two or more weeks, I went to the doctors again on the 21st, to get a fresh dose of pills and to have a breakdown. My near-death experience on the Toll Road, may have been caused due to the Citalopram kicking in and giving me the thoughts, apparently, it takes two to three weeks for Citalopram to take effect, suicide is a side effect, that's good to know!

As I'd never suffered from a Mental Health issue before, I had no idea how bad it really is!

I spent Christmas Day with Mum and Perry which was lovely; I usually have Daz Boxing Day, but for a treat, Cheryl and Bernard took him to a Bristol City at a home game instead, he loved it! I however stayed home, as I wanted to be on my own and wrote more of this book. I had Daz on the 27th instead, so another day was spent at Mum and Perry's; Cheryl and Bernard, Ryan and Holly, Adam, Abbie, Ky and Esme, Daz and myself had an awesome day. I'd got Daz a nice big photobook of his entire life, mainly with Abbie as they've grown up together for the last twenty-seven years, luckily I'd bought it before my breakdown and he loved it. Cheryl and Bernard got Daz and I matching drum T-shirts, Mine had Drummer printed on it, and Daz's had Drummers Son. Mum and Perry got me a Lambretta Harrington.

I spent New Year's Eve writing this book until quarter to midnight, then I grabbed a can of thatchers and took a walk to the seafront, and said Happy New Year to an empty beach and the heavens.

Inner City with Dave Cairns from Secret Affair

Mark Feltham and Dennis Greaves acoustic night

CHAPTER 11

I CAN'T BELIEVE WHAT YOU SAY, OR BELIEVE WHAT YOU DO!

After a bad ending to 2018, it was time to be more positive and think ahead.

I went to see the doctor on the 9th of January, and I was back to work on the 12th; I told the doc it was what I wanted to do as I was starting to feel lonely. It was great going back; everyone was really nice to me as they all knew what I'd been through, well some did anyway. All the bosses had been fantastic; Carl was always there and always checked on me, the main boss Dan, phoned me from time to time to make sure I was ok, and other postie's had also stayed in touch whilst I was off from work.

It was tough once I was out on the road with plenty of thinking time in my job; I had to pause on more than one occasion to take a deep breath, whilst a few tears welled up in the base of my eyes, but still, I got back into the flow of work ok, and did my best to get Sharon out of my system; the Citalopram helped a lot.

What also helped, was a new venture I'd been looking forward to getting involved with. In the last chapter I spoke of Angie Wells, well, on the 20th of January; a Daz-free weekend, we spent the day together at a proper Utility Warehouse presentation day, at The Webbington Hotel.

It was a lovely day with lots of people there and I mean hundreds! On a good note, I bumped into a good friend that I'd not seen for a long time, Andy Harger; along with Richard who works at Hutton Moore Leisure centre, it was great to have a catch-up. It really did help to see them both, as Angie is a very popular lady and kept disappearing to talk to people; at that time I still wasn't very comfortable with masses of people. I did learn a lot that day, and it was great hearing the success stories that Utility Warehouse had created; seriously if you know of people in this trade then you really should check it out.

On the 25th of January, I'd been in touch with Sharon to say hi; she was now single and was off work sick with the flu and was going for a walk along the seafront; I joined her so that was nice. We walked the whole length of the seafront and back again, having a lovely chat, stopping at The Bay Cafe, at the Tropicana to enjoy a couple of hot drinks. It was at that time, that I presented her with a small gift; it was the Peugeot keyring I'd got her for Christmas, she loved it and I was happy she finally had it. After we finished our second hot drink, we made our way back to the cars where I gave her another gift, but this time it was the CDs and she loved them too. It was a really nice ending to a lovely morning; we shared a nice hug; I pecked her on the cheek and we parted; I was just really happy that we had been for the walk.

The rest of the month I just worked, had Daz on the weekend with the usual Treats lunch, and a visit to Nan and Pop Perry before dropping him home, then back to work again on Monday.

Thursday was an interesting day on my post-round; I was out on a Worle round with Scotty Hurman who was the driver, he dropped me and I went on my way with my pouch of mail. It had been snowing the night before, so roads and pavements were dodgy and it was very cold. I was coming to the end of a cul-de-sac, when a vehicle delivering home medication for the NHS, span in, he delivered to a house I'd already been to, but all this whilst talking on his mobile phone. I crossed over to carry on my way, and I was nearing the end of the loop, whilst entering a drive, I noticed the same vehicle, now enter the same drive as the one I was in; I'd just posted the mail so was now leaving and walking towards his van. He was still on the phone, and I made a comment on using the phone whilst driving, his return was, "What the fuck's it got to do with you!" I don't like being spoken to like that, so I just casually said, "You're a twat," he got angry and asked what I'd said, so I walked back down the drive, put my forehead on his and said, "I called you a twat!" His response was a very week left hook, it felt like I'd bitten my lip. His mistake was doing it when his phone number was all over his van, so I just dialled the number and heard how he was suspended until further notice. No charges were pressed, and I have seen him driving the same van since.

That night was definitely a great one; Anita had been in touch, she informed me that she still had the Jethro tickets for the playhouse, that she'd purchased for us both. So as the snow once again fell, quite hard and fast, Anita and I went for an awesome night of entertainment. Unfortunately, due to the heavy snow, the show was cut short as Jethro had to travel. Niece Abbie was working at the playhouse that night, she informed us that Jethro will be out the back loading his van ready to go, we said our goodbyes and safely scuttled around the back. He was loading the van, so we said a quick hello, took a selfie each, left him to it and went home. It was a great end to a strange day.

The week later and now in February, I was out with Mick to see some live music in the Back Bar; it was clearly a great night as I have no clue what band we saw, but at the same time we spent time with some great mates; Jamie and his brother Carl Critchlow, Jamie's missus Claire, taxi driver mate Steve Wintle; even Stell was out with other friends I'd not seen for ages, Ella and Hannah. Followed on the Sunday by a mega breakfast at Treats, after eating I made my way to visit great friends and my proofreader Caz and Niall.

By the Monday my tooth had become a bit painful; I made a call and a visit to the dentist was arranged; I was told a root canal and cap will be needed, so three further appointments were made. The Tuesday evening my Facebook messenger went ping, it was a wave sent from my latest friend add, Ellie, the girl I met in Treats; I sent a wave back and we started the messages, finishing the chat with a date sorted for her to come to mine the following day. A lovely evening was had on Wednesday as we got to know more about each other, I had the Thursday off work and went to the dentist again as I also needed two fillings. I made up for it that night as Ellie came round again, and it was also her birthday, my mouth was swollen until late so we talked and she left later. The next night and feeling much better, I took Ellie for a curry at the Viceroy for a birthday treat, we stopped for a quick drink in the Waverly on the way home; that was great, as ex-school best buddy Sean Thomas was also in there, with his good lady Katherine; after a couple of drinks, we went back to mine.

Saturday I had a lay-in, as Daz was being dropped with me at four, the day was spent with Ellie and her daughters and when Daz arrived we all went to Pizza Hut. We ordered a nice few pizzas for takeaways, then went next door to McDonald's for coffees and milkshakes while we waited for our pizza; we picked it up when it was ready and we all went back to mine to enjoy it.

The next day I took Daz to Treats and visited Mum and Perry, after dropping Daz home later I made my way to Caz and Niall's for a coffee, catch up and a new laptop. Back to work on the Monday and Inner City rehearsal's in the evening which was nice, I had a day off on Tuesday as did Ellie, so we were able to spend the day together which was lovely.

Back to work on Wednesday and I took a fall, I lost my footing on a step and was falling backwards, now in my work you DO NOT want to drop that bundle of mail! So to save the mail I fell on my left elbow and base of my back, it bloody hurt I can tell you, but still, I stood proud, gritted my teeth, and continued until I was out of sight; then I rubbed my elbow like crazy holding back the tears, whilst letting out a couple of quiet screams. Now with a very swollen elbow, I carried on my day and was better later after another night in with Ellie and Co.

Valentine's Day, I woke with a very stiff neck but still I carried on, I got up for work and popped a couple of painkillers. After what seemed like a really long day, turned out well, Ellie had made a lovely Valentine's meal for us, she cooked tea a few times that week, so on Saturday I treated her and her youngest to a Treats, in the evening I took Ellie to meet my parents and my sister. Now I was moving on and not wasting my time thinking about Sharon, although I had sent her a Valentine's card as I had it made a while back. After a lovely weekend, I was back to being a postie on the Monday and Inner City rehearsal later that night. I'd received a text from Sharon to say hi and thank me for the card; she also informed me that she was a little upset, as I'd changed my Facebook status to in a relationship, and had posted pictures of Ellie and I enjoying curry at the Viceroy, the Pizza Hut visit and the Valentine's meal, but after everything I'd just been through, I didn't care; or did I?

Well, it didn't take long, and yes, Sharon was back in my head full time! I had a counselling session on Tuesday afternoon for fifty minutes; I was able to talk about my situation and feelings, it was good to talk and let my emotions out. That night I had toad in the hole made by Ellie. The next day was a day off, so I went to see Caz and Niall, and we had a good chat about my life. I saw Ellie later, and she came to me for a sleepover, as I had the next day off, Ellie was between jobs so we had a great day, as we both blitzed Daz's bedroom, it was a long time overdue. We filled black bags with stuff that was pointless to keep and filled boxes with stuff for charity shops; once that was done, it was back to Ellie's for tea.

Now, what I did leave out, was the fact that whilst I was enjoying Ellie's company, Sharon and I had been communicating a lot; so much so that Sharon made it clear she really wanted me back and wanted us to try again. The Friday, after Sharon finished work and was home, I went to her flat for a good chat. It was awesome, for the first time in a long time we actually had a great connection; we talked and drank coffee, and I made the decision to end it with Ellie that night. We shared the best kiss and then I went home to text Ellie, no, not to dump her that's wrong, to invite her over as I had to do it properly.

We spent an hour or two talking, then Ellie soon walked out gutted; I got on the phone and Sharon came straight round, she left early hours and I was once again one very happy man. It wasn't the best timing as I had Daz the following day, and also Inner City had a gig to play in Cirencester at The Vaults. It was only for forty-five minutes, but to a great audience and another gig smashed by Inner City.

Cheryl's birthday had passed on Friday; she had a meal organised at The Duke of Oxford on Sunday. It was all a bit weird as nobody knew that I'd split with Ellie, and definitely, nobody knew I was back with Sharon. Anita was invited as now she'd become a friend with my family and was asking to meet Ellie; I said nothing just enjoyed the day with family and friends, Holly sang which was lovely and Daz got up to sing with her for a song or two. That was me in tears as the Frozen song came bellowing out, I love that boy!

We enter another week, there were no rehearsal's but a hard week for me all the same, I had an easy day in Weston on the Monday, a day off Tuesday, a laugh on Wednesday with Jake posting in Avonmouth, but then paying for it Thursday and Friday in Easton, Bristol. Sunday afternoon, I spent time with my family and Abbie's friends at the Viceroy; Abbie had organised a charity lunch; it was different, and a great day was had.

From the 4th of March I had two weeks off work, I met mum in town for a coffee on Monday, I told her all about getting back with Sharon, she knew I still loved her and she was happy with whatever I decided to do, but she still warned me to be careful as a good mum would! Tuesday was my last fifty-minute counselling session in town, and again I was able to tell him my feelings about Sharon, and how my head was feeling so much stronger, should it not go my way. After I had left the session, I met with Sharon and Keanu and we went for a coffee in town.

I just enjoyed my holiday time; I chilled until the Saturday, and that night I made arrangements to meet my nephew Ryan at Olea, ex-Imperial for a few drinks; Holly arrived later, and we eventually made our way up to Claremont Vaults, to meet Holly's dad Rob and his wife. We drank more cider and played some pool; a great night was had. The next day, I was picking Daz up and taking him for a Pizza Hut pizza for his usual birthday treat; he was happy.

Now into my second week's holiday, my tooth had become very painful, so I concentrated on that; by Wednesday I was having my root canal drilled out, now that was not pleasant. I kept moaning that our relationship was no different than before, and Sharon soon ended it.

I got on with things the best I could, I went to work when I should and went home all fed up every night. Nearing the end of March, Inner City played another blinding gig in Cheltenham for Punkfest, and we still made it back in time to get to the Brit Bar in Weston, to see ska legends and good friend's Skacasm and Daz came too, a complete night all round.

Then it was back to work and home fed up, but at the same time I'd been in touch with Ellie and told her I could do with a shoulder to cry on; she was a great listener; also, she still had her tub of hot chocolate that I'd not used; she'd pop round on occasion for a chat.

The postie's had been looking forward to the weekend, as a quiz night had been arranged at the Conservative Club. We sat in groups; I joined Steve Davies (ex-Hunt's driver), Dawn Richardson, Paul Simmons, Ian Dicker, and Darryl Palmer; we didn't win but didn't lose either. A few of us left and made our way to the Back Bar for some live tunes and more cider, then home in the early hours, and up for a busy Sunday after a Treats to soak up the night before.

Late Sunday afternoon, a meal at The Nut Tree had been organised for the Mums in the group, as it was Mothering Sunday; it was lovely when I arrived, as Daz was sat with his mum and her family. We all enjoyed a lovely meal and catch up, and we soon went our separate ways. I'd had a birthday card made by MoonPig for Sharon for a while, I posted it on the 1st of April; I spent the rest of the week working during the days, and at night, either lonely texting Sharon in hope, or sat having a shoulder to cry on with Ellie.

Monday the 8th, I was delivering mail on Weston seafront, I had a parcel for Mark Coombes, he was my best friend during the school days and after, he was in the car that took Steve's life and he's also Darren's godfather. I knocked on his window as I didn't know if his doorbell worked, it had also been a very long time since I last saw him. I was all ready to say, "Hi Mark hope you're well mate, I'm so sorry to hear about your mum," and give him a handshake. Instead, he opened the door and proceeded to wave his finger at me; whilst giving me an ear full about sleeping with someone behind his back; a name I'd never heard of, I'd never done that to any mate anyway, it's not what I do. So I just said "sign here, nice to see you and take care," he slammed the door and I carried on with my day.

I was on a really heavy round all week but with a great colleague Debbie Burrison who is the wife to Dale, a long-time friend and scrap yard owner.

Saturday was a day to remember. Literally midday, my Facebook messenger went ping, I was loaded up with mail, and with a heavy pouch on my shoulder, I struggled to get my phone out just in case it was something important; it was Scott Dickenson the drummer from Skacasm, asking if Inner City were free for a gig that night, in Weston's Tropicana supporting Bad Manners. Of course, I said yes, I'd been texting people all week to try and get that support slot, to no avail. After I'd said yes, I soon got another phone call from Astro (Bad Manners manager) to ask the same question, then as soon as I ended the call MJR group were calling me, to confirm the booking and to inform me, we needed to be there by three (the whole band). Suddenly the pressure was on, I had a lot to do. First I text Steve to tell him to round the boys up, then I rang my boss Ian, to let him know once I was done I was out of there; I then continued to run for the rest of my working day to get a heavy round done quickly.

I was at home by two, and the rush was on; first I got all the cased drums and put them in the hall from the stairs to the front door, as Steve had been in touch and he was picking me up at two fifty-five. I headed upstairs for a shower and to pick the right clothes; by the time I'd done all that, it was only about two-thirty, I still had plenty of time so I calmed down a bit. I made a coffee and a sandwich then sat watching some TV, whilst feeling happy with myself that I'd got everything done in good time, and also looking forward to working with Bad Manners and Buster again, after fifteen years. I popped upstairs as I'd left my house keys up there, and by now Steve was about to turn up. Making my way slowly downstairs and now with my drums in the way at the bottom and rather a few jackets on the bottom banister, I misplaced the bottom stair and was heading for a fall. I'd quickly put my arm out at full stretch, so I wouldn't smash my head on a partition; a noise came from my shoulder and I was suddenly in excruciating pain. I seriously thought I'd snapped my shoulder; I danced around, I was screaming and going white, when there was a knock on the door. I let Steve in, who in seconds was worried as I didn't look well, I told him what had happened and said I'd still play no matter what, he loaded the kit for me and off we went with me still in agony!

Once we got to the Tropicana and unloaded the car, I set my kit up one-handed and then just sat massaging my shoulder, the best I could to relieve the pain. I text Ellie and invited her. We all had an awesome night, and despite the excruciating pain I suffered, Inner City played a blinding set to a packed crowd and many friends. What the rather large audience couldn't see, were the tears that rolled from my eyes with the pain throughout the whole performance. Once the night was over, and we'd spent more time once again with Buster and Co, Ellie took me home and Steve brought the kit for me. The pain was too much, and I was unable to get comfy, by now my shoulder was throbbing, I sent Ellie on her way. By noon Sunday I was calling her back, we then spent an hour or so, in the Casualty Department to sort my still painful shoulder. After an X-ray and not a very long wait, it was shown to me that I had a very tiny fracture in the shoulder bone; I was handed painkillers and was sent on our way. Monday I got up as usual for work and did my morning routine, but when it came to putting my jacket on it was impossible, the pain was tear-jerking. I made the call and phoned in sick; late that afternoon I was once again sat in the dentist chair having my root canal inserted. Tuesday was my day off that week, so I stayed in bed all day to recuperate.

Wednesday, I filled myself up with painkillers and went back to work, I worry about being off sick too much. It was very painful every day, but I just carried on and suffered the burn. The following Sunday, Inner City were playing at Jacs in Aberdare, straight after "5:15" pulled off an awesome set; my shoulder was in agony but still, the show must go on! Two weeks later, Inner City were back over the Severn Bridge, to play a wedding do for Myra and Carl John, two of our biggest fans when we play Jacs; it was again very painful; but nice to see Wayne Bending, the bass player for Skacasm who was also a guest. That weekend was the spring bank holiday weekend, so again, Inner City played the Back Bar on Sunday afternoon to many scooterists', it was Weston Scooter Rally weekend too; my shoulder was still, in pain; I had to do things a little different to make it less painful, but still I got through. The following Saturday and The Stanley's were playing their last gig ever, (again), so on Friday night Jordan, Stell, Eddy, and I got together at Ed's studio for a mini rehearsal, it had been a while since we last played together. We played a couple of songs, chatted, and jammed playing songs we'd never played before. The following night, I changed my bass drum skin from Inner City to The Stanley's and set the gear up in the Brit Bar. Another awesome, very packed with drunk and happy punters gig was nailed. It killed my shoulder, but from then it was four weeks until the next gig with Inner City, so I only had work to deal with.

That's what I did, I spent the next two weeks working hard and coping with the pain. Ellie was popping round on an occasional evening for a good chin wag, and generally keeping me happy. We never became that close again even though I'd often ask just in case. Towards the end of May, Sharon had been in touch, so I took her and Keanu for a coffee to talk. It was my long weekend off work, so I blitzed the kitchen on Friday and cleaned the entire house the next day. After tea and not really knowing what to do with myself, I decided at ten-thirty to take a walk to the Back Bar and check out what band was on. I have no clue who it was, but I did get very drunk. Stell was out, a mate I worked with at Smart Systems Anthony Dunn was also out, and I'd not seen him since 2010, Richard Hocking, who Sarah lived next to many years ago was out too, I spent until two with him on a mini club crawl; only to realise that we were both too old for the night club lark. I bumped into Wayne Bell at the taxi rank and we shared a taxi home, a great night was had.

I just worked for the next couple of weeks; Ellie was still popping around on occasion, Sharon and I were also still communicating; now and again we'd meet at Costa for a late evening cappuccino. I was sat with Ellie one evening, and I gave her Sharon's number and said, "Text her and get her out of my head!" A big mistake that was, I'd basically lied to Sharon and told her I'd not heard from Ellie, yet Ellie was at my house most nights; even though Ellie and I were just friends, I lost them both. By mid-June, Inner City were playing the Moorland Mayhem Scooter Weekend in Buckfastleigh; it was a Friday night and the weather was pants, still we pulled off an awesome gig to many drunk and happy scooterists, then we made it safely home the same night ready for a weekend with Daz.

The following Saturday was a night out with Mick; we had a night of entertainment at the Winter Gardens to see the awesome "Neville Staple Band," followed by The Specials Jerry Dammers, doing a memorable set on the decks'. Just about every mate from my life was there, from Steve and Janet Parker to Steve Shelley, Aaron Fear, even Vicki Britton from my local Tesco Express, we drank, we skanked and we had a great time. As it was over by eleven PM, a few of us made our way to the Back Bar to sink some more cider and listen to music, that I didn't take note of. Long-time friend Simon Smale was out with his wife Jayne, and Phil Manville who I'd not seen for a while was out with Gary; once the awesome night was over, we jumped in a taxi and went our separate ways. Treats the next day for a mega fry up.

By now I was still worried about my shoulder; the pain was still really uncomfortable, and it was starting to get me down! It was only a tiny chip for god's sake; it should've been pain-free or at least better. I made more appointments with doctors and then a specialist, to be told after rotating my arm painfully, that an MRI scan is necessary. By the end of June, I was spending a Saturday afternoon in a tube having my MRI done; the same evening I was enjoying a meal at the Nut Tree for Ryan's birthday treat. It was whilst looking at the paperwork I realised my MoT was about to expire, so I got some new tyres fitted and booked in for a wheel bearing change the following week. I had the final dentist visit for my cap fitting, once that was done, I carried on with work. At some stage whilst doing my job one day, my phone was ringing and it was Sharon, telling me that Keanu had an accident at school and was being rushed to hospital in Bristol, she was on her way there too. She later called to inform me he'd broken his wrist in a fall. On the 8th of July, I took Sharon and Keanu to Bristol for his next X-ray appointment as I had another week off work, unfortunately, my car kept overheating. It was nearing my birthday which I shared with my awesome postie friend Chezney, so on the 11th Chez came and picked me up, and we went to the Cabot for a brunch, Happy Birthday to us.

My birthday weekend I had Daz, so Mick and I went out on Friday night to celebrate instead of the Saturday, a great move that was, as Rude Awakening were playing in the Back Bar. Their drummer is ex-Eastertown drummer Gary Widlake who I'd not seen for yonks, the bass player was Paul Newton, Eastertown's now bass player so we had a great night listening to an awesome cover's band.

I finally woke Saturday and Daz was with me by four, it was the Sunday that we'd been waiting for. It's a knockout was organised, with plenty of teams competing, including two teams for Royal Mail. I took Daz for a great day out with plenty going on; my postie friend's that weren't taking part, all stood chatting and cheering for our teams racing against the clock. Daz was in his element; the Grand Pier were also competing, and the day was organised by them; as Daz has spent probably a quarter of his life on the pier, he knew everybody; which was just as well as it was a really hot day and I had no sun cream, they did and Daz spent most of the rest of our time there with the girls' from the pier. That night instead of dropping him home I was to drop him at the pier, as they were having a party to celebrate the day, which made Daz even happier; I could go home and put my feet up and rest ready to go to work the next day.

Thursday was my day off the next week, and also the day of my MRI results; I booked in the hospital and waited to see the doctor. Jo Weymouth works in this section, and it's always nice to see someone you've known for years but don't see a lot. After a short wait and seeing the specialist, I was shown that during my fall before the Bad Manners gig in April, I had in fact, torn the tendon right at the top of the shoulder in my right arm. I was told that surgery will be required, but it could be fixed; now I had answers, and the wait was on for the next step.

I took my car for its MoT, and it failed badly, mainly on rust and brake pads. I'd swapped my future holiday week with a fellow postie, so I was once again on annual leave. I started the procedures on the car, bought the appropriate brake pads and anti-roll link, then went home to do the job. The rod was old and would not budge, so I made a call to my good mate Mick, he soon arrived with cutting tools, a heat gun, and every other tool I didn't have. He cut it off after a lot of hard work and I fitted the new one; then I found I'd been supplied the wrong brake pads; we jumped in Mick's car and took a quick trip to Spartan car parts for the correct one's; then the job was done! Wednesday I met up with mum, we went for our weekly coffee and a bite to eat at Brunel Lounge on Weston seafront, the rest of the week I spent searching the internet for a quality but cheap welder, as my car needed some serious work.

Sharon and I would often exchange texts', and we'd still meet for a Costa on an occasional evening. The last Sunday of the month and Inner City were playing The Sound of the Cotswolds once more; Steve took my drums, I went up with Mick as he takes me and my gear everywhere, and Reeves jumped in with Nick; it works well so we stick with it. Another great gig smashed for Gerry and Mandy Watkins and a happy audience too; some we've all become great friends with, especially Gary and Caroline Parker, Dudley Dunning, Del Tyler, Bob Enef Entwistle, and his good wife, Chris Carnew, Lisa Barry, and the gorgeous Caroline

Waters. We'd played the gig, said our goodbyes, and were ready to leave, when I bit down on a sandwich and my false tooth popped out; it could have been worse, it did it after and not before the gig. Day off Monday and back to work Tuesday followed by another visit to the dentist to have my denture glued back in.

The Thursday was a sad day, Sally Wadsworth in previous weeks had been diagnosed with cancer; within weeks she passed on. The 1st of August was the day of her funeral; she was a very well-known young lady, and was the mother of Ryan's girlfriend Holly and her sister Beth. I wasn't able to get to the funeral service due to work commitments, but after finishing work and going home for a shower and change, I made my way to Olea where I was greeted by a very busy pub. She really was well known, so many were there to give their condolences and it left a lot of people very sad. A majority of people at the wake were stage performers and singers, so a few of Sally's favourite songs were sung in memory, it was lovely to be part of the day. I spent most of it talking with fellow drummer Martin Dykes who is Adrian's brother, Adrian is Sally's partner and Paul Newton from Eastertown and Rude Awakening, as well as Mum, Perry, and other family members, after a quick snack from the prepared food, I gave my condolences and left them all to it. Rest in Peace Sally!

What a memorable workday Saturday became; after getting to work and sorting our delivery for two hours, Lisa and I made our way out to Mead Vale to deliver our mail. We were stopped at a set of red lights, waiting to turn right onto the main road with a postie van in front of us and two cars' in front of them all going the same way; the lights turned green, but it appeared that the front car had indeed run out of fuel and was going nowhere. I saw no movement, so I immediately jumped out and aided the poor guy to push his car over to the nearby garage, I couldn't believe it, a bloke came running from right over the other side to help, but no one right near us would help. I heard a thank you as he rolled into the petrol station, I jumped back in the van with Lisa and we carried on our way.

It was a good day for a Saturday; the weather was nice, the mail wasn't too heavy and I was working with Lisa, who I do always get on great with and we always have a good laugh. The day was going well until

I had a parcel I really wanted to get rid of; no postie wants to be writing a seven-three-nine, especially on a Saturday, I knocked on three doors desperate to not take this parcel back to the office. It was after knocking on the third door; I heard several loud bumps and then silence. I was worried at this point as I couldn't see or hear anything, then suddenly, the door handle started moving and I could hear keys jangling; it finally opened, for me to see an elderly lady, laid on the floor struggling to try and get up. I threw my stuff down and got her in a good hug, then lifted her up placing her zimmer frame to hold; I walked her to her lounge and talked to make sure she was ok. She explained, that after hearing the doorbell and heading for the stairs, she'd slipped on the third (carpeted) stair down, and then stair surfed on the base of her spine to the wooden floor at the bottom. After a minute or two, I went and knocked on her neighbour's door, the daughter came out and went to look after her; they also took the parcel. Then it was home for the usual housework and a quiet night in. Sunday was another afternoon trip to Treats, then onto the Duke of Oxford to see Holly sing for an hour or so.

I finally booked my car in for welding, and not too far from my house but not until the next week. I was home after work on Friday when I received a message from Dave Allen (The Stanley's manager), to ask if Inner City would be interested in supporting XSLF, (ex-Stiff Little Fingers) in six weeks time at the Brit Bar. Once I'd messaged the boys it was a yes from us, by seven-thirty I was meeting Sharon and master K at Costa for our usual chat and to share my happy news. Mid-month, I was at Costa again, but this time with March of Time legend and long time friend Mike Headington, we drank coffee and discussed a band idea I'd had; he liked the idea and we'll see how that works out. Two days later and I was at Costa again, this time with the Inner City guys, having a meeting about the rest of the year gigs'. Friday and I loaded my mountain bike into the back of my Vectra, and I made my way to the garage to get the welding done; I cycled to work and back, Sharon picked me up later, so we could go for a Costa. I was on holiday again, so the Monday after Sharon finished work and K dude was home from school, I treated them to a Subway, I also received a call from Phil's Autos, where my car was, to be told the jobs were done and it now has an MoT; four hundred and sixty-seven pounds that cost me, that's more than the car's worth for god's sake! I had Daz Saturday and Sunday, so I went to the Back Bar for a lonely night on Friday, just to get drunk! By this time, I'd also been told that the murderer had been released from prison; I could have done without knowing that to be honest.

The bank holiday weekend was spent with Daz; the Isle of Wight scooter rally was a thing of the past now. I was back to work on Tuesday, on Wednesday I received a call from Cheryl. Mum and Perry were in Dartmouth on their boat for the Regatta, as they were for a couple of weeks every year; Cheryl and the rest of the family had been staying there too. She was ringing to inform me that Perry, had a fall and had broken his wrist, they were at Torbay Hospital all day having it put right; I was now worried as I was miles away and not able to be with them.

On the Friday after work, I received a call from my dad Denis, for him to inform me that on Wednesday, two days before, he was rushed into a hospital after suffering a stroke. "Oh my god," I couldn't believe it, my dad and my stepdad taken down on the same day; he was in Exeter Hospital, only twenty-two miles away from Perry in Torbay Hospital; you couldn't make this stuff up I tell you!

Although I was now worried about my family members who were too far away for me to get too, my car kept overheating so I didn't want to use it for long journeys and I'd have to get trains and book time off work.

I had however, bought online back in July, a ticket for myself to see "Madness" on the downs in Bristol. On Sunday the 1st of September, I got up and had a healthy Treats mega breakfast, then a hair cut and home for the right clothing, before catching a bus to Bristol. Emma Longstaff text me, to inform me she was also at the gig; she is a best friend of my cousin Karyn, luckily I found her very quickly, along with other great friends, Simon Phillips, Sara Redding, Steve Shelley, Darren Harvey and all amongst thousands of people. It was awesome, we were right near the front and it was the first time I'd seen Madness properly; after the show, I shared a taxi home with Simon, Sara and Elaine, Simons partner; it was a long wait but worth it in the end. Back to work on Monday to chat about the great gig I'd just seen, by Wednesday I was having a couple of days off, so I met Mum for a coffee in the afternoon and rehearsed with Inner City in the evening.

By Thursday I was having my pre-op, even though I'd still not had a date for an operation by then.

I made my way to work on Saturday morning but my car seemed to be a bit chuggy, I thought I'd better pop to Tesco first and get some fuel as it was low. I rolled up to the pump and treated it to twenty pounds instead of the usual ten I put in. I do very little mileage so I use very little fuel. Anyhoo, after paying the bill, I got in the car and turned the key but to no avail, that car was going nowhere! Then I was in panic mode; I had to get to work, only to find, for the first time in my life I'd left my phone at home. Luckily for me, a man at another pump loaned me his phone; he also helped me push my car into the store car park; then I had to get a taxi home to pick up my phone, then back to work, that was another seven quid gone. I finally got to work, but now twenty-seven pounds shorter and now carless too.

I did my day's work and phoned Mick, who came and helped me tow the car as we still had no luck starting it. Of course, neither of us had tow bars, so after a quick Facebook beg, the lovely Teresa Wadman had one I could borrow; she only lives a couple of hundred yards away. After getting it home and still having no luck starting it, we decided to go out for a night on the town instead.

The following Thursday the 19th was the date Inner City couldn't wait for; we were playing the support for "XSLF," it was a very busy night and packed pub. Original "Stiff Little Fingers" frontman and songwriter, Henry Cluney, blasted out the classic tunes, after our awesome forty-five-minute set. Fergus Jack got up on stage and sang with them which was great, I don't think I'd ever seen Ferg so happy.

On the 21st we had a top night; I took Daz to see "Momentum" at the Electric Banana; Duncan Parkes plays the guitar, with excellence in that band, he's also a great postie mate. The week later, Inner City were gracing the same stage, for an awesome night with the Sounds of the Jam.

I took Daz to the Brit Bar the week later and saw Skacasm again, a great night and plenty of friends were out; followed the next day with taking Daz to the Pier so he could work for an hour, then enjoy the Go-karts before going for lunch at good old Treats.

I'd spent plenty of time over the weeks' with Mick, looking over the car to see if we could get it going to no avail. I'd borrowed a fuel pump from Glynn Smith to suck the fuel through; we changed fuses, Mick had to take the battery for recharge at one point, but still, the car sat outside my house motionless and straight after spending five hundred quid on the MoT.

During the working week and the following weekend, my shoulder had become a lot more painful; by the time I woke Monday for work, I could barely move the arm, as it had become ten times worse. I phoned in sick at work, then made appointments for the doctors, the pain killers I was using just weren't killing anything. I myself phoned the hospital operation booking line, to try and get the op done as soon as possible. I became a lot more relieved, knowing that they were trying to push it through as quickly as possible.

I'd been invited to a long-time great buddy, Errol Flynn's 50th Birthday Party at the Parish Pump in Weston, by his good wife Marcella. It was on Saturday so I jumped in a taxi and made my way out there, it was brilliant to see so many people, mainly mates from cruising the seafront days. I was filled with pain killers so only had a couple of pints of coke, my mate Gary Watts, also a long-time friend of Errol's was there; he was also my lift home by ten-thirty.

Now I was off work sick for a while and waiting for the operation date, I cancelled all gigs' for Inner City for the rest of the year; I was also gutted, as great mate Vespa Marcus, had asked the Stanley's to play his, and Lyndsey Smith's Birthday bash at the King's Head at the end of November, so I had to ask the boys to source another drummer for that one.

Gary had been round for a cuppa one afternoon to say hi and keep me company, as had Sarah-Jane my postie mate.

It had been literally two weeks since I last spoke to the hospital team when they called to inform me there'd been a cancellation, and I could have my operation on the 6th of November in a weeks time, I was well chuffed as I could have waited for another four to six weeks.

Wednesday arrived and I got a taxi to the hospital for seven-thirty. I had to sit and wait until the doors opened at eight, then spent a further few hours seeing different people, before finally getting to put my surgical gown on; then another half an hour of joking with the nurse's Wendy and co, before being put out and under the knife. It was just over an hour, and I eventually woke up to cups of tea and biscuits; I'd not eaten since eleven the night before. The surgeon also had to inject my arm to numb it for twenty-four hours, as it would still be painful when I woke after the operation. Mum and Perry were contacted, and they soon arrived to pick me up, I spent that night at Mum's in a single bed but just couldn't sleep; especially as by one o'clock my arm finally came back to life, it really hurt too. I sat and watched TV sobbing softly until seven in the morning. After a bowl of cereal and a cup of tea, Mum and Peb's dropped me home. The next night wasn't much better to be fair but home comforts like my cats made the night more bearable. Cheryl and Bernard popped round with loads of shopping for me and she washed my hair as I didn't want to get things wet; for the next week sleep was still uncomfortable, I had to sleep with a sling on and could only sleep on my left when I've always slept on my right.

In the last week things had really been getting to me, I had to visit the doctor as things had become so bad, now I was on a stronger dose of Citalopram and what with my shoulder, a broken-down car I'd just paid hundreds to MoT and Sharon in a new relationship, I was again low.

Mick came to see me and give me a lift to the doctor's, we also made arrangements to go to the King's Head on Saturday. That night, the 23rd was The Stanley's gig I couldn't play, ex-school buddy and great drummer mate Matt Stevenson depped for me; it was also Vespa Marcus and Lindsay Smith's (landlady) birthday party, Mick picked me up at eight and we made our way to the King's Head and met up with everyone. Marcus was dressed as Danny from Grease; his better-half Lisa was dressed as Sandy, Glynn and Lindsay had 70's gear on as did many others. I was only going for an hour to see everyone and say hi; I had a thatchers Haze, then a couple more and I really enjoyed the night. Senna Weekes did a great solo act followed by an awesome Stanley's set; with Matt on drums and Leo Parsons on bass, as Eddy wasn't available. After the first set, we said our goodbyes, jumped in Mick's car and went home; my shoulder was still painful, but I'd managed to avoid getting bumped into all night. Unfortunately, due to a couple of ciders, I sent some stupid texts' to Sharon; I still wanted to be with her but she still never replied.

Monday the 25th and by ten-fifteen AM, I was picked up by Mum and Perry and we went straight to the hospital to have my stitches removed. The appointment was ten forty-five and I was finally seen at twelve-fifteen. During the wait, Mum went and grabbed us a Costa each and after a chat I sent them home, I got a taxi when I was done. Thankfully, it was great friend Jo Weymouth who had the pleasure of pulling the then, nineteen days old stitches free and I didn't feel a thing. As my arm had been in the same position for nearly three weeks, and I'd been sleeping with a sling on; made it very uncomfortable at night for me to get any sleep. I carried on with painful sleep anyway; Gizmo would always make sure to cuddle up to me all night, and Sparky would be flat out on the floor next to the bed.

Apart from physio on the 28th, things stayed boring for a couple of weeks as I'd also gained a full-on head cold too. I was stressed that I couldn't work or play the drums, I'd look out the window and see a car that just cost me five-hundred quid and it won't go; I was still paying to keep it insured and taxed. I have permanent tinnitus in both ears full time, but different tones in each ear, I didn't want to see people, I wouldn't leave the house and I was popping pills for everything to stop all the pains and to stop my anxieties'.

Now into the second week of December, the 9th was another visit to the hospital, first for the surgeon to inform me I was doing well, considering it was such an awkward operation. I then went for my second Physio visit to be shown my next stretching move, it helped but it still hurt.

I was up early the following day; I was planning on popping into work for an hour to show my face, due to another horrific night sleep, I phoned my boss Geoff and told him I'd see him the next day.

Wednesday and I was at the Post Office by midday to have a chat about how my shoulder was healing, the rest of the week was at home alone; I was preferring that to be honest. The weekend was a Daz weekend, and he was all that could make me smile, of course, with no car I couldn't take him to see Mum and Perry and I'd have to send him home in a taxi if no one was available for a lift.

I just spent my days and nights doing my physio exercise's and watching box set after box set of DVDs, whether it was Mark Cherry's "Desperate Housewives," "Smallville," "CHiPs," or my favourite, "The Duke's of Hazzard." The week before Christmas and I was back at the hospital for another surgeon visit, to be told I was doing really well and once again to physio for some more progressive exercises.

I had Christmas Day on my own, don't worry I love Chrimbo alone, I can watch what I want on TV, I can stay in my pyjamas all day, I cook the biggest meal I cook all year and I drink plenty of thatchers.

Of course, Boxing Day is really my Christmas Day as I spend it with my family and most importantly, Darren Day is Boxing Day. Perry came and got me; Daz's mum had dropped him off at my mum's for me. We enjoyed a lovely meal followed by pressies. After we ate and had a sit down to digest, we soon took a walk a few hundred yards down the road to Cheryl and Bernards house, Adrian Dykes was there and a couple of other friends of theirs; Adam soon arrived as did Ryan and Holly, then Auntie Val and Graham, Tracey and Fred Hooper and their kids' popped in for an hour, there was loads of great food to enjoy and take home too, I had my thatchers, My son and my family, life was as it should be; great!

Daz and myself went home later, Graham was visiting his laundrette around the corner from my house so offered us a lift, Daz was in bed at eleven and I sat up until three AM writing this book.

Adam came and picked his cousin up for me on Sunday and took him home. That night after Daz went home, I cracked open the thatchers and scrolled Facebook. I noticed a post from Peter "Dougal" Butler, that he was hosting an event in London on the 25th of January. Now, Peter has been a friend on my Facebook for a few years; for those of you who have no idea who he is; you wouldn't believe how happy I was, when I booked two tickets to the said event. Peter was in fact Keith Moon (The Who's) bouncer and friend; he was hosting a night in honour of Keith but also, Annette Walter-Lax, Keiths girlfriend at the time of his death, and Richard Barnes who was a great long-time friend of The Who, as well as an author, were also there. Annette had written a book, "The Last Four Years," her life with Keith which I'd already purchased.

As Mick had become a best friend over the years, and we'd done a lot of nights out together; as well as him being my own personal driver for rehearsals' and gigs'. I chose to offer him the other ticket as a gift, also, as he's a Londoner he knows where is where, and he booked us a cheap hotel in Kensington too!

Inner City support Bad Manners

The Stanley's at The Brit Bar

CHAPTER 12

FROM MIDLIFE CRISIS
TO MOD LIFE CRISIS!

I saw the New Year in with the housemate Mike, posting my end of year poem on Facebook too; else I just spent my days cleaning the house, doing my physio exercises and watching rubbish on television.

I did make a few eBay purchases, like a couple of pairs of Ox Blood Dr Martens and five brand new pairs of quality Next, Ben Sherman and Firetrap jeans, as well as a couple of CDs and a present for mum.

My shoulder seemed to be improving, so I had a quick play on my electric drums to a Kaiser Chiefs' classic "Ruby," I'd not played this song since Off the Record split. I put on my new Ben Sherman shirt, my bowling shoes and filmed me playing Ruby. My shoulder didn't hurt whilst playing the drums, but it was uncomfortable towards the end of the song. I'd also been in touch with a female friend Emma, and we made a date for the following week.

I was back to the hospital a few days later for another physio appointment; I wasn't in there long to be fair, just to be shown my next move's to strengthen my shoulder. Soon after coming out, Mick came and got me and we went for a Treats, I had a nice Treats Combo rather than a big fry-up, made by the owner and great mate Ricky; Mick had a mini breakfast but the hour parking soon ran out, so we made our way back to mine for more catching up over a cuppa. The next day, Caz popped in for a coffee, catch up, and the updated memory stick; she was my proofreader, and I'd not given her a copy for a while. After Caz left, I cracked open the cider and with one properly usable arm, I did a job that had been a long time waiting. I moved my three-door wardrobe, hoovered behind it, and retrieved my gold necklace, which had fallen down inside it a couple of years before; I also found a lump of solid pot, that also must have been down there for a couple of years. As I'd not smoked anything but a Vape since the 23rd of July 2019, I put the tiny lump in a tub in the drawer. After a busy day and my shoulder now more painful than uncomfortable, I popped some painkillers, drank some cider, and sat and watched more crap on television whilst back feeling sorry for myself.

Although my shoulder was still causing me to have an uncomfortable night, I was starting to get anything up to four or five hours of sleep at night. Of course, I'd been on the cider and was taking pain killers and antidepressants which probably helped.

I didn't drink Saturday day time, Daz was being dropped with me at four and we were going to a party anyway that night; I did pop into town for a mega breakfast at Treats, as I knew I'd be having a few ciders that night. Once home from town, I thought I'd get in touch with The Stanley's guys as I'd not heard from any of them for some time. I'd sent them a video of me playing the Kaiser Chiefs song, stating that I was ready should they want me; especially for Dave Allen's, up-and-coming 70th birthday bash, we were playing at the Brit Bar in April. They still hadn't replied after a few hours, by which time I was getting annoyed; I messaged Dave Allen and he informed me that he'd spoken with Jordan, unfortunately, I was no longer required in the band. I was upset but kept a calm head.

Daz was dropped off at four and the preparations started for our night out. I got us both showered, shaved, dressed, and ready to go, we ate first then made our way to the pier for Stuart Davies's 50th birthday bash. Even though there were no rides open at night; Daz was so happy to see his pier buddies again. We soon found the party that was now in full flow, and busy with a load of friends from old; most of which I'd seen at Errol's 50th a few months before. One of the highlights of the night was seeing an ex-school friend Nigel Hudson, I'd not seen Nigel in seventeen-plus years since he left for a new life in the USA. He was back visiting family and thankfully couldn't miss Stu's party. He soon returned to Los Angeles to continue his career in the film industry.

I remember back in 2003 when I had Sky fitted, I was watching Jackass every night on MTV. Well, one night I spat my coffee out when I saw Nigel on the screen, he'd just floored a huge guy in one punch for the show; I was proud to see he was doing well. He went on to do choreography for fight scenes in films, which brings me to another coffee-spitting moment. I was sat watching Mr & Mrs Smith with Brad Pitt and Angelina Jolie, within the first ten minutes of the film, Brad is chatting to a mate whilst being thrown around a boxing ring; well, he happens to be struggling with none other than Nigel Hudson; who's now the CEO and Founder at Easy Peasy Films in LA California. So as you can imagine, it was awesome to see him and let him know I was proud of him. Daz and I mingled and chatted with a lot of other mates, and we finally sat with a great taxi driver mate Paul "Ziggy" as he was on his own. By eleven o'clock and five pints of thatchers later, we left and got a taxi home.

Once Daz was in bed, I drank more cider and scrolled my Facebook, but still upset about no longer being in The Stanley's after ten years. My vision was blurry, and I went text crazy to Sharon, I have no idea what I wrote as I'd deleted every text after I sent it.

After falling asleep on the sofa for a few hours, I got up and sorted a bowl of cereal and cups of tea for Daz and I. We showered, and Daz played on his keyboard whilst I sat and checked out the pictures on Facebook from the night before. I also looked at Stanley's gig photos and videos that brought things flooding back. It was then that I remembered I'd text Sharon during the night. I had no memory of how bad, or even how many messages I'd sent during the early hours. I did send a really sorry text anyway!

Now into a new week. I met Mum in town for a coffee and small snack which was always lovely, then on Tuesday, I was back at the hospital for an early morning physio appointment. Thirty minutes later when I was leaving the hospital, I bumped into my boss Ian Gregory and his good wife, they offered me a lift home.

I only drank a couple of ciders that afternoon, not just for pain relief I hence to add, but for a bit of dutch courage as I was going on a date with Emma that evening. I've known Emma for about thirty years, and she also worked for many years at a playgroup that Darren attended during the school holidays. Even though we'd known each other for a long time, we never really knew each other at all and thought it would be nice for us to get together and see where it goes.

We met and we had a great hour plus, catching up and chatting about life in general, before finishing our drinks and taking a walk to the taxi rank so she could go home. I offered her the comfort of my nice kingsize bed but to no avail; we shared a lovely kiss, and I waved goodbye. I took a walk home and opened a cider, It wasn't long before I received a text from Emma, to say she'd changed her mind and would love to share my bed. So after another taxi journey, she came back to mine; we kissed and cuddled which was lovely, in the morning she jumped in a taxi and went on her way. I soon got up and showered, with music playing loud I got on and cleaned the house, still one-handed as my shoulder was still uncomfortable at times.

That night I chose to have a spliff, using the pot I found behind the wardrobe. Even though I had been tempted in the past few months as weed is a good pain killer, I chose not to go back down that road. Well, after hoovering and bumping my shoulder, I got my pot grinder out and I ground the lump of pot until it was like dark sand. The lump in the first place was only the size of a twenty-pence piece round, by the time I'd put it through the grinder, the lump was now the size of a five-pence piece round. I'd only smoked a Vape in the past six months, so I asked my housemate for a bit of tobacco and some rizla papers and I rolled a spliff, using very little of the pot. After building the four-inch fag, I flicked the lighter and I took a drag. I coughed a little, then took another drag, after the third drag my head started spinning, I felt sick and was as white as a sheet. I did nothing but turn the tele off and crawl upstairs before falling into bed, luckily I had my pyjamas on, else I would've slept in whatever I had on! The room was still spinning what with the cider as well, but still, I wasn't sick and dropped off to sleep with no hesitation.

For the first time in three months, I finally had an undisturbed sleep, until eight-thirty AM that is. At first, I wasn't sure if I woke hearing things and soon snuggled back into my warm pillow, but then, there were four very loud, side of the fist bangs on my front door; even I know bailiffs don't knock that loud. I leapt out of bed and didn't even put my dressing gown on; as I was coming down the stairs, I could see through the window above the front door, a police car parked in clear view. After looking out the front room window, I noticed another police car and saw four coppers', stood waiting for me to let them in.

I let them in, and after telling them my name, I was arrested for harassment for the texts' I'd sent to Sharon. After getting dressed in police presence and feeding the cats, I was cuffed and led out to the waiting car. We had a half-hour drive to Bridgwater Police station where I spent thirteen hours locked up, I had a poxy pasta for lunch and a crappy cottage pie for tea, I drank plenty of disgusting machine coffee and read an entire copy of a magazine I don't even remember!

I was arrested at eight-thirty AM and by ten-thirty PM I was finally interviewed. As it was late and for some strange reason, the solicitor (whom I only just met) said, "I can see you're a guy that likes to talk, I advise you to answer no comment to everything." That's what I did, but it was a task that was hard to do, I could've answered most of the questions but I just wanted to get out of there; me going on like I do, meant we would've been in there until three in the morning. They also read a couple of the messages I'd sent, I was holding back tears as they were vile and I didn't even know what I was sending.

After the complete no comment questionnaire was finished, I was led back to cell thirty-one, where I sat alone for another hour with a coffee. Midnight came and the bolts made their noise, the cell door opened and it was time for my release. I was stood chatting to the WPC that interviewed me, whilst waiting for my wallet and keys, she informed me that my house had been completely searched and many items have been removed; including my laptop, computer tower, any paperwork to do with this book; they also kept my phone. They expected me to take a thirteen-mile walk home! I had no money for a taxi, and it was too late for buses or trains. After I said I was going to walk to the motorway bridge and jump off, they gave me a lift home.

The first thing I was greeted with on entry, was a broken glass panel of the inside front door. I walked into the kitchen quietly and opened a can of cold thatchers then sat in thought; I had no phone, no laptop and there was a space where my computer tower once stood. I was gutted that I'd let things get so far, I was now on bail with conditions and waiting for the Crown Prosecution Service to make their decision.

The police had left things tidy to be fair, but when removing the computer tower, they unplugged a memory stick with the full book on it; they took the tower but left the memory stick! They also took the tiny lump of pot that I found like five days before, but they left the grinder sat right next to it and still full of the pot too! Once I checked the bedroom, I noticed my tonfa had gone from under my bedside cabinet, yet they left two swords; a tonfa is a two-foot piece of wood with a handle, similar to an American police truncheon; it's actually part of my martial art arsenal from the old days. It would fit quite snug under the cabinet, and it was my protection, should I get broken into. They'd also taken every photo I had of Sharon and Co, every piece of paper which had the book on it and a lump of pot worth about two pounds fifty. As they left me the pot in the grinder, I had another good sleep in the end!

When I finally woke, I made my way into town to the EE shop as I now needed a new phone. Luckily, being on a contract I was due an upgrade, so after a phone call, a new phone was ordered. I paid extra to have it delivered the next day as it was a weekend, but it didn't turn up; so after using the housemate Mike's phone, I was told I had to wait until Monday. Thankfully I had a drawer of old phones that the cops once again missed, I was able to use an old one of those to log into Facebook but not for calls.

I had a ten-thirty physio appointment on Monday and was told by DPD that my phone would be delivered between eight-thirty and ten-thirty. Panic was on when it finally turned up at ten-fifteen, I signed his PDA and then ran to a nearby phone box so I could phone a taxi. I made it on time to see the surgeon, what a great result to be told he didn't need to see me for another year, as my shoulder was doing really well; then it was home to sort out my new phone. Tuesday I had a dentist appointment, to be told I needed to have two old fillings refilled and by Wednesday I was heading back to work after three months off sick. It was like I'd never been away, but it was great to be back to some sort of normality. That night, Mick came to me as Inner City rehearsals were back on too. My life was as good as back to normal. The rest of the week was tough but great as it was the Saturday Mick and I had been looking forward to. He picked me up at three o'clock and we were on our way to London; the motorway's were clear, so we arrived just after five and booked straight into Lily's Hotel, overlooking a big empty space that was where Earls Court once stood.

We went up to our room and had a drink that Mick had brought with him, and relaxed for half an hour before getting our smart togs on and making our way to the venue. It was only a ten-minute walk, so we made our way and bought a round in a very busy pub. We were slightly early, so we chatted for a bit; mainly about how we in the Southwest moan about paying over four-quid for a pint of thatchers, yet a few miles up the road, it's seven-pound a pint.

It was only a ten-minute wait, so we made our way down the stairs, as the event was starting to a very crammed, hot, and sweaty cellar bar; the youngsters had got there early and had the only table with seats; being stood up was very uncomfortable for us oldie's after a while. It really didn't matter, the stories from Peter, Annette, and Richard, about their antics and lives with Keith Moon and The Who were great. Sure, I may have read about them in some of the magazines' or books' I've collected over the years, but to hear the stories from the horses mouth's was awesome. We met them all afterward when the night came to a close. We got some selfies and autographs and we also became friends with a couple of other mods, Daniel Sheilds and Jeffrey Munday who is a known London DJ. We said our goodbyes and made our way to the small pizza parlour next door to the venue, I ordered a massive pizza and walked back to the hotel with Mick, happily discussing the stories we'd heard.

After leaving a slice of the greasy pizza and getting our pyjamas on, we went to our separate beds' and attempted to sleep, on what can only be described as, something more uncomfortable than thirteen-hours in cell thirty-one! One rock hard pillow and what felt like a mattress of lead! So after not much sleep, we got dressed and made our way down for the fried breakfast, well, two fried eggs', baked beans, and eight-triangles of toast between us; the pot of tea was worth it.

After a quick snack, we grabbed our things and checked out. I asked

Mick if he minded popping to Carnaby Street as I'd not been there for years and he obliged. Ok, so nothing was open as it was a Sunday, but I took some pictures and jumped back in the car. We took some wrong turns, ending up down some dodgy lane behind Soho, where we had the pleasure of witnessing a topless bird being photographed. Then we left and headed home, but not before Mick treated me to a drive-through Windsor, up to the Castle gates where I was able to get a quick selfie with the guide, I jumped back in with Mick, and two-hours later we were home.

Into another new week, a week working with a long-time mate, Lee O'Shaughnessy, delivering in Mead Vale. Lee's usual working partner was John, and he was off on long-time sick leave, so I covered this route for a few months. It was the normal week with the Tuesday off to meet my mum for a brunch. I'd see plenty of friends on this particular round on most days; I used Darren and Lisa Gibbs's toilet often, or sometimes I'd knock on Paul Hatton's door for a chat. Remember Sarah? (after Lisa before Louise 05) Well, it was lovely to bump into her as I delivered her mail too. She still looked so young and pretty, even fifteen years later; she hadn't changed a bit. She introduced me to her fifteen-year-old son, and he's a good-looking lad, I still wonder!

On Saturday we worked that little bit harder, as I had to be home for three-thirty, to make sure I was home when Daz got dropped off by his carer. We'd finished our deliveries and Lee offered to run me home as my car was still off the road. As we were leaving Mead Vale, I noticed a group of older people desperately struggling to help an old man back up, after he'd fallen in his garden. I shouted to Lee, and he spun the van around and drove back to the house. We leapt out the van and grabbed hold of the old fella, whilst the others backed off, I only had one good arm so I grabbed the back of his trousers, Lee aided his balance and we hoisted him on to his feet, then leant him against the wall to gain his balance; they all thanked us, and we went on our way. Daz turned up about ten minutes after I got home, it was a great end to a busy week.

After a quiet night on a Saturday night and a day of cleaning and a Treats mega on Sunday, it was back to work on Monday and Tuesday, with the mid-week two days off. I met mum in town by midday on Wednesday, and we had brunch in the coffee shop we use a lot. My days off were soon over, and the rest of the working week was busy, I had the normal rush home from work on Saturday, Daz was staying with me for the weekend, another standard Sunday cleaning and Treats was had.

It's funny you know; I'd worked somewhere for two years, I was walking or catching a taxi to work every day since September, yet work colleague and good friend Paul Simmons lived about two hundred yards from my house. That was lucky as on Monday we were sharing a route and our working week shift patterns were the same.

Tuesday, I was with Rob, delivering a route I'd not done for a while. It was nice as I got to see the ex-Anita and little excited Freddie, it was lovely to have a chat. The Wednesday I was supposed to be visiting Bridgwater Police Station for more questioning and possible results, the week before I'd received an email, to inform me that the date had now moved to April the 14th due to Covid 19. I met mum instead and worked the rest of the week covering different rounds with different fellow postie's; I was with Louise one day, Jordan the next, then Andy House to finish the week. Just like the next week working with Mike Gardener on Monday and Tuesday, Yvonne Wednesday and Thursday, and a nice long weekend off work. They only come round every four weeks, so I try and make the most of them. Inner City rehearsal's were on Friday night, I cleaned Saturday until Daz arrived at four, then we had a pizza delivered from Delights Kebab House. Sunday I spent an hour digging the sealant from the edge of the bath, before cleaning and resealing it all, rewarded with a Treats, and Daz went home in a taxi later that evening.

March had suddenly come around, and it was soon to be Darren's 30th birthday. It was my mid-week off; I worked for two days, then I met Mum on Wednesday, Caz came round for a coffee and chin wag the next day. I was back at work to finish the week off, then Saturday night it was Daz's pre-birthday treat to Pizza Hut, it was lovely as the place was empty. Daz and I enjoyed plenty of non-stop salad and a huge meat feast pizza each, of course, I ate loads with the garlic bread as well, but it didn't stop us going for a mega breakfast on the Sunday in Treats.

Daz went home in a taxi Sunday evening; I sat and caught the book up to date with no work for a week, as I was on annual leave.

A nice lay in on the Monday followed by a ceiling renovation in the bathroom, as a hole had appeared next to the switch for the extractor fan. I got the step ladder and filler I needed and got to it, I also sanded down some bacterial spots on the ceiling ready for painting. I met Mum in town on the Tuesday which was the usual, coffee and catch up on the weekly family gossip. It was also one of those days I saw just about everybody I'd not seen for a while, first Dave Harvey who drove the bin trucks when I did, he'd recently had a heart attack but was looking well. I also bumped into the lovely Michelle Lee; I used to deliver her post on occasion and became friends, I'd not seen her for a while. Mum and I also popped over to the Playhouse Theatre, to check tickets on an up and coming 80's show; we found they had seats available, so Mum bought two tickets for Darren's birthday that I was taking him to.

Soon after, Mum caught her bus home and I took a walk, the weather was lovely and as I was off work for a week I thought I'd better get some exercise.

Tuesday night was the best, Mick and Bev picked me up at five PM and we made our way to my top man Darren's house; Traci had prepared a party for him. The last I'd heard, no one from my family could make it, so I was happy to see them all there on arrival, Mum and Perry, Cheryl and Bernard, Abbie and little Esme, Ryan and Adam, Traci's mum and dad, Sandra and Dennis were all there. Rob was away, but his sister Jo, her son Lewis and their mum Pam were there, as was Chelsea, Daz's half sister.

Daz opened his cards' and presents', to find lots of tickets for shows; including Shrek the stage show, that Cheryl was taking him too the following night; an 80's show that I was taking him to at the end of March; the play Nine to Five with other family members in April, and Showaddywaddy at the end of July with loads of us; that was my 50th birthday treat from my sister too. We all ate plenty of food, I as good as cleared the table; as well as a few cans of thatchers. Music played, and people danced, we all had a top night; Traci did Darren proud.

Wednesday and Thursday were chill days with a bit of housework, my week off was coming to a close and with the Corona Virus on the scene I was safer at home. Friday was lovely after a nice lay-in, Gary Watts came and picked me up and we went for an all you can eat, afternoon Chinese at Dragon Kiss in Westons Regent Street. After eating far too much, as well as a couple of cold pints of thatchers, we soon went back to my house for more chin wagging over coffee.

No sooner had Gary left and Mick turned up to get me for Inner City rehearsals. Off we went to 13 Sound Studio's in Kewstoke, for another great night belting out plenty of Jam classics'. It was our last get together before our gig the next weekend in Swindon. After a great hot and sweaty night, I went home and put my feet up with a cold can of thatchers, and watched the Shane Meadows classic, "This is England" which had just started on TV.

I had a quiet day and a night in on Saturday, even though I found the Corona Virus to be a bit over the top I stayed out of the way of it all. I braved the open air on Sunday and made my way for a Treats breakfast in the afternoon with a quick visit around town; I bumped into and had a good chat with good mate Simon Phillips; then made my way home to get my stuff ready to go back to work the next day.

Just like a lot of people I had no idea how serious the Covid virus was about to become. After returning to work on the Monday, I realised then that things were already changing! The whole office had become a one-way system, with printed arrows everywhere, the shift patterns were also about to change, as too many postal workers couldn't be close together. I opted to work the later shift starting at eleven instead of eight and finishing by six instead of three, I didn't mind those hours as it meant a lay-in and I like my bed! I still went out with Mike Gardener that day as the rota's hadn't been changed at that point.

It was then the hard thinking started again! Walking the streets all day gives you plenty of time to think. All I could think about was how fed up I was, that the Sharon situation had turned so bad! I also couldn't help thinking, "Right now Sharon must be having a nightmare, she'll be alone and locked in." Like a hopeless fool I found myself texting her. She replied straight away to say I'd really upset her and also to thank me for caring, we exchanged a few texts and I carried on with my job until it was all done. I drove Mike and myself back to the yard to find I'd missed my chance of a lift with Paul, luckily Dawn was still there and was about to leave, so she dropped me home.

In the last few weeks, I'd been searching Google and sent emails to various book publishing companies. Well, this one particular evening after sitting down with a coffee, my phone rang; I don't always answer numbers I don't recognize but chose to answer this one. It was a publication company, who I then spent over thirty-minutes talking with. It was all so positive, and within minutes I'd received emails from them, with package details and other information. The ball was now in motion; I was very happy but somehow I needed to come up with funds to start the publication process.

No sooner had I started reading their email, when my phone again rang but this time it was Sharon, of course, I answered it and we spoke for an hour, she also informed me that she'd split with her boyfriend a few months before.

The next day I was back at work and still going out as a pair of postie's, but now with Yvonne for two days. That was great as we had a good laugh, her other half postie Paul gave me a lift home on occasion too.

Wednesday evening after another hard day at work, I looked at my ringing phone to see Sharon was calling again and we had another fifty minute chat. During this week, I was also informed by the Inner City boys', that the Swindon gig on Saturday and all future gigs will be cancelled due to Covid 19. We'd had one practice since my shoulder operation and now everything was having to change.

Now into the last week of March and life was becoming weird, I couldn't see my mum because she has COPD and was high risk, I couldn't see my son either. I still had to work, even though a massive population of the country was about to be paid eighty percent of their usual earnings, whilst sitting at home doing nothing all day, just like my house mate, there were no gigs for a while either.

Work was tough, but it did seem better now as I was going out alone, I could do the delivery my way. I tried my best to make a positive out of a horrible situation, by the Saturday, I went out as a postie, but this time dressed full on as Spiderman. My sister had dropped me a bag with a selection of wigs and fancy dress. It felt great, people were happy to see me dressed up, especially the kids, after a hot day I got home and peeled the suit off. Around this time I met and became friends with Jayne and Martin; they have a Scooby Doo Mystery Machine van and they let me borrow a Batman and a Robin costume for further postal rounds. I wasn't having Daz at weekends, but we still spoke on the phone on Sunday's, when I wasn't at work I self isolated accept a walk to Tesco express every couple of days.

Monday was nice, one of my delivery spots had left a Freddo chocolate bar for the postie. Later the same day and coming close to the end of the round, I took a fall after slipping on wet leaves, my left arm went out to stop the fall, unfortunately, the only thing to my left was a thistle bush. I had cuts and scratches all down my arm and also now a pain in my lower back; I got up and carried on.

Tuesday I got up and relaxed as it was my day off, the sun was shining so I decided to not waste the day. I spent a few hours moving piles of old rubbish in my back yard. It was a great result at the end, as I pulled my scooter out, from where it had been stored for the last ten years! It looked awful, dirty and sad, anything that was chrome in the past was now rusty, there were a couple of rust holes, paint was faded and was flaking. I took a few pictures, then sat and made a list of things I needed to buy, my car was still broken down outside and I needed some transport; from that moment I knew my scooter was the way forward!

The rest of the week was the usual at work, although now I'd been put on a bigger route than I'd been on for the previous couple of weeks. I didn't mind, it was on the flat with no hills, it was a hot week as the sun had been shining, as it still was on the Saturday. After finishing work and returning home, my neighbour's Aimee and Rose had been outside drinking in their front garden, after I'd grabbed a bite to eat, I took some thatchers out the fridge and joined them; it was a lovely end to a hot and heavy week.

Housework was the usual Sunday routine and even though my shoulder was still uncomfortable, I still found myself playing my electric drums and filming it too. Then in the evening I could sit and edit the video's and upload them on Facebook for everyone to see. It wasn't the same when the Inner City boys weren't there, but at least I could still play and entertain. Monday was another day off, so I got to work on the scooter and spent plenty of time rubbing down parts ready to spray. I primered most of the bits that needed doing and filled some holes in the frame, a productive day was had.

Tuesday, however, was a completely different story, it was the day I was off to Bridgwater Police Station, to see where the Sharon case was going. Mick offered to drive me there and we got there for eleven, I waited patiently in my mask and gloves before two police officers came and got me. I was led into a room where I was told that I was being formally charged for Harassment, with the same bail conditions. after a mini tantrum I just stormed out; I climbed into Mick's car and spent the journey home speaking about how gutted I was.

Mick dropped me off and I sank a couple of ciders' and thought about what happens next!

It was nice to receive a card the following morning from Royal Mail head office, there was also a letter to inform me, a customer had sent an email, to say how happy they were that I was doing a top job, also keeping the streets entertained whilst dressed as Spiderman. After the horrific day I'd had before, it was a lovely thing to receive. The following day was a hot one; people were sat outside their houses enjoying the lockdown in the heat. I already knew a lot of people on this particular round, but I was now starting to meet new people. I'd just delivered to one house that were long-time friends Gary and Barbara, they were outside with their daughter Sam. Barb had got me a nice cold glass of blackcurrant and after downing the drink, I walked on to their neighbours house, I tripped on a small step, "Boom," I went straight down, putting a graze on my knee and causing me to walk on with a limp. It hurt, but there were people about, so I looked brave and walked on, screaming and rubbing it like crazy when there was no one in sight. I finished the day and went home, eight o'clock saw me out the front of the house, with the whole street clapping for the key workers and the NHS.

For a couple of weeks, the Saturday mail deliveries changed. There had been such a massive surge on parcels, as the public were sat home all day ordering from the internet, we were only delivering packets on Saturdays to enable a catch up. That Saturday I chose to do my packet round dressed once again as Spiderman, it got me a lot of laughs and if truth be told it kept me upbeat too. The Sunday was spent getting lot's more done on the scooter. A few years ago, housemate Mike was given about ten aerosol cans of Vauxhall midnight blue; he was never going to use them, so I thought that would be the colour of my scoot! I got to it and started spraying bits, before I knew it the Vespa was starting to look like a Vespa again. Everything I did was a step closer to me being on the road. Monday was another day off, so I rubbed more panels down and primered them ready for spraying blue; some of the cans didn't work as they were old, so I had to throw them out! The spray started to run out, and I still had so much to do. I got on eBay and searched and searched; I had the colour code on the blue paint I'd been using, but unfortunately, the code was for midnight black not blue! What I was using was old stock with the wrong colour code. Now I had a two-tone blue scooter.

I didn't get stressed as there was nothing I could do straight away, so I decided to have a shower and do something else instead. As my hair hadn't been cut for a long time, I now had a mass of grey hair, so after my shower I put my hair all funny and made a video. I put on a bright shirt and with my silly hair cut, I did a mime to the song "I'm a nut," by Roger Miller. You can find it on YouTube.

Back to work on the Tuesday and Wednesday, but by Thursday decided to go to work as Batman this time. There were two reasons behind this, someone I met en route, Anna, had on a previous day put a hop scotch along the pavement for people to hop on, as it had washed off due to a rainy day, I said I'd do it Thursday if she did a new one. It was better to do it as Batman rather than just a postie for more entertainment. Also, someone had informed me that it was a young lads birthday in her street, and he was a massive super hero fan. That was it, first I did the hop scotch, I clapped, I span, I touched the pavement and even shook my tooshie; to hear the kids screaming with laughter made me feel like I was making a difference out there. Even better was when I entered the next road. I was heading to a front door to wish a young lad a happy birthday; all I could hear from the house was a very excited screech, "Batman's outside, Batman's outside" and when I knocked it got louder, "Batman's at the door, Batman's at the door." I wished him a happy birthday and went on my way, listening, as the lad shared his happiness with his family. That night was the eight o'clock clapping as usual.

Friday was a boiling hot day, not a great day to be walking the streets. It was more than helpful when long-time friend Dianne and her son Jamie brought me an ice lolly, just like the Saturday when ex-school mate Dominic brought me out a can of cold coke. I usually had a chat with long-time pals Carl and Tracey Manaton, as I delivered their mail daily and my last road was Andrea's house, I often see her and Weston music legend Mike Headington. I also became acquainted with Karen, a young lady I'd seen many times over the years, but never actually knew her.

I was now on annual leave from work again, as mum's 80th was in the week, I had plans to spend a lot of time with her. By the end of Sunday, the rear end of the scooter was sprayed, it looked really good. Monday I sprayed a set of wheel rims, then dug through a pile of tyres and came across three brand-new ones. I relaxed in the evening and got on to Moonpig, I ordered Mum a massive card with pictures of her through the years printed on the front. Ryan and Holly were making a video for Mum, so I put a nice top on and made Mum a birthday video for Ryan and Hol's to add to what they had.

As I never had the spray sorted for the scooter, I kept her in the kitchen until I decided what the next move was and did other things instead. Through the week I did some housework and I made up a bass drum panel, with "Support the NHS" on it. The electric bass trigger didn't seem to be full on, so I'd recently pulled my acoustic bass drum from its case and was using that drum with the electric kit. I have "M Peoples" greatest hits on CD, so I put "Search for the Hero" on and filmed myself playing the drums along to it five times, once dressed as a postie, then Spiderman, then Batman, followed by Robin and finishing in an NHS tunic, my neighbour Aimee had leant me. You can see it on YouTube.

Thursday was Mum's birthday, but I couldn't see her, I was upset about that. My mum is my rock; I had the week off to spend loads of time with her but couldn't. Luckily for me, a long-time postie friend Nick Cooper knew of my pain; he was also on annual leave, and he lives around the corner from my house so he offered to run me out to Milton. I was made up, I was able to see my mum, even though we couldn't cuddle; I still got to see her and wish her a happy birthday to her face.

I spent the week sorting the electric's out on the scooter, I also sourced a midnight blue on eBay, I only ordered one can, as I needed to see the match with the midnight blue, I'd sprayed the entire rear end in. For many years, I knew I had a big job with the tool box as it was so rotten, where it had been rained on for the last ten years. Well, on the weekend I decided I couldn't afford to buy a new one, so the filler came out, to be honest I was very happy with my repair work!

The paint turned up and I spent every evening after work rubbing down and spraying the front end, the colour wasn't a match but it was a lovely blue. I got on eBay to order more of that blue, to find out they'd sold out and it was a blue that wasn't the same as anywhere else, I know this as I ordered two other midnight blues to find they were different again! The Vespa was again at another dead end!

Another week off and mainly housework and doing what I could to the scooter, I could now see Daz again so I had the pleasure of him staying with me from the Wednesday until the Friday; there wasn't a lot we could really do, but it didn't matter as I was able to be with him. Some other things were changing for the better, the local Chinese also reopened, so Saturday saw me ordering a lovely special curry. Sunday was a hot day and my neighbour Mary had bought a new pool, I dragged my compressor round to her back garden, blew it up, I filled it with water and enjoyed a nice cold can of cider, that Mary had for me.

I was back to work on the Monday for the usual daily routine, and once home I was on eBay ordering any parts I needed, brake shoes one minute, ignition switch the next, then more paint became available, I ordered more, only to find, I could only order one tin. I'd been posting things on Facebook to say how the scooter rebuild was going, and a great long time mate Nick Taylor, who was also the same guy that did all my chrome over the years, got in touch to inform me, that he had a load of bits I could have. These bits included spot lights', mod mirrors', some air horn's and a back rest; by Friday he turned up in his van with a box full of dirty bits. Over the weekend I cleaned everything up and made good any bolts that were rusty, a set of three of the lights were pooped, so I stripped them down and resprayed them grey, I polished the chrome rims back to a shine, then made three discs to go inside. I got some colourful pens and drew a target on each and the three words, "Mod Life Crisis," as this was the name of the scoot.

We were now approaching the end of May and work was getting heavier, I couldn't see my mum, I still had the Sharon situation pending and I had a housemate on furlough. I ordered an amplifier for my scoot as I had speakers and wanted to rig my phone to play the tunes. I then spent my nights' downloading my CDs ready for playlists. I spent an hour with my neighbour Mary having a catch up and topping up the tan in her garden on the Sunday.

Tuesday was my day off, but as the post office was struggling, I chose to work my days off, I needed some extra cash what with the scooter and solicitor fees to pay. Thursday night was brill for me; I decided to build the front rack for my scooter; I spent a couple of hours, adding nine spot lights', eight mirrors' and the set of air horn's, Mod Life Crisis was coming together nicely. I ordered another set of air horn's as the front rack now looked odd; Daz stayed for the weekend and as well as the usual housework, I made Daz and I a six egg omelette and beans each.

Mike went back to work on the Monday and I just continued in the normal way, working every day and doing the scooter; well, what I could do in the evenings! Apart from eBay and music downloads I'd not turned the laptop on, so the book didn't even get a look in. During the week the paint arrived so I was able to spray the necessary parts, now she started to match. My new air horns arrived, but they were red, so I had to spray those with chrome spray before I could fit them; through the next week I wired all the electrics for my extras', I could do that in the comfort of my kitchen.

Daz was with me for the weekend and now as I wasn't starting work until eleven, he stayed until Monday morning, then it was work, work and more work, as well as connecting the cables on my scoot, and any other jobs I could do once I was home.

Saturday was another packet only day and very heavy!

Sunday, I decided that my music corner needed a good proper clean and believe me that is a long job to do. I started it, but by lunch time I had to drop tools, I was being picked up to go to Ryan's surprise birthday party. Adrian came and got me; we arrived to a few guests, mainly family and a couple of friends. Daz was dropped off to, which was nice, although only a few days before, his gran, Sandra (Traci's mum) had lost her fight to cancer and passed away, as you can imagine he was very upset. A great surprise party was organised, and I sank a couple of ciders as well as eating loads of food. When Holly and Beth's dad Rob was leaving, I jumped in his car as he lives near me, I then went home to finish drum corner, but now a little tipsy after cider and Pimm's. The job was done, and I put my feet up and relaxed before another busy day at work.

It was my court date on the Tuesday, Mick came and picked me up and we made our way to Weston Magistrates Court. We weren't there long to be honest, after a quick chat with the solicitor; he said, "wait here, I'm going to get this adjourned," sure enough, he was gone for twenty minutes, then returned to tell me to wait for another hearing date. I still had a fee to pay, but I was happy knowing things were about to make a change for the better. I jumped in Mick's car and went home smiling, I spent the rest of the day sorting the electrics on the scooter.

The working week was as expected, heavy and hot and by the weekend I was graced with Daz's presence. He went home Monday morning, and I carried on my week at work. More sad news, we'd heard that long-time postie and great bloke, Bob Layden, had also lost his fight with cancer and he passed on.

I ordered a new seat for the scoot and worked hard all week, by Saturday I was to finish for another week of annual leave, as my 50th birthday was only days away. My seat arrived on the Friday and thanks to Sally my neighbour for taking it in for me. Saturday and the seat was fitted, now the scoot was looking good and I had no work for a week. Monday and the Vespa was running, I sorted out the lights but there was a problem with the indicators' and horn. I pushed her in the kitchen once more and left it for another day. Midnight turned, and I opened the birthday cards I already had, I'd had cards from Carl and Tracey Manaton on my post round and long time friend's, also a card from Anna also a customer on my post round. Tuesday and I woke up a year older, my phone was pinging all day, Mum and Perry popped round with cards and cash, my sister popped round with a few more cards, a new wallet and more cash. Gary Watts popped round with a card and ten cans of thatchers, and later that evening both neighbours, Aimee and Mary popped in with cards, a cake and eight more cans of thatchers. I'd also had a card pushed through the door from other side neighbour Sally with some cash, a good day was had. It wasn't how it was supposed to be but still I had a great day. Wednesday I had the Vespa horn sorted and by Thursday three out of four indicators were working. That day, my cousin Jonnie had been in touch, and he soon turned up with four cans of thatchers for my birthday. Friday I was up early, I had a hair appointment booked at Anson's Barber shop, I'd not seen Gary for some time, so it was nice to have a catch up. Later that day was Bobs funeral, as a great gesture, most of the Weston posties' all met at the crematorium and lined the streets with postal vans, followed by a sea of red postie T-shirts. It was a very sad occasion, but lovely to see so many people showing respect for a great man. Rest in Peace Bob!

Daz was with me by twelve on the Saturday; I spent the day doing housework and the Sunday doing the yearly tree chop down, and clearing as much rubbish I could in the back yard. I had a lovely visit from Ryan and Holly, as they'd popped round a birthday card and ten more cans of thatchers, I was happy and Daz was too as he got to see them both.

Traci turned up at nine-thirty Monday morning to pick up Daz, but unfortunately, this was the day of Sandras funeral, so it wasn't a joyful goodbye. I went back to work and carried on my day. A group of people I'd meet on a daily basis, that became known as the "Arnor Close Clan," gave me a nice surprise. I was handed a card signed by the whole street and ten more cans of thatchers, how nice was that! I spent the day thinking how my court case the next day was going to go; well, I'll tell you how it went, I wasn't due in court until two PM and by ten-thirty AM I'd received a call from the solicitor, to inform me that the Magistrates were taking the case no further! I was so happy that it was finally over. I continued my day a very happy man! I dismantled the brake light switch on my scoot, cleaned it and fitted it back on; whilst I swigged thatchers happily in the sun!

What I had noticed, was a lump that had appeared on the right side of Sparkys face. I was concerned, although she'd been doing everything as normal like eating. By Friday she wasn't interested in food and now I was really worried, she could eat a horse on a normal day! I spoke to Mum, and they organised to take her to the Vet for me, so I could still work.

Paul, who used to give me a lift to work, had bought a new car. He offered me his convertible Vauxhall Astra 1.8 05 plate for a great price, I could pay what I want when I want. How great was that. I worked the Saturday after Mum and Perry came and picked Sparky up to take her to the vets. Mum rang later to inform me Sparky had an abscess, and it had been removed, they dropped her back to Mike where she spent the day asleep. Bless her fluffy little feet, she knew things weren't right, when I put the cat box down she just walked into it and laid down, in fact she loved that box so much, for the next week she wouldn't sleep anywhere else but in the box. When I got home from work, I spent time on the computer, sorting to have the registration number from my broken car put on retention, this I did and made a call to another mate, Mark Penfold, to arrange collection of the wreck that had been sat outside my house for nearly a year.

As the end of July was approaching and time was moving too fast, the world had gone Covid crazy, beaches were packed with people not caring about social distance, wear a mask, don't wear a mask; supermarket security telling us to follow the arrows, that's why I worked and went home and I stayed there until I had to leave.

Work on the Monday was the best; Paul came to me and handed me the documents for his car, and I picked it up after work as he lived on my way home. I was now a happy bunny; I'd had no transport for ten plus months, then suddenly I had a new car and I'd rebuilt a scooter that was nearly ready to ride!

It was time to start being happy with my life. I finished work on the Saturday and now in August with a new car, I was finally able to pick Daz up instead of having him dropped with me. After we loaded his bag in the car and a five minute chat with Traci, we made our way to McDonalds for a drive through tea; that was our first visit to Maccy D's in a long time, a lovely change it made too!

The car did need a couple of things doing to it; it had a blowing exhaust and the electric roof didn't work, along with the passenger window. Sunday I dragged the hoover out to the car and gave it a good polish too. I made Daz and I the Sunday omelette each, and I ordered a new bag for work as mine had fallen apart. That's the trouble with having to take bottles of frozen drink, a towel, food, a brolly hat and something to wee in, to work every day!

Mark turned up on the Tuesday and collected my old car, that was nice to see it was gone on my return from work and an extra parking space too. The rest of the week was a hot and heavy one, but it really didn't matter as my long weekend off work was ahead! I worked the

Friday on overtime as I needed a new exhaust centre pipe as soon as possible. I did the usual housework on Saturday and chilled for the whole weekend, Mum and Perry went to the boat in Dartmouth to do some cleaning, as they'd not been down that way for a month or so. I was back to work on the Tuesday for a full week and happy knowing I was again on annual leave the following week! A great friend Scott had let me know that he could sort me an exhaust for my car, so I ordered it ready to fit at the weekend. I picked Daz up after work on the Saturday and picked up two lots of fish and chips for our tea from the local Chinese.

Perry had given me his old car ramps a few years before, I finally got to use them on the Sunday as I changed the exhaust. Within thirty minutes the old exhaust was off, putting it back on was a different story. Yes, the car was reversed up the ramps, but the front end was still low, the pain in my shoulder was still unbearable at times but the job needed doing, so I suffered the pain. I eventually gave in and asked for Mike's help. After we were able to get it in place and tighten the bolts, I then found, that the welded nuts were a different thread to what I'd taken out, so I left her on the ramps and went in to think how to solve the problem!

As I was on work holiday, Daz stayed with me until Monday evening, Perry had dropped his drill with me the following morning; so I was able to fit the tailpipe on the car.

Cheryl had found a book at a book fair and bought it for me, she'd dropped it through my door but I didn't hear her knock; which was a shame as Daz was with me. The book was "Scooter Boy's" by Gareth Brown, on the front cover was a long-time friend Garry Griffiths. Cheryl had said to Bernard, "Tim will love this book and he'll probably know people in it;" she'd known Garry as long as I have and didn't even notice him on the cover, I called to thank her, and we discussed meeting on the Sunday for an ice cream on Weston sea front.

By three-thirty Sunday, Daz was excited as we were about to meet Auntie Cheryl for ice creams. No sooner had we sat in the car to make our way to the meet; bearing in mind it had been a blistering hot day, the clouds opened and it just didn't stop raining. We took a drive along Weston sea front, to see hundreds of half-dressed people dashing about hunting for cover. We drove around dry, but at the same time gutted, there was no chance we were having ice creams! So we went back home.

Cheryl and Bernard soon came to us with Barley (Abbies dog), a lemon drizzle cake and a bag of fruit tarts; as time was getting on, Daz packed his bag and spent the rest of his time with his auntie and uncle, they ran him home at six o'clock. I did some chores on the Tuesday, then spent from four PM until two AM writing the book to catch it up to date.

It was the best Friday in a long time, the Inner City boys got together for the first time since Covid kicked in, we practiced hard and it sounded awesome; like we'd never been apart.

The following Thursday after fixing the last faulty indicator, I started the scooter and rode with pride; to Bridge Motorcycles owned by great friend's Steve and Sue; I later picked her up with an MoT. I also popped to Claron Graphics to collect my new "Mod Life Crisis" discs.

I went home and fitted my new mod front rack, I stood proud as now the scooter was ready for the cover photo. Despite the worry about Covid 19, I myself am happy that I can end the book with a new car and my Vespa back on the road.

Adam and Ryan celebrating Daz turning 30

Happy 80th Mum

CHAPTER 13

IN CONCLUSION!

Everyone has their own story; if ever you're feeling so low you could end it, switch on a computer or grab a pen, and lots of paper and get your story down. Keep your memories as I have over the years, every wedding invite, every funeral invite, tickets to every gig I've been too, set lists for nearly every gig I've played and invites to every birthday party I've attended. I didn't keep many diarys over the years but I'd noted important things only in the one's I did have and as I wrote the end of the book up to chapter 10 at the end of 2018, I kept a diary every day of 2019 and wrote chapter 11 at the end of 2019 and into 2020, it's made me feel great and thinking so positive, so if you're on a low then let your life story flow.

I would like to add, that if you have read this book and enjoyed it, then thank you. Most of all, as the ending of the book took place in 2020 and despite Covid 19 ruining the year, My top lad turned thirty, Mum turned eighty and I turned fifty. Nothing would make me happier; than to know I'd finally made my mum really proud, of something I'd done before it was too late. I love you mum X

Printed and bound by CPI Group (UK) Ltd, Croydon, CR0 4YY